THE IRISH IN POWER

The Men And Women Who Helped Build A Superpower

JOHN JOE McGINLEY

GLASSAGH PUBLISHING

Published in 2022 by Glassagh Publishing Glassagh, Derrybeg
Letterkenny, County Donegal Republic of Ireland

Telephone 00353 83 1818 437 Email: info@glassaghpublishing.ie Web
www.glassaghpublishing.ie ISBN 978–1–3999–0102–4
© Text copyright John Joe McGinley and Glassagh Publishing

While every effort has been made to ensure the accuracy of all
information contained in this book, neither the author nor the publisher
accepts liability for any errors or omissions made.

Book design and production by Joe Coyle

CONTENTS

ACKNOWLEDGMENTS

This book is dedicated to my wife Eileen and children James, Nathan, Ronan and Joseph. Without their support and encouragement these ideas would still be in my head and the stories of these interesting men and women would not be written.

I hope you enjoy the lives of men and women who each in their own way made life better for their fellow Irish. Some did so out of duty, some out of ambition and a fair few out of a burning desire to escape poverty and oppression.

During my research I came across men and woman whose families had fled Ireland, which was at the time a land suffering under the twin calamities of famine and foreign oppression. They found a new home in America and as part of the Irish diaspora, they assimilated into every day American life. They began climbing the greasy pole of politics.

I want to acknowledge the courage, determination and public spirit of the men and woman in this book, who all at some time in their careers helped make

America a better place and helped build a superpower. I enjoyed writing about these people and I hope you find pleasure in my take on their stories.

CHAPTER 1
FROM SURVIVAL TO POWER

S hortly before the Easter Rising of 1916, Cecil Spring Rice the British ambassador in Washington reported back to the British foreign office that:

> "The best politicians in the country are Irish, and the professional Irish politician is against us."

It had been a long difficult road, but the Irish American political establishment was well rooted in American society. It was confident in its ability and after many hard years of struggle, it was now determined to have its voice listened to.

The influence of Irish men and women in American politics was nothing new, they had played a prominent part in the US political system even before the foundation of the United States of America.

The first wave of Irish emigrants, in the 18th and early 19th century were predominantly of the protestant faith. They sought religious freedom and had embraced their new home, using their ingenuity and work ethic to enjoy economic success, which in turn led to involvement in all levels of the American political system.

This was apparent, when in July of 1776 fifty-six men came together to pledge their "lives, fortunes and sacred honour" to form a new country where "all men are created equal" and entitled to "life, liberty and the pursuit of happiness".

Among the brave citizens who signed what could have been a death warrant, were at least eight of Irish blood and three who had been born in Ireland – James Smith, Matthew Thornton and George Taylor.

James Smith was born in Dublin 1719 and moved to America at a young age with his family, eventually settling in Pennsylvania. He studied law and emerged as a leading lawyer of his day. He rose to prominence with his legal opinions that denied the constitutional power and moral right of Great Britain over the colonies in America. He also urged, as Jonathan Swift would also do in Ireland, an end to the import of British goods.

He signed the Declaration of Independence when he was 57 years old and went on to serve as a Colonel of the Pennsylvania militia and a member of the Continental Congress.

The unit he commanded had so many Irish recruits, that one General quipped that that it should more properly be designated as "the Line of Ireland".

Matthew Thornton was born in County Limerick in 1714 and emigrated with his family as a four-year-old child in the passage of five ships carrying 120 Irish families from the Bann Valley.

A prominent physician, he more than once stepped away from his lucrative medical practice to serve the people of his community. Prior to joining the Continental Congress, he had previously volunteered as an Army Surgeon during the French and Indian War.

He signed the Declaration on behalf of New Hampshire when he was 62 and served as a Colonel of the New Hampshire Militia, 1775-1783.

George Taylor from County Antrim was born in 1716 and he emigrated to America when he was 20 years old. He came to the United States as a "redemptioner" (indentured servant) who was first employed in the backbreaking task of stoking coal into a blast furnace at an Iron foundry.

As would be typical of succeeding generations of Irish immigrants, Taylor through his own efforts and hard work prospered, eventually becoming a foundry master himself. He was a member of the Committee of

Correspondence, 1774-1776, and of the Continental Congress, 1776-1777.

Amidst the gentleman farmers and professionals of the Continental Congress, Irish American George Taylor was a self-made working man. His Durham furnace in Pennsylvania was a major supplier of shot and shell for George Washington's army.

It could be said that there were Irish fingerprints all over the declaration of independence. The Secretary of the Continental Congress who incorporate the final revisions to Jefferson's Declaration was an immigrant from County Derry, Charles Thomson.

An Immigrant from County Tyrone first printed the Declaration, John Dunlap and it was first read in public by Lieutenant Colonel John Nixon the son of an immigrant from Wexford.

Those millions who crossed the Atlantic aboard coffin ships, swapped famine for the lottery of months at sea, enduring hunger thirst and cold in a quest to survive. These ships were hell on the sea, where up to 15% of immigrant passengers would not survive the crowded and unsanitary conditions.

Once they docked in New York and Boston and the other cities of the eastern seaboard the Irish poured into the slums of the cities. The New York Tribune wrote in 1851:

"It is really lamentable to see the vast number of

unfortunate creatures that are almost daily cast on our shores, penniless and without physical energy to earn a day's living."

In New York, the Irish settled in the already over-crowded rat infested and violent slums. Between 1868 and 1875 roughly half of New York's population lived in crumbling tenements which despite their dilapidated state where an improvement on some of the hovels they had left behind in Ireland.

One of the most notorious of these Irish enclaves was the Five points area in lower Manhattan where every tenement was home to poverty, disease, drug abuse and extreme violence.

This was highlighted by Charles Dickens who visited the area in 1842 when he wrote:

"Poverty, wretchedness, and vice, are rife enough where we are going now. This is the place: these narrow ways, diverging to the right and left, and reeking everywhere with dirt and filth... Debauchery has made the very houses prematurely old. See how the rotten beams are tumbling down, and how the patched and broken windows seem to scowl dimly, like eyes that have been hurt in drunken frays... So far, nearly every house is a low tavern; and on the barroom walls, are coloured prints of Washington, and Queen Victoria of England, and the American

eagle. Among the pigeon-holes that hold the bottles, are pieces of plate-glass and coloured paper, for there is, in some sort, a taste for decoration, even here...

What place is this, to which the squalid street conducts us? A kind of square of leprous houses, some of which are attainable only by crazy wooden stairs without. What lies beyond this tottering flight of steps, that creak beneath our tread? A miserable room, lighted by one dim candle, and destitute of all comfort, save that which may be hidden in a wretched bed. Beside it, sits a man, his elbows on his knees, his forehead hidden in his hands..."

Source: Charles Dickens, American Notes

The Irish desperate to work filled the most menial and dangerous jobs, usually for low pay and in many cases for unscrupulous employers looking to exploit the new immigrants. They cut canals. They dug trenches for water and sewer pipes. They laid the expanding rail lines. They cleaned houses. They slaved in textile mills. They worked as stevedores, stable workers and black-smiths. Thousands would also toil in the coal mines of Pennsylvania and Virginia.

Not only did working-class Americans and espe-cially the descendants of the Protestant first wave of emigrants see the cheaper laborers taking their jobs they feared their religion.

The Roman Catholic Irish were particularly vilified by the country's Anglo-Saxon Protestants whose ancestors had explicitly made their exodus across the ocean to find a refuge from what they perceived as papism and ensure their worship was cleansed of any remaining Catholic vestiges.

It was true that conflict between Protestants and Catholics in the United States was nothing new and had taken place before the second wave of the famine immigration.

Anti-Catholic and anti-Irish mobs in Philadelphia destroyed houses and torched churches in the deadly 'Bible Riots' of 1844.

New York Archbishop John Hughes determined to protect his flock and church responded by building a wall of his own around Old St. Patrick's Cathedral to protect it from those angry at the rise in Catholic emigration, and he stationed musket-wielding members of the Ancient Order of Hibernians to guard the city's other Roman Catholic churches.

As the famine ravaged Ireland and with immigration controls left primarily to the states and cities, the Irish poured through this porous border.

Boston, a city of a little more than 100,000 people, saw 37,000 Irish arrive in the matter of just a few years.

Such numbers made integration difficult, and the

Irish in Boston were according to the historian Oscar
Handlin in his book Boston's Immigrants, 1790-1880: A
Study in Acculturation.

> "Fated to remain a massive lump in the commu-
> nity, undigested, undigestible."

As the young nation began to tear itself apart in civil
war, the Irish played their part with 200,000 men and
some women fighting in the conflict. 150,000 for the
Union and 50,000 for the Confederacy.

As America emerged from the civil war the Irish in
every city they settled understood the importance of
building a better life for themselves and their families.
Slowly like the first wave of Protestant emigrants before
them, the millions of Roman Catholic Irish began to be
involved with their communities at every level, especially politics.

Over time the downtrodden realised they had power
in numbers and helped found the political machines
that would go on to dominate and seize control of major
American cities such as Boston, New York and Chicago.

By the third wave of major Irish immigration to
America in the early 20th century, Irish Americans had
risen to political office as mayors, representatives, senators, governors, and even running for the presidency.

Irish Americans would go on to participate and, in

many cases, dominate the political life of major cities and eventually national politics.

While the stories of the major players like JFK, Joe Biden and others such as Tip O'Neil are well known, others who were just as influential deserve their stories told. Irish American men and women whose lives will be told in 'The Irish in power,' individuals such as:

- Richard 'Boss' Croker who rose to the top of the corrupt Democratic Tammany Hall organisation in New York and at the height of his powers received bribe money from the owners of brothels, saloons and illegal gambling dens.
- James "Old Buck" Buchanan was the 15th President of the United States of America and the man many blames for failing to stop his nation from falling into the catastrophic mire of civil war and is ranked as the worst President in American History. He was also the only President from Pennsylvania before the victory of his fellow Irish American Joseph Biden in 2020. Buchanan is often portrayed as a man whose belief in the rights of every state to determine their own destiny within the union was a contributing factor to the bloody civil war that ripped the young

America apart and threatened to end the union.

- Chester A. Arthur was a lawyer, soldier and politician who was elected the 20th Vice president of the United States but who became Americas 21st President in September 1881 when President James A. Garfield was shot by Charles Julius Guiteau and died two months later from infections related to the wounds.

- Mary Harris Jones was a teacher, seamstress, labour activist and union organiser. A champion of the underdog and the working-class Jones was a campaigner for the United Mine Workers Union, founded the Social Democratic Party and helped establish the Industrial Workers of the World. Mary was an inspirational icon for any distressed strikers and used to clad herself in typical black Victorian dresses, which made her look older than she was. She was given the title of 'Mother Jones,' by striking miners grateful for the support and leadership she had shown them. Jones in turn referred to the miners as 'my boys.' During one of her numerous trials for labour activism, a US Attorney once called Jones the 'most dangerous woman in America.'

- James Michael Curley who will always be remembered as one of the most flamboyant and controversial politicians in American history. Dragged up in the slums of Boston he was beloved by his fellow Irish emigrants and the working class of all nationalities. So much so they elected him Mayor of Boston 4 times, Governor of Massachusetts once and Curley was twice elected to the US House of Representatives.

- John Francis Fitzgerald was the first American born; Irish American Roman Catholic elected as Mayor of Boston. He was also a state Senator, US Congressman and made several unsuccessful runs for Governor of Massachusetts. Fitzgerald maintained a high profile in the city whether in or out of office, and his theatrical style of campaigning and charisma earned him the nickname "Honey Fitz". However, his greatest claim to fame, was that he mentored and began the political career of his grandson John Fitzgerald Kennedy, the 35th President of the United States of America.

- William Randolph Hearst is best remembered as one of America's richest businessmen, a media mogul and the main inspiration for Charles Foster Kane, the lead character in

Orson Welles's 1941 film Citizen Kane. He would build up the nation's largest newspaper chain and whose methods profoundly influenced American journalism and not always positively. However, like many rich and powerful men he also believed he should be president and he also had a controversial political life.

- Al Smith was the dominant force in New York State politics for over 20 years. He was the first politician of national stature to rise from the ranks of urban Irish American Roman Catholic immigrants, in his case, the Irish American immigrants of downtown Manhattan. He served 4 terms as New York State governor. He ran unsuccessfully as the Democratic candidate for president as the first Roman Catholic nominated by a major party. After his career in politics ended, he became the president of Empire State, Inc., the corporation that built and operated the Empire State Building.

- Richard Joseph Daley was Mayor of Chicago from 1955 until his death in 1976. Daley played a major role in the history of the United States Democratic Party, especially with his support of John F. Kennedy in 1960 and of Hubert Humphrey in 1968. He would

be the longest-serving mayor in Chicago
history until his record was broken by his
own son Richard M. Daley in 2011.

- Jane Margaret Byrne, the first woman to be
  elected Mayor of Chicago the second largest
  city in the United States at the time, who
  finally broke the glass ceiling in the windy
  city to become the first female mayor of any
  major American city.

- James Aloysius "Jim" Farley, one of the first
  Irish Catholic politicians to achieve success on
  a national level who became postmaster
  general and brought Coca Cola to Europe. He
  was also a Knight of Malta and a political
  kingmaker who was President Franklin
  Delano Roosevelt's campaign manager for all
  his major elections, including his presidential
  victories in 1932 and 1936.

- Daniel Patrick Moynihan who was known to
  his friends and family as Pat, was a man who
  rose from humble Irish American origins in
  Hell's kitchen in New York to become a
  Harvard Professor, United States Senator,
  Ambassador to India and Ambassador to the
  United Nations. He also served in the cabinets
  and inner circle of Presidents Kennedy,
  Johnson and surprisingly for a Democrat,
  Republican Presidents Richard Nixon and

Gerald Ford. This made Moynihan the sole individual in the nation's history to be appointed, in succession, to four presidential cabinets: Kennedy, Johnson, Nixon, and Ford.

- Eugene McCarthy ran for the presidency 5 times and never secured the nomination. As a liberal he was not afraid to call out the anti-communist paranoia of Senator Joseph McCarthy and helped end the presidential career of Lyndon B. Johnson when he ran on in an anti-war platform in the 1968 Democratic presidential primaries. He was also one of the most prominent Reagan Democrats who endorsed the republican presidential candidate, Ronald Reagan.

In the early 1950s America was gripped by a paranoid fear of all things allegedly Soviet and many innocent men and women were smeared with the tag of communists or soviet sympathisers. One man personified that era even giving his name to the tactics used to out and ostracise alleged communist party members. This man was Senator Joseph McCarthy and his reckless and, in many cases, unsubstantiated accusations and public attacks on fellow politicians, actors, film makers and government officials would become known as 'McCarthyism.'

Many years have rolled on since Al Smith became

the first Catholic nominee of a major party and in 2020 Joseph Robinette Biden Jr. son of the Blewitts from County Mayo and the Finnegans from County Louth became the 46th President of the United States of America.

The Irish Americans have now truly arrived at the pinnacle of US politics, but as we will see in the chapters ahead it has been a long and eventful journey for the Irish in power.

CHAPTER 2
RICHARD CROCKER
THE BOSS OF TAMMANY HALL AND EPSOM DERBY WINNER

I t was said of Richard 'Boss' Croker that he was an honest politician, because when he was bought, he stayed bought!

Richard Croker was an Irish American politician who never took high office, but who controlled the Democratic Tammany Hall operation in New York for nearly 20 years dispensing political patronage and influencing elections at every level including presidential.

He would also go on to amass a vast fortune, which he used to build a horse racing operation as effective as his political machine, which would go on to win the English Derby.

Richard Welsted Croker was born on the 23rd of November 1841 in the townland of Ballyva, in the parish of Ardfield near Clonakilty, County Cork. His parents were Eyre Coote Croker an Army officer and Florence

Croker, daughter of John Welsted of Ballywalter, County Cork.

The Croker's were Church of Ireland land owing minor gentry who claimed to have arrived in Ireland with Oliver Cromwell, not a claim to endear you to the Roman Catholic local population.

Richards Father was a restless spirit who after squandering his inheritance on a range of failed business ventures decided to resign his army commission and try his luck across the Atlantic in America.

The family, including young Richard, embarked from Cobh for a new life. They were not typical of the thousands crossing the ocean for a new life. Firstly, they were not Roman Catholic and secondly, they were not destitute landless previous tenants escaping hunger and oppression. The Croker's were instead leaving in genteel poverty, after selling the family estate in Arfield in southwest Cork. When the family arrived in America, they settled in New York and soon faced the spectre of poverty. However, Eyre Croker who had served in the British Army and had an extensive experience of horses, soon rebranded himself as a veterinary surgeon, or more accurately, a horse doctor.

He would go on to serve as a Union army veterinary officer during the American Civil War.

Whilst not prosperous by any means, this employment stabilised the family's fortunes and allowed Croker and his siblings to attend public school.

Richard Croker, whilst an intelligent boy, was not academically minded and in 1853, he left school at the age of 12, beginning an apprenticeship as a machinist in the workshops of the New York central railroad.

In common with many young men of his age in the Irish enclaves of New York, he soon sought out the camaraderie and in most cases safety of gang membership. He joined a local street one, the Fourth Avenue tunnel gang.

They engaged in several rackets around the Harlem Lines freight depot, robbing drunks, supporting or breaking strikes and demanding protection money from every business in the area.

This usually involved violence and Richard was not afraid to get involved. His fighting prowess marked him out as a man to watch, and in just a few years, he was the gang's leader, ready for the next rung up the economic ladder in New York.

This was to be in 1863 as part of a volunteer fire department, becoming an engineer of one of the engine companies. The New York fire department in the early 1860's was the ultimate boys club, with gangs of rival firefighters, with their own volunteer 'runners', racing to fires as though in a sports competition. It was not uncommon for fighting to erupt between rival fire units or for fires to mysteriously erupt if kickbacks were not forthcoming to the local mob or political bosses, who were usually the same people.

As an engineer of one of the engine companies, his leadership qualities and fighting prowess soon brought him to the attention of the Tammany Hall operation which controlled the Democratic party in New York City who were always looking for new recruits. In 1865, Jimmy O'Brien, a local ward boss saw Richard fight in an illegal back street bare knuckle boxing bout. This was against fellow Irishman and renowned pugilist Dick Lynch. It was a particularly violent bout, where Richard knocked out all of Lynch's teeth.

An impressed O'Brien immediately hired Richard as a political enforcer, and 'repeater.' This was someone who would as the name suggests, vote repeatedly and illegally at elections. Richard had reached the first rung on the Tammany Hall ladder. If he were to climb any further, he would have to make a major change and later that year he converted to Catholicism and his rise in politics was about to begin.

In 1868 he became an Alderman of the city, but trouble was brewing for Tammany Hall.

The organisation was led by the notoriously corrupt giant of New York politics William M. Tweed more commonly known as 'Boss Tweed,' whose financial voraciousness and appetite for corruption, knew no limits. He participated in every aspect of commerce in New York where his patronage allocated jobs and contracts.

At one stage he was the third-largest landowner in

New York City, a director of the Erie Railroad, a director of the Tenth National Bank, a director of the New-York Printing Company and the proprietor of the Metropolitan Hotel. He was also a significant stockholder in iron mines and gas companies, a board member of the Harlem Gas Light Company, the Third Avenue Railway Company, the Brooklyn Bridge Company, and the president of the Guardian Savings Bank.

The rampant and conspicuous corruption as practised by Tweed was drawing condemnation from those who advocated cleaning up politics and the populace who could tolerate some levels of corruption but not on this scale.

Some clever operators in Tammany Hall knew that the winds of change were blowing, and that different tactics and behaviour were needed.

Richard Croker was one of these men, and he now split from Tweed's faction and aligned himself instead with the Young Democracy faction led by 'Honest' John Kelly, who despite the name, was far from honest, but much more careful than Tweed.

1873 was to prove a momentous year for Croker. The first event was his marriage to Elizabeth Fraser, they would go on to have seven children. He was then elected as a New York County Coroner on the Tammany Hall ticket. This was a purely political appointment, given his only medical experience was beating people to a pulp in the boxing ring. However, it did provide a lucrative salary of $25,000 a year which cemented Crocker's financial security.

In January, Boss Tweed was sent for trial on corruption charges. The trial ended when a jury, which many believe was bribed, was unable to provide a verdict. Despite being a free man for now, with a retrial set for November, Tweeds time as the boss of Tammany Hall was over and he was replaced by the man Crocker supported 'Honest' John Kelly. Tweeds retrial was convened, and a jury convicted him on 204 of 220 counts of corruption, bribery, and coercion. He was given a fine of $12,750 and sentenced to 12 years, which was reduced to 1 year on appeal.

Despite his downfall, Tweed still had a strong cohort of supporters within Tammany Hall, and they rallied to oppose the new leader Kelly's slate at the next election in 1874.

This would bring Crocker into conflict with his old mentor Jimmy O'Brien, who was running for Congress on a Tweed slate in opposition to a Kelly nominee, Abraham. S. Hewitt.

Despite his role as County Coroner, Crocker still relished the politics of enforcement and was drawn into a confrontation with one of O'Brien's aides, John McKenna at a polling station. An argument started, guns were drawn, shots fired and while Crocker remained standing McKenna lay dead at his feet.

Richard was arrested on the testimony of numerous witnesses for the murder and sent for trial. However, the power of Tammany Hall came to his rescue and the jury returned a hung verdict of 6 v 6, after a high-profile visit to the trial of Tammany Hall Boss John Kelly.

Richard was acquitted by the judge, again likely to have been on the Tammany Hall payroll.

The newly free Croker returned to his role as County Coroner, a position he would be re-elected to for another three-year term in 1876.

In 1880 now financially secure, but seeking further advancement, he continued as a key member of the Kelly Tammany Hall operation, he set up home with his growing family in Harrison New York.

In 1883 he became a New York Fire Commissioner, whilst acting as number 2 to John Kelly in Tammany Hall.

John Kelly was in ill health and decided to resign and in 1886 Richard Croker became the most powerful politician in New York city and state politics and assumed the nickname he would have for the rest of his life 'Boss Croker'.

Richard Croker the Irish immigrant who had run with the street gangs of New York, fought for money in brutal bare-knuckle fights and who had been tried for murder, was now at the helm of the most powerful political machine in 19th century America.

While leadership of Tammany Hall didn't provide a

salary in itself, it was the route to a series of lucrative income streams. Croker now received bribe money from the owners of brothels, saloons and illegal gambling dens, all keen to avoid prosecution and conduct their illegal activities unhindered by regulation or oversight.

Croker was also aware of the large profits available from kickbacks and commission from the sales of land and buildings owned by New York City. Keen to get his slice of the pie, he created a real estate firm with his friend Peter F. Myer. The new firm, Myer and Croker soon made millions from property deals.

The money just kept on coming. The city police were receiving large payoffs from the emerging Irish and Italian crime gangs and Tammany and then ultimately Croker wetted their beak in this tsunami of corruption.

Legitimate companies also wanted to ensure Tammany protection and favours and Richard began to amass stock in a variety of streetcar, railway and transit companies that were springing up all over New York City and State.

Just a year into his leadership of Tammany Hall, Croker faced his first major crisis. The 1886 mayoral election was the first to be contested under Croker's leadership of the Tammany Hall faction and they needed a strong candidate to take on the popular political economist Henry George, who was standing for the United Labor Party.

George wished to realign politics along class lines

rather than race and this was a threat to the Irish dominated Tammany Hall organisation.

Croker lined up the Tammany Hall political machine behind US Congressman Abram S. Hewitt. This was a strange choice as Hewitt was staunchly against further Irish immigration into America and was now the leader of the anti-Tammany Hall faction in New York City.

Croker was being pragmatic; he knew that a victory for Henry George could mean that class rather than race would be the major factor in future elections. Tammany Hall depended upon the loyalty and votes of the Irish who had flooded into New York and were determined to retain their power at all costs, even if it meant backing a candidate they could not control.

They gambled on Hewitt being a non-controversial mayor and they ensured he secured the Democratic nomination. With the help of Tammany Hall, Hewitt went on to defeat Henry George and a certain Theodore Roosevelt who was the Republican candidate.

Hewitt proved to be a problem for Tammany Hall and his reforming colleagues encouraged him to deny Croker the control of the patronage appointments that was a massive part of his power. Hewitt's fate was sealed when he refused to review the 1887 St Patricks Day parade. Croker and Tammany Hall withdrew their support and Hewitt lost the mayoral race of 1888 to the Tammany Hall candidate Hugh John Grant, who was only the 2nd Roman Catholic mayor of New York (after

William Russell Grace in 1885). Grant who had initially opposed Tammany Hall, was now an enthusiastic supporter and in thanks for receiving backing to become Mayor appointed Croker to the lucrative post of City Chamberlain.

At the height of his powers and feeling politically invincible Croker opposed Grover Cleveland's campaign to be re-elected President in 1888.

The 1888 general election was a close-run affair with the election on a knife edge. Cleveland won the popular vote by almost 1%, but Harrison won the electoral college 233 to 168 and with it the presidency.

Whilst not completely to blame for Cleveland's defeat, Croker's opposition ensured New York went for Harrison by a slim margin.

Ever the pragmatist and eager for financial reward, Croker would go on to help Cleveland regain the presidency in 1892, helped by a financial sweetener to encourage his support.

Tammany Hall and Croker ensured that their candidates secured the position of New York City Mayor, first with Hugh John Grant from 1889 to 1892 and then Thomas F. Gilroy from 1892 to 1894.

This allowed Croker to amass a fortune of $8 million from the rackets that Tammany controlled. Property and planning frauds, protection rackets, prostitution, and saloons all fell under his control.

A story is told that Croker even tried his hand at

being a building contractor. He did this because there was a multi-million-dollar contract to re-pave the streets up for grabs.

Croker submitted a tender that was at least 50% below the other bids. This combined with his Tammany Hall influence ensured he won the contract.

He was now required to provide a new even street, and he still managed to make himself a fortune, by brazenly turning the existing slabs upside down!

Despite the vast amount of money flowing into Croker's pockets, no one ever proved any illegality and not for the want of trying. Reform politicians, including many of the growing Irish political class were opposed to the rampant corruption of Tammany Hall and several investigative committees were formed with the hope of bringing the organisation to heel.

In 1890, a probe by the New York state Senate was set up to finally go after Croker and Tammany Hall. An investigative committee was established under the chairmanship of the Republican J Sloan Fassett.

The Fassett committee as it became known, was looking for evidence of bribery among appointed officials and the Board of Aldermen. Most of these were Democrats under the leadership of Croker and his appointee as Mayor, Hugh Grant.

There was some sensational testimony, especially from Croker's brother-in-law, Patrick H. McCann who claimed that Grant, before he became Mayor, once made a present of $25,000 to Croker's six-year-old daughter, Flossie. McCann claimed the Croker's used this to purchase a new house.

He also claimed that, on another occasion, in 1884, Croker dropped in on McCann and showed him a bag with

$180,000, explaining that it was cash for bribing the Aldermen so that Grant would be approved as Commissioner of Public Works.

Despite these lurid accusations, no indictments were ever brought forward, and Grant went on to win the 1892 mayoral race and Croker maintained his position of profitable power.

However, the tide of reform was flowing stronger and in 1894, despite Sligo born Thomas Francis Gilroy another Tammany Hall figure winning the election for mayor, the pressure for reform was becoming unstoppable.

In 1892 Charles Henry Pankhurst a clergy man with a zeal for social and political reform had begun preaching sermons heavily critical of Croker and the corruption of Tammany Hall. Under pressure from Pankhurst, Republican members of the New York state Senate began an investigation in 1894 which was to be known as the Lexow committee, headed up by Republican State Senator Clarence Lexow.

Croker rather than submit to the indignity of the investigations, relinquished his leadership of Tammany

Hall to John C. Sheahan and decided that a vacation was in order, a long one.

He did this without his wife Elizabeth as they had now separated. As a Roman Catholic, Elizabeth would not consent to a divorce, but was happy for them to live separate life's.

Croker purchased a country estate in England, in the Vale of the white horse in Berkshire. He now styled himself as 'Richard Welsted Croker Esquire,' gentleman and horse breeder.

However, his dreams of being accepted by the wealthy country set were dashed when he was shunned by his neighbours who referred to him as a 'New York Gangster.'

Richard, then undertook a tour of the continent before returning to his English estate where he continued to train his horses and even began to breed pigs. He took great delight in naming his pigs after his neighbours and political enemies back in New York.

Meanwhile across the Atlantic, the Lexow committee was undertaking a probe into police corruption and the Tammany Hall operation. The hours of testimony ran to over 10,000 pages. The committee, ironically headquartered at the Tweed Courthouse on Chambers Street, examined evidence from Parkhurst's city vigilance league, as well as conducting its own investigations.

The Committee uncovered police involvement in extortion, bribery, counterfeiting, voter intimidation, election fraud, brutality, and various money-making scams.

It was discovered that the promotion of police officers was dependent on the payment of bribes, and that that payment was recovered from the protection of vice businesses including prostitution.

A Captain Timothy J. Creedon testified that he paid $15,000 to obtain a captain's rank.

He did not achieve this rank prior to this payment even though his examination score for promotion was 97.82.

Originally, he was quoted a price of $12,000, but his Tammany district leader, John W. Reppenhagen, told Creedon that another officer had already come up with that amount and the new price was $15,000, which Creedon paid.

Creedon also revealed, that a portion of that cost was paid by local businesses. The committee also revealed that when the police did go after prostitutes, they were independent street walkers, and even then, Tammany made a profit with its control of the bail system.

Croker relaxing across the Atlantic, escaped the scandal and backlash against Tammany Hall, which resulted in the election of the reform candidate for New York mayor William Lafayette Strong.

Strong's victory was optimistically hailed by the New York press as an epic defeat of Tammany Hall's "fraud, chicane, trickery, double-dealing and contempt for the moral sense of the community."

He was the last mayor of New York City before the consolidation of the City of Greater New York on January 1st, 1898.

The City of Greater New York was the term used by many politicians and scholars for the expanded City of New York created by consolidating the existing city with Brooklyn, western Queens County, and Staten Island.

This was an opportunity for Tammany Hall to rise again and regain its position of power, so Croker returned from the continent to assume the leadership of Tammany Hall once more.

Croker swung the full support of the Tammany Hall organisation behind Peter Van Wyck the New York Chief Justice.

Van Wyck was seen as the ideal candidate to take on the reforming faction that had now lost popularity. His legal background and lack of baggage was ideal for Tammany Hall, which ensured he secured the Democratic nomination and he went on to become the first mayor of the newly consolidated New York City. Croker and Tammany Hall were back.

During Van Wyck's term Croker dominated the political landscape of New York, further enriching himself and his Tammany Hall colleagues as the city began construction of the interborough rapid transit, the first subway in Manhattan, and the Brooklyn Tunnel.

Van Wyck's administration was brought down by the so-called 'Ice Trust' scandal of 1900. The newspaper New York World reported that the American Ice Company of Charles W. Morse planned to double the price of ice, from 30 to 60 cents per hundred pounds.

In the era before refrigeration, this had potentially fatal effects, as the ice was the only preservative available to keep food, milk, and medicines fresh. The high price would have put ice beyond the reach of many of the city's poor which were Tammany's main power base in the years of waves of immigration.

American Ice was forced to reverse its decision due to the public outcry. Van Wyck's political rivals forced an investigation into the issue. It revealed that American Ice had secured an effective monopoly over the supply of its product to the city. This was because it was the only company with rights to land ice at New York piers and would have dramatically increased its profits at the new price.

To make matters worse, Van Wyck, whose salary as mayor was only $15,000, owned and had not paid for,

$680,000 worth of American Ice stock. Croker also had shares worth $250,000!

The Ice Trust scandal destroyed Van Wyck's political career. Tammany Hall was forced to drop him, and their candidate Edward M. Shepard lost the 1901 election to the reformist slate led by Seth Low.

Croker once again thought that the political tide had

turned, and he decided to take the money (lots of it) and run. He resigned as leader of Tammany Hall, not to spend more time with his family but his mistress and racehorses! Horse racing had always been his passion and he had established a stable of thoroughbred racehorses in the states and these had been sent over to his estate in Berkshire.

It was again to England in 1903 that Corker went when he bade farewell to Tammany Hall. He was determined to avoid the fate of the great Tammany Hall politician William 'Boss' Tweed who had died penniless in jail. This was not to be the legacy of Richard 'Boss' Croker who was now focussed on becoming a successful racehorse breeder and owner.

He wanted to have his horses trained at Newmarket, but he first needed the permission of the ultimate establishment gentlemen's organisation, the Jockey Club.

Croker was perceived as a brash newcomer, flush with money and an old reputation for crime and corruption.

The venerable men of the Jockey club headed up by Brigadier-General Edward William David Baird, decided Croker was not the sort they wanted and refused him permission to train his horses at Newmarket.

Undaunted by this rejection, Croker sold his estate in England and moved his entire horse breeding operation and £25m fortune to Ireland.

In 1905, Richard bought the 51-acre Glencairn estate in Sandyford County Dublin. Richard believed this was the ideal venue for his horse breeding vision, as it was close to Leopardstown racecourse. In time he would add another 500 acres to the estate.

He hired the renowned trainer J. J. Parkinson and became the leading owner in Ireland in 1905 and 1906. However, Croker's autocratic manner led to a fall out, and he soon employed Col. F. F. MacCabe to train his stable. Richard had a burning desire to not only breed successful horses, but to show the Jockey club who was the real boss! The prize Richard craved was the Derby, and in 1907 his horse Orby, ridden by American jockey John Reiff, sensationally won the prestigious race at Epson by a distance of two lengths and at a great price for gamblers at 100 to 6.

Orby became the first Irish-trained horse, and the third owned by an American, to win The Derby.

Orby was a superb animal and sired both Diadem who won the 1917 1,000 Guineas and Grand Parade, also bred by Croker who would go on to win the Derby in 1919.

This was a moment of great pride for Richard, he had shown the snobs in the Jockey Club that he was no amateur. His victory was also all the sweeter, as the second placed horse was owned by the very man who had blocked his request to train his horses at Newmarket, Brigadier-General Edward William David Baird.

Orby's Derby win was celebrated with great pride in Ireland, bonfires were lit across the country and cheering crowds praised both the horse and owner.

The horse and owner were paraded through the streets of Dublin, where one old lady was heard to exclaim:

"Thank God we have lived to see a Catholic horse win the Derby!"

It would have been churlish, to point out that the horse's owner was, in fact, born and raised a Protestant.

In 1908, the Dublin Corporation voted 27-13 to make Richard Croker a Freeman of the City of Dublin.

Later that year Orby's half-sister, Rhodora, captured the English 1,000 Guineas for Croker. He then insisted on incestuously mating his two champions; the result was a horribly deformed foal and the death of the mare. His stable later won two Irish Oaks and he was again leading owner in Ireland in 1911.

As for Orby, he would go on to win the Irish Derby and be set out to stud, but this was a short career and he died of heart failure soon after.

Throughout his tenure at Glencairn, Richard had a loving relationship with a woman who was described for appearances sake as his housekeeper, Stella Beaumont.

Stella died on the 24th of January 1914 and was buried in the grounds of his estate.

In August 1914, Richards estranged wife Elizabeth died while on holiday in Austria. Croker arranged for the body to be brought back to America and he attended her grand funeral on the 6th of October.

Just seven weeks later, Richard who had lost both his long-term lover and estranged wife married a small-time actress almost 50 years his junior. This woman was Bula Benton Edmundson, she claimed to be 1/8th Cherokee and was styled by Richard detractors, who included his estranged children, as the 'Indian princess'.

His surviving children believed he had lost his mind and in 1920 they sought an injunction against their father, claiming that they were likely to be deprived of their due inheritance because he had fallen entirely under the influence of their stepmother. They lost the case, but they were right, Richard changed his will and left everything to his new wife.

Richard and Bula spent what he would describe as 8 happy years between their homes in Palm Springs, which Richard called 'Wig Wam' and his beloved Glen-cairn in Ireland. Bula often said Richard was the only saint she had met in her life.

For a man, whose life was dominated by political intrigue, Richards life in Ireland was remarkably politi-cally uneventful; however, he probably provided monetary support, if not arms, to republicans in the years leading up to independence.

Boss Croker died on the 29th of April 1922, aged 80 from a thrombosis, at his home Glencairn House. His funeral was attended by the great and the good of Dublin.

His funeral mass was celebrated by Bishop William Miller and his coffin was taken to his resting place in the grounds of his estate, by among others Arthur Griffith, the President of Dáil Éireann; Laurence O'Neill, the Lord Mayor of Dublin; Oliver St. John Gogarty; Joseph MacDonagh; A.H. Flauley, of Chicago; and J.E. Tierney.

Michael Collins, Chairman of the Provisional Government of the Irish Free State, was represented by Kevin O'Shiel.

The Lord Lieutenant of Ireland, Edmund Bernard FitzAlan-Howard, 1st Viscount FitzAlan of Derwent, was represented by his under-secretary, James MacMahon.

Richard was buried near the lake at Glencairn. But this would not be his place of eternal rest, as some years later his remains were removed to a nearby graveyard because the new owners wanted "vacant possession".

However, many locals claim to this day that over the years they have seen the ghost of Richard Croker. There have been sightings of a burly frock coated figure, in his trademark bowler hat, wandering the grounds of his previous home. Perhaps seeking his old resting place.

Croker left his estate to his wife Bula, but again his children challenged the will.

They claimed that their father was of unsound mind and unduly influenced by his wife. They also claimed that the 1914 marriage was void, as Bula was already married to someone else in Massachusetts, one Guy R. Marone and thus she was not her father's lawful wife.

In a 12-day hearing in the High Court in Dublin, Bula gave lengthy evidence and was cross-examined by Serjeant Sullivan, the barrister for Richard Croker Jr.

At the end of the case the jury found in her favour, and she inherited a further £3 million from Croker's estate, much to the dismay of Croker's children who had once again failed to overturn their fathers will.

Richard Croker born into genteel poverty ended his life a wealthy and respected man, a politician, racehorse breeder and in his own words an honest politician because when he was bought, he stayed bought!

66

Buchanan spent most of his time in retirement defending his administration and his own record in response to public criticism and blame for the war that many referred to as 'Buchanan's War'

CHAPTER 3
JAMES BUCHANAN
MISUNDERSTOOD OR AN ABJECT FAILURE?

James "Old Buck" Buchanan was the 15th president of the United States of America and the man many blames for failing to stop his nation from falling into the catastrophic mire of civil war and is ranked as the worst president in American history.

He was also the only president from Pennsylvania before the victory of his fellow Irish American Joseph Biden in 2020.

Buchanan is often portrayed as a man whose belief in the rights of every state to determine their own destiny within the Union was a contributing factor to the bloody civil war that ripped the young America apart and threatened to destroy the country.

The reality is of course more complex. Buchanan as we shall see was a man of his time, who was morally opposed to slavery, but who believed it was protected by the US Constitution.

He also believed it was the manifest destiny of the American people to expand their territory to grow the United States.

He never married and his love life was the subject of much conjecture, with some historians believing that he was either gay or even asexual.

When James Buchanan's father left his home in Ramelton in county Donegal to join his Uncle Joshua in Pennsylvania, little did he know that his eldest son and namesake would go on to become the 15th president of the United States of America.

James settled well in his new home and bought a trading post which he renamed 'Stoney Batter' after his grand parents' home in Ireland. He met and married an Irish woman Elizabeth Speer and bought a farm outside Mercersburg in rural Pennsylvania. It was here that James Buchanan junior was born on April the 23rd 1791. He would be the last president to be born in the eighteenth century.

While the infant Buchanan was born in a log cabin, within months the family would move into a town house in Mercersburg, as James senior began to become the wealthiest man in town as a merchant, farmer and real estate investor. The American public has a fascination with their presidents being born in a log cabin. Many such as William Henry Harrison, James Knox

Polk and of course the most famous of all Abraham Lincoln used their birth in a log cabin on the campaign trail.

This is psychological as voters love to see an underdog rise from poverty to reach the White House. Former President Bill Clinton, joked in 2012, that former Democratic National Convention Chairman Bob Strauss used to say that every politician wants every voter to believe he was born in a log cabin he built himself.

Whilst being born in a log cabin, James Buchanan never experienced poverty. Despite his parents going on to have 11 children, his father's business acumen, ensured that the young James would benefit from a comfortable upbringing and an excellent education.

As a boy James attended school in Mercersburg, but as his father's wealth increased his mother who was extremely ambitious for her eldest son arranged for James to attend Dickinson College in Carlisle, which was seventy miles from home.

A spirited and mischievous teenager, Buchanan was twice threatened with expulsion but his father's influence and his own plea for a second chance ensured he graduated with honours in September 1809. He then decided to pursue a legal career and moved to the then state capital Lancaster. His father arranged for him to gain a place in a leading law firm, and he was admitted to the Pennsylvanian bar in 1812.

That same year war broke out between America and

the United Kingdom over British attempts to restrict US trade, the Royal Navy's capture of American seamen and America's own desire to expand its territory.

As the war progressed and the British invaded Maryland, Buchanan enlisted in the Pennsylvanian militia and served at the defence of Baltimore. As a private, Buchanan is the only US president with military service not to have been an officer.

Returning to Lancaster, Buchanan set about creating his own law firm and began to display a legal brain and talent for the profession that soon amassed him a substantial fortune.

As with many lawyers, he entered politics and was elected to the Pennsylvania House of Representatives as a member of the Federalist Party in 1814. The Federalists called for a strong national government that promoted economic growth and fostered friendly relationships with Great Britain in opposition to revolutionary France.

Buchanan himself supported federally funded improvements, high import tariffs and a national bank. Being a member of the state legislator helped Buchanan expand his legal practice as did becoming a freemason. He would go on to become the Master of masonic lodge no 43 in Lancaster and a district Deputy Grand Master of the Grand Lodge of Pennsylvania.

In 1818, as his term in the state legislature was ending, James met Anne Caroline Coleman at a ball in Lancaster. Coleman was the daughter of a wealthy industrialist. She was also the sister-in-law of Phil-adelphia judge Joseph Hemphill, one of Buchanan's colleagues. James set out to win her hand.

While Ann's family initially opposed the match, they eventually relented, but due to Buchanan's workload the couple spent little time together.

Rumours spread that James was only interested in Anne for her money. However, this is unlikely as by the time they met Buchanan was worth well over quarter of a million dollars himself. Gossips also spread rumours that while James worked in the legislature and in his legal practice, he was seeing other women.

Whilst no evidence existed, word of this gossip reached Anne who broke off the engagement in a distraught letter.

Anne Coleman was known as a shy, sensitive and exceptionally beautiful young woman and when she broke off her engagement with James, she went to visit relatives in Philadelphia,

There on December 9th, 1819, she died mysteriously, and her death has long been speculated to be a suicide.

The records of a Dr. Chapman, who looked after her in her final hours, and who said just after her death that this was "the first instance he ever knew of hysteria producing death", reveal that he theorised, despite the absence of any valid evidence, that Anne's death was caused by an overdose of laudanum, a concentrated tincture of opium.

James Buchanan lost in his grief said afterwards that: "I have lost the only earthy object of my affection without whom life presents to me a dreary blank. My prospects are all cut off and I feel that my happiness will be buried with her in the grave."

The Coleman family held James Buchanan responsible for Anne's death and this was this was made clear when they returned unopened Buchanan's request to be permitted to take part in the funeral services.

The experience severely shook Buchanan; he vowed he would remain unmarried, and he never became seriously involved with any other woman for the rest of his life, though he carried on many flirtations. He would be the nation's first and only bachelor president and as we will see later the subject of speculation surrounding his sex life. The tragic death of his fiancée and the fact he was barred from attending her funeral had a lasting impact on Buchanan. The immediate effect was that he threw himself into his work and political life.

Leaving behind the Pennsylvanian state legislator he ran successfully for a seat in the US House of Representatives. He served in Congress from 1821 until 1831.

As a congressman, he used his legal training to establish a reputation as a constitutional expert gaining a place on the House Judiciary committee.

Despite being elected from Pennsylvania, Buchanan was more comfortable and politically aligned with southern congressmen rather than his New England neighbours, whom he viewed as being political radicals.

Despite being elected as a Federalist, the party was on its last legs and Buchanan knew that his career would falter unless he obtained a new political home. He would soon find this in the coalition led by the charismatic war hero and future president Andrew Jackson. This movement would soon evolve into the Democratic party.

Buchanan was an ardent supporter of Jackson and his Democratic party and soon became its leader in Pennsylvania. He swung his supporters behind Jacksons successful bid for the presidency in 1828.

He helped re-elect President Jackson in 1832 and was rewarded with an appointment as the US Ambassador to Russia.

Initially reluctant to leave America, Buchanan eventually agreed to leave for St Petersburg.

He served as ambassador for 18 months, and yet again his legal training proved invaluable. America and the Russians had been unable to negotiate a trade treaty, and Buchanan's diplomacy and eye for detail enabled him to push an agreement through. During his time in Russia, he took time to learn French which was the trade language of diplomacy in the nineteenth century.

On his return from St Petersburg in 1833 Buchanan quickly won a US Senate seat representing his native Pennsylvania.

In the short time he was away, slavery had become the dominant issue in US political life.

Buchanan was morally opposed to the concept of slavery, but as a keen student of the constitution, he believed that it upheld the right of southerners to own slaves and saw it as America's duty to protect slavery in the South. He was also disdainful of the abolitionist movement, viewing them as troublemakers and as a greater threat to the union than the institution of slavery.

Buchanan would remain sympathetic to the southern cause throughout his political career. So much so, that in the Senate he soon became known as a 'doughface,' which as a derogatory term used by other northern politicians for those, they believed to be sympathetic to the South and slavery.

While in the Senate, he served on and eventually chaired, the Foreign Relations committee.

He also opposed a gag rule sponsored by Senator John C. Calhoun that would have suppressed anti-slavery petitions.

Buchanan also argued for the annexation of both Texas and the Oregon.

Now firmly established in the Senate Buchanan attempted to position himself for a run for the presidency. However, he lost the nomination to James K. Polk who went on to win the general election of 1844.

As one of the most prominent Democrats in the

Senate, Buchanan was in a strong position for promotion. President James K. Polk offered him the choice of a seat on the Supreme Court or Secretary of State. As Buchan still harboured presidential ambitions, he decided on the State Department and became Secretary of State in the Polk administration.

During Buchanan's tenure, which lasted until 1849, American territory grew by more than one-third and extended across the continent for the first time. The United States annexed Texas, acquired California and much of the present-day southwest, during the Mexican American war and secured what would become the Oregon Territory after settling a boundary dispute with Great Britain.

The question of whether to extend slavery to America's newly acquired territories, as well as the moral legitimacy of slavery as an institution, became increasingly divisive issues across the United States.

In 1846, Buchanan sided with southerners who successfully blocked the Wilmot Proviso, which proposed banning slavery in any territory acquired from Mexico in the Mexican American war. Buchanan later supported the 'Compromise of 1850', a series of congressional acts that admitted California as a free state, but let the new western territories decide whether they would allow slavery before applying for statehood, a concept that became known as popular sovereignty.

Polk despite leading the country to victory in the

Mexican-American war, had always promised to serve only one term. True to his word, Polk declined to seek re-election.

James did not overtly campaign for the nomination, but did attempt to secure this behind the scenes, only to be thwarted once again when Senator Lewis Cass of Michigan was nominated.

However, the war had made heroes of its victorious generals, and one of them, Zachary Taylor, running as a Whig, won the subsequent presidential election of 1848.

With the 1848 election of President Zachary Taylor, Buchanan returned to Lancaster and his legal practice. He bought the house of Wheatland on the outskirts of Lancaster and enjoyed the life of a wealthy patrician, while maintaining a watching brief on the events in Washington.

In 1852, he was named president of the board of trustees of Franklin and Marshall College in Lancaster, and he served in this capacity until 1866.

Politics was in his blood and despite losing the nomination twice he plotted to secure the Democratic presidential nomination in 1852.

Standing in his way was Senator Stephen A. Douglas, a pugnacious and extremely able young politician from Illinois. With tremendous public speaking skills.

As the convention drew out in Baltimore, Buchanan and Douglas fought for the nomination. After 34 ballots they were still deadlocked, and party officers turned to a compromise candidate.

This was the little-known New Englander who offended no one, Franklin Pierce of New Hampshire, who secured the nomination on the forty-eighth ballot.

Buchanan had been denied the White House yet again and would never forgive Douglas.

Pierce tried to persuade Buchanan to be his running mate, but Buchanan declined and went back to Lancaster to lick his wounds and plot his next move, which would be unknown to him, across the Atlantic.

Franklin Pierce won the 1852 election, and like Polk before him he wanted to utilise the skills and experience of Buchanan in his administration.

In 1853, Pierce offered Buchanan the critical post of Minister to Great Britain where he would remain for three years. Buchanan helped draft the 1854 'Ostend Manifesto', a plan for America to acquire Cuba from Spain. Although never acted upon, the proposal generated protests from anti-slavery northerners and others in the United States who feared Cuba would become a slave state.

James acceptance of the ambassador's role would prove to be an astute move as it removed him from the American political stage just when the controversy of states' rights and slavery was about to boil over in the disastrous 'Kansas-Nebraska Act.'

In 1854, Senator Stephen Douglas of Illinois

proposed a bill to organize the territory of Nebraska, a vast area of land that would become Kansas, Nebraska, Montana and the Dakotas. Known as the 'Kansas-Nebraska Act,' the controversial bill raised the possibility that slavery could be extended into territories where it had once been banned. Its passage intensified the bitter debate over slavery in the United States, which would later explode into the Civil War. On his return to America, Buchanan now 65 and popularly known as "Old Buck," knew that 1856 would be his last chance at the presidential prize he had coveted for so long.

The 1856 Democratic National Convention was held from June 2nd to June 6th in Cincinnati, Ohio.

Buchanan was up against two main competitors for the nomination, the sitting President Franklin Pierce seeking re-election and his old enemy and nemesis from the 1852 convention, Stephen A. Douglas.

While Douglas had strong support, President Pierce's standing with the public had been severely damaged by "Bleeding Kansas,". This was the term given to the civil strife in Kansas Territory over slavery because of the 1854, Kansas-Nebraska Act, which created two new territories and allowed settlers to determine whether they would enter the Union as free states or slave states.

The fallout from 'Bleeding Kansas,' had damaged the Democrats in the midterm elections of 1854–1855. The convention was eager to seek out a compromise candidate untainted by the recent past.

This was ideal for Buchanan who had been in England as Pierce's ambassador to Britain and had avoided the controversy over 'Bleeding Kansas.'

On the first ballot, President Pierce received 122 votes, many of them from the South to Buchanan's 135, with Douglas and Lewis Cass receiving the remaining votes. By the following morning fourteen ballots had been completed, but none of the three main candidates were able to get two-thirds of the vote.

The convention now began to abandon President Pierce and others on the political centre lined up behind Douglas. Buchanan who had led from the first ballot was slowly growing his support on subsequent votes, leading Pierce to withdraw, and he instructed his delegates to back Douglas. A protracted round of voting now began, but as deadlock loomed once again, Douglas agreed to withdraw his name after receiving assurances that Buchanan would not seek re-election in 1860, allowing Buchanan to clinch the nomination on the seventeenth ballot.

Franklin Pierce became the first and only elected president, who was an active candidate for re-election, to be denied his party's nomination for a second term.

As a compromise, the vice-presidential nomination was given to John C. Breckinridge of Kentucky, who was an ally of Pierce and Douglas.

James Buchanan the son of Ramelton in Donegal was now the Democratic candidate for president and determined to win the White House.

Buchanan's two main opponents in the November 1856 presidential election, were former President Millard Fillmore who ran for the American Party also known as the Know Nothing party and John Fremont the explorer and Californian senator, who was the first ever Republican candidate, the party having been established in 1854.

Slavery was the main topic of the election with the nation split over the issue. The choice was clear, Buchanan held to his belief that slavery was an issue to be decided by individual states and territories. He also supported the Kansas-Nebraska act which allowed slavery in states where it had been previously banned by the Missouri Compromise of 1820.

His Republican opponent, John C. Fremont was unequivocal in his assertion that federal government should ban slavery in all US territories.

In the election James Buchanan received 45 per cent of the popular vote, but 174 electoral college votes, winning every slave state except for Maryland and just five states in which slavery was banned, including his home state of Pennsylvania.

Fremont took 114 votes, while Fillmore, who focused on an anti-immigration platform and did not focus on slavery, received just 8 votes.

This victory made Buchanan the first president from Pennsylvania and its only White House occupant until the 2020 victory of Joe Biden.

A buoyant Buchanan gave a pugnacious victory speech and attacked his defeated Republican rivals, branding them a dangerous group that had unfairly attacked the South.

In a more conciliatory note, he set out his main objective of his coming administration as being:

"To restore harmony to the union under a
national and conservative government."

Unfortunately, harmony would soon be in short supply. Buchanan was inaugurated on March 4th, 1857, taking the oath of office from Chief Justice Roger B. Taney. In his inaugural address, Buchanan committed himself to serving only one term, as his predecessor had done.

President Buchanan held tightly to his conviction that although slavery might be morally wrong, the Federal Government lacked the right to interfere with States' rights. In his inaugural address, Buchanan called the question of slavery in the territories "happily, a matter of but little practical importance."

Buchanan's vice president was John Breckinridge, a US congressman from Kentucky. Breckinridge was 35 when elected, making him the youngest vice president in US history.

At time of Buchanan's inauguration, the Dred Scott issue was still pending at the Supreme Court.

Dred Scott was an enslaved African American man, who had sued for his freedom, because he had lived in states and territories where slavery was illegal. Scott had won his freedom in the lower courts but after several appeals the case had reached the Supreme Court.

After his election and prior to his inauguration, Buchanan had lobbied the Supreme Court behind the scenes regarding the case. He wanted to use it as a turning point for a triumphant program of national harmony.

Two days after Buchanan's inauguration, the Supreme Court released their infamous Dred Scott decision.

The Supreme Court ruled that the US Congress had no authority to regulate slavery within states and that African American people, free or slaves, "were not and could never become citizens of the United States".

Reaction to the decision was swift and negative in the North. In a speech criticising the decision a certain Abraham Lincoln stated:

"The Republicans inculcate, that the negro is a man; that his bondage is cruelly wrong, and that the field of his oppression ought not to be enlarged. The Democrats deny his manhood; crush all sympathy for him, and…compliment themselves as Union-savers for doing so."

Frederick Douglass, the leading abolitionist, believed the Dred Scott decision would strengthen the abolitionist movement. And it did. The movement continued to grow as northerners believed the Supreme Court decision legalised slavery everywhere in the United States, even where it was currently banned.

The Dred Scott decision is considered the worst Supreme Court decision in its history. While Buchanan did not write it, he lobbied for the result and supported it, forever tainting his presidency.

As for Dred Scott himself, despite losing the case, he was released from slavery. He lived for 18 months as a free man until dying of tuberculosis. The issue of citizenship was resolved with the passage of the 14th amendment about 10 years later. Section 1 of that amendment reads "All persons born or naturalized in the United States, and subject to the jurisdiction thereof, are citizens of the United States and of the State wherein they reside."

Once in office, James Buchanan appointed a cabinet composed of both northerners and southerners and hoped to keep peace between the country's pro-slavery and anti-slavery factions. Instead, the national debate over slavery only intensified, and the new president was seen by many people as being more sympathetic to southern interests.

Buchanan is the only US president who never married. And during Buchanan's time in the White House, his niece, Harriet Lane, assumed the social duties of first lady and became a popular figure, with journalists frequently describing her as the "Fair First Lady of the Land." Although it was not an official title at the time, Harriet is now considered to be the original 'First Lady.'

Buchanan's lifelong bachelorhood after Anne Coleman's death has drawn interest and speculation. One of Buchanan's biographers, Jean Baker, suggests that he may have been celibate, if not asexual.

Buchanan also had a close relationship with William Rufus King, which became a popular target of gossip. King was an Alabama politician who briefly served as vice president under Franklin Pierce. Buchanan and King lived together in a Washington boarding house and attended social functions together, from 1834 until 1844.

As Buchanan took power, the US economy was on the brink of recession and events soon took a turn for the worse and a financial panic soon began. This started with a loss of confidence in an Ohio bank but spread as railroads failed.

Fears mounted that the federal government would

be unable to pay its debts. 1,400 state banks and more than 5,000 American businesses failed within a year, and unemployment was accompanied by protest meetings across the land.

Buchanan believed that speculation was the root cause of the panic and decided against an interventionist policy. He concentrated on reform and hoped the market would do the rest.

While the overall economic downturn was brief, the recovery was unequal, and the lasting impact was more political than economic. No recovery was evident in the northern parts of the United States for a year and a half, and the full impact did not dissipate until the Civil War.

While a financial panic is a major problem to deal with this was soon to be just one of Buchanan's worries and a comedy of errors resulted in what would become known as the 'Utah War.'

Sensitive to Republican charges that Democrats favoured the "twin relics of barbarism—polygamy and slavery," President James Buchanan moved quickly after his inauguration to find a non-Mormon governor for Utah. This decision resulted in a costly, disruptive and unnecessary confrontation between the Mormon people in Utah Territory and the government and army of the United States. It resulted from misunderstandings that transformed a simple decision to give Utah Territory a new governor into a year-long comedy of errors with tragic potential.

Influenced by reports from Judge W. W. Drummond and other former territorial officials, he and his cabinet decided that the Mormons would resist the replacement of Governor Brigham Young.

At the same time, the contract for the mail service from Washington to Utah was cancelled and not renewed.

A 2,500-man military force was ordered to accompany the new Governor Alfred Cumming to Great Salt Lake City. While a letter stating this intent was written it was not sent and in the absence of formal notification of administration intentions, Young and other Mormon leaders interpreted the army's coming as religious persecution and prepared for conflict.

The Mormon governor Brigham Young declared martial law and deployed the local militia, the Nauvoo Legion, to delay the troops. Harassing actions included burning three supply trains and driving hundreds of government cattle to the Great Salt Lake valley. The "scorched earth" tactics forced Albert Sidney Johnston's Utah Expedition and the accompanying civil officials to improvise winter quarters at Camp Scott and Eckelsville, near burned-out Fort Bridger, while the nation now feared the worst.

Brigham Young hoped for a diplomatic solution and sent an appeal to Thomas L. Kane, the influential Pennsylvanian who had for ten years been a friend of the Mormons. Communications and personal problems delayed Kane's approach to Buchanan, and not until after Christmas did, he receive permission to go to Utah as an unofficial emissary. He reached Salt Lake City late in February, via Panama and California, and found the Mormon leadership ready for peace.

On 23rd March, Young announced that the time had come to implement the "Sebastopol" policy, a plan named after a strategic Russian retreat during the Crimean War. All the Mormon settlements in northern Utah would be abandoned and prepared for burning. Initially conceived as permanent, the evacuation began to be seen by the Mormon leadership as tactical and temporary as soon as word came that Kane was bringing Cumming to Salt Lake City without the army.

Despite this, 30,000 people moved fifty miles or more to Provo and the other towns in central and southern Utah. There they remained in shared and improvised housing while the outcome of the 'Utah War,' was being determined. Kane and Cumming came to the Mormon capital in early April. Young immediately surrendered the gubernatorial title and soon established a comfortable working relationship with his successor, the costly and bizarrely comical conflict was finally over.

The debate around slavery raged throughout Buchanan's presidency. The controversial Kansas Nebraska Act of 1854 created the Kansas Territory and allowed settlers there to decide whether to allow slavery. This led to violence between free soil (anti-slavery) and pro slavery settlers.

On May 21st, 1856, hundreds of men crossed the border between Missouri and Kansas and entered the town of Lawrence, setting fire to buildings and destroying the printing press of an abolitionist newspaper.

While no one was killed, the Republican press labelled this event as the "Sack of Lawrence," which officially ignited a guerrilla war between pro-slavery settlers aided by border raiders and their anti-slavery counterparts.

The violence surrounding 'Bleeding Kansas,' even made its way to Washington D.C.

On May 19th and 20th, 1856, on the Senate floor, Senator Charles Sumner (Republican-Massachusetts) gave an impassioned, yet carefully rehearsed speech entitled "the Crime Against Kansas." In this speech, Sumner denounced popular sovereignty and described 'Bleeding Kansas,' as "the rape of a virgin territory, compelling it to the hateful embrace of slavery." Sumner accused Senators Stephen Douglas (Democrat-Illinois) and Andrew Pickens Butler (Democrat-South Carolina) of this crime and claimed they were personally responsible for the horrific crimes perpetrated in Kansas as they co-authored the Kansas Nebraska Act.

Sumner also made lurid personal and insulting remarks against the two senators.

Butler was absent for Sumner's speech; however, his cousin Representative Preston Brooks (Democrat-South Carolina) was present for these remarks. On May 22nd, 1856, in retaliation for the degrading remarks made against his cousin, Brooks entered the Senate chambers and accosted Sumner at his desk, beating him unconscious with a cane!

Buchanan hoped the admission of Kansas as a state would remove the issue of slavery in the territories from public attention. Buchanan urged Congress to accept a constitution drawn up by a pro-slavery group meeting in Lecompton, though the pro-slavery men were outnumbered four to one in the territory. His proposal angered Republicans and even members of his own party and Congress refused.

Buchanan backed the 1858 English bill, which offered Kansas immediate statehood and vast public lands in exchange for accepting the Lecompton Constitution. In August 1858, the people of Kansas strongly rejected the Lecompton Constitution in a referendum.

Kansas did not achieve statehood until 1861, remaining a sore reminder of the fractured nation.

In 1858, Buchanan ordered the Paraguay expedition to punish Paraguay for firing on the USS Water Witch, and the expedition resulted in a Paraguayan apology and payment of compensation.

The division between northern and southern Democrats helped the Republicans to win a majority in the

House during the mid-term elections and allowed them to block most of Buchanan's agenda.

In October 1859, abolitionist John Brown tried unsuccessfully to stage a massive slave uprising by raiding the federal arsenal at Harpers Ferry, Virginia (now West Virginia). After Brown was convicted of treason and hanged, hostilities between the North and South continued to escalate.

By the end of 1859, the federal government was in near paralysis. Republicans and northern Democrats dominated the House. Southern votes in the Senate and presidential vetoes blocked any legislation passed by the House. The North was still depressed following the Panic of 1857, and John Brown's anti-slavery raid on the federal arsenal at Harpers Ferry brought sectional tension to a boil.

In March 1860, the US House of Representatives formed the 'Covode Committee, to discuss impeaching Buchanan. They accused him and some in his administration of alleged impeachable offenses, such as bribery and extortion of representatives.

The committee, three Republicans and two Democrats, was accused by Buchanan's supporters of being nakedly partisan; they charged its chairman, Republican Representative John Covode, with acting on a personal grudge from a disputed land grant designed to benefit Covode's railroad company.

Despite their best efforts, the committee was unable to establish grounds for impeaching Buchanan.

A majority report issued on June 17th, did however allege corruption and abuse of power among members of his cabinet.

The report also included accusations from Republicans that Buchanan had attempted to bribe members of Congress, in connection with the pro-slavery Lecompton Constitution of Kansas. The Democrats pointed out that evidence was scarce but did not refute the allegations.

Buchanan claimed to have "passed triumphantly through this ordeal" with complete vindication.

Republicans later distributed thousands of copies of the Covode Committee report throughout the nation as campaign material during the 1860 presidential election.

Upholding a promise, he had made in his inaugural address, James Buchanan did not seek re-election in 1860. At their national convention, the Democrats were split over their choice for a nominee, with northern Democrats selecting Buchanan's old rival Senator Stephen Douglas of Illinois and southern Democrats picking Vice President Breckinridge. Buchanan refused to ensure one unified candidate due to his long-standing hatred of Douglas. This would result in two Democratic candidates and a split in the Democratic vote, handing the election to the Republicans.

The Republicans chose Abraham Lincoln (Though his name did not even appear on the ballot in any southern state), and the Constitutional Union party nominated John Bell. Lincoln won 180 electoral votes and a little less than 40 percent of the popular vote, while his challengers garnered a combined total of electoral 123 votes.

On December 20th, 1860, in response to Lincoln's victory, South Carolina seceded from the Union. By the time of Lincolns inauguration on March 4th, 1861, six more states, Mississippi, Florida, Alabama, Georgia, Louisiana and Texas had also seceded and formed the Confederate States of America.

While still president, Buchanan asserted that these states did not have the right to secede; however, he also believed he had no constitutional power to stop them.

During Buchanan's remaining months in office, he made repeated but unsuccessful efforts to compromise with the secessionists. Early in 1861, Buchanan finally took stronger measures to uphold federal authority. He sent an unarmed merchant ship with reinforcements and supplies to relieve the beleaguered garrison at Fort Sumter, in Charleston Harbor. When South Carolina batteries drove the ship away, he refused to evacuate the fort, though he made no further efforts to resupply it.

This stalemate only briefly averted the outbreak of war. On his final day as President on March 4th, 1861, he remarked to the incoming Lincoln, "If you are as happy in entering the White House as I shall feel on returning to Wheatland, you are a happy man."

On April 12th, 1861, a little over a month after Buchanan left office and retired to Wheatland, Confederate forces fired on Fort Sumter in South Carolina and the Civil War began. Despite his previous support of states' rights and the southern right to slavery Buchanan supported the Union cause.

James Buchanan never married and is the only US President not to do so. He lived with his "little family," his two wards, niece Harriet Lane and nephew James Buchanan Henry.

He spent most of his time in retirement defending his administration and his own record in response to public criticism and blame for the war that many referred to as 'Buchanan's War.'

This defence resulted in his memoirs, published in 1867 'Mr Buchanan's Administration on the Eve of the Rebellion'. In May 1868 he became ill with a cold, which quickly worsened, and he died at his beloved Wheatland home outside Lancaster, Pennsylvania, on June 1st, 1868, at the age of 77.

When reviewing the life of James Buchanan, I was left with the feeling that two things drove him. The first was a burning desire to become president and the second was his passionate belief as a lawyer in the US constitution and the union.

While he certainly achieved the first, that success

nearly resulted in the destruction of the union he so loved. While morally opposed to slavery, his support of the rights of southern states, undoubtably emboldened them in their pursuit of secession. His feud with Stephen Douglas also weakened the Democratic party and inadvertently ushered in the presidency of Abraham Lincoln, who would save the union and end slavery.

CHAPTER 4
CHESTER A. ARTHUR
THE ACCIDENTAL PRESIDENT

While John F. Kennedy was the first Roman Catholic Irish American President, many others who held that office could claim Irish heritage, including Chester Alan Arthur, whose father was born in Dreen Cullybacky County Antrim, a Presbyterian with Scot's Irish decent.

Chester A. Arthur was a lawyer, soldier and politician who was elected the 20th Vice president of the United States but who became Americas 21st president in September 1881. This was when President James A Garfield was shot by Charles Julius Guiteau and died two months later from medical negligence and infections related to the wounds.

Chester Arthur was born on October 5th, 1829, in Fairfield Vermont. His father was William Arthur who had immigrated to from Ireland to Canada in 1819.

Chester's mother was Malvina Stone whose grandfather had fought with the Continental army during the American war of Independence.

William Arthur had graduated from college in Belfast and then decided to make a new life for himself in Canada. He met his future wife Malvina when he was a young teacher in Dunham Quebec near the Vermont border. They married in April 1861, and they would go on to have nine children.

Baby Chester was the fifth of these nine children and named after the Dr who delivered him, a family friend by the name of Chester Abell.

William Arthur with a growing family left teaching to study law but then decided to become a Presbyterian minister in the Free Will Baptists. As a Minister, William became an outspoken opponent of slavery and a committed abolitionist.

This stance made him unpopular with some members of his congregations and may have contributed to the nomadic lifestyle of the family as they moved to churches in several towns in Vermont and upstate New York. The family would eventually put down roots and settle for good in the Schenectady area of New York State. The name "Schenectady" is derived from the Mohawk word skahnéhtati, meaning "beyond the pines".

The movement of the Arthur family would have ramifications for Chester in later years. As you will see, the presidency of Chester Arthur had many parallels with the tenure of modern office holders such as Trump and Obama.

In common with Barrack Obama the 44th holder of the presidency, Chester was also accused of not being born in America.

The Arthur family's frequent moves as William upped sticks and took his wife and young family to a series of new parishes, would later spawn accusations that Chester Arthur was not a natural-born citizen of the United States. When Arthur was nominated for vice president in 1880, a New York attorney and political opponent, Arthur P. Hinman, tried to spread a ridiculous rumour that Arthur was born in Ireland and did not come to the United States until he was fourteen years old.

This was obviously ludicrous, but if true, opponents might have argued that Arthur was ineligible for the vice presidency under the United States constitution's natural-born-citizen clause.

When Hinman's original story did not take root, he persisted and spread a new rumour that Arthur was born in Canada. Whilst this was at least a bit more credible, given the Arthur families ties to Quebec, this claim, was also quickly shown to be false. I guess the message here is that fake news is not just a modern-day political tactic.

Anyway, back to the growing Chester Arthur who

was home schooled before enrolling in the local school where one of his first teachers said of him that he was:

"Frank and open in manners and genial in disposition."

Source: Reeves, Thomas C. (1975). Gentleman Boss: The Life of Chester A. Arthur

It was now that a young Chester Arthur developed his first political leanings and began to favour the Whig Party which was one of the two major parties (the other being the Democrats) in the United States between the late 1830s and the early 1850s prior to the emergence of the Republican party. Passionate about politics, a young Chester even participated in a brawl between young Whigs supporting their candidate, Henry Clay against fellow students who supported the Democratic candidate and future president, James K. Polk.

Proud of his Irish roots, Arthur also supported the Fenian Brotherhood, an Irish republican organisation founded in America. He showed this support to fellow students by defiantly wearing a green coat.

Chester enrolled at Schenectady's Union College in 1845. As a senior, he was president of the debating society and was elected as the college president of Phi Beta Kappa. The Phi Beta Kappa society is the oldest academic honour society in the United States, and is often described as its most prestigious one. Phi Beta Kappa aims to promote and advocate excellence in the liberal arts and sciences, and to induct the most outstanding students of arts and sciences at American colleges and universities.

During his winter breaks, he served as a teacher at a school in Schaghticoke in Rensselaer County New York.

After graduating in 1848, Arthur returned to Schaghticoke and became a full-time teacher but soon began to pursue a career in the legal profession. He had clear goals, he was determined to be a lawyer soon and live a wonderful independent life. In 1854 he passed the bar exam and left to practice law in New York City. He was on his way to achieving these goals.

Now aged 24, Chester was a junior partner at the Culver, Parker and Arthur law firm where Arthur handled and worked mostly with cases concerning the African American community.

In his second year with the firm, he successfully represented Lizzie Jennings, who was forcibly removed from a streetcar in 1854 because of her skin colour. Chester and his client sued a Brooklyn streetcar company for forcing her off a car reserved for whites.

When Chester Arthur defended Lizzie Jennings, he earned a lot of money from the public transportation company and from the court. More importantly, he defended the rights of African American people and made it a legal agreement never to discriminate against them again on New York public transportation.

Chester was heavily influenced by his father's abolitionist views and he also successfully pleaded the case of a slave who sued for his freedom on the grounds that his master had brought him temporarily to the free state of New York. When he won the case, he drew the attention of prominent law firms who wanted his service, and more importantly he gained connections to several high-profile politicians.

Now a successful lawyer and a rising star in New York legal circles in 1856, Arthur met the woman who would be the love of his life, Ellen Herndon, who was the daughter of William Lewis Herndon, a Virginia naval officer and one of the United States Navy's outstanding explorers and seamen.

In 1851 Herndon led a United States expedition to the Valley of the Amazon, and prepared a report published in 1854 and distributed widely as 'Exploration of the Valley of the Amazon'.

The young couple were soon engaged to be married.

Chester had a thirst for adventure and decided to start a new law partnership with his great friend Henry D. Gardiner. The young men travelled to Kansas with a plan to set up a law firm in the state.

Kansas in the 1850s was in turmoil with a battle between pro and anti-slavery factions.

The Abolitionist Arthur was firmly aligned to the

anti-slavery movement. However, the frontier life far from the genteel pleasures of New York did not agree with Chester and his partner and the pair soon returned east. On his return tragedy struck Chester's Fiancé Ellen, when her father was lost at sea in the sinking of SS Central America. Survivors of the disaster reported last seeing Commander Herndon in full uniform, standing by the wheelhouse with his hand on the rail, hat off and in his hand, with his head bowed in prayer as the ship gave a lurch and went down.

The S.S. Central America was given the nickname "Ship of Gold" for her famous cargo which was tons of gold from the San Francisco mint and various other gold coins, ingots, gold dust, and bullion from the California gold rush. The sinking of the S.S. Central America has been described as the greatest economic catastrophe in US maritime history, contributing to the economic panic of 1857 and leading to a severe US recession.

In 1859 Chester and Ellen finally married at Calvary Episcopal church in Manhattan. The couple would go on to have three children.

After his marriage, Arthur devoted his efforts to building his law practice, but also found time to engage in Republican party politics. In addition, he indulged his military interest by becoming Judge Advocate General heading the legal arm of the United States Army for the Second Brigade of the New York militia.

As the threat of civil war raged, Arthur was

appointed by the New York Republican Governor Edwin D. Morgan to the post of engineer in chief on the states military staff. This was a purely political post and didn't in any way suggest Arthur had any engineering experiences or prowess. This was in recognition of his political loyalty and Morgan had picked out Chester Arthur as a man to watch and nurture in the Republican party.

However, in April 1861 when the cold war between the states heated up and hostilities began, Arthurs logistical and organisational skills were recognised and in demand as the New York leadership were faced with the task of raising and equipping an army to help defend the union.

Arthur was commissioned as a brigadier general and assigned to the state militia's quartermaster department. He was so efficient at housing and outfitting the troops that poured into New York City, that he was promoted to inspector general of the state militia in March 1862, and then to quartermaster general 4 months later in July.

Despite being desk-bound, Chester Arthur did have several opportunities to serve at the front line. The first came when the 9th New York volunteer infantry regiment made him their commander electing him with the rank of Colonel. Chester turned down this opportunity at the request of Governor Morgan who judged him too valuable to the war effort in New York.

The second opportunity came when he turned down the command of four New York City regiments who had been reorganised as the Metropolitan Brigade, again this was at the request of his mentor Governor Morgan.

The closest Arthur came to the carnage of the front-line, was on an inspection trip, when he reviewed New York troops near Fredericksburg, Virginia, in May 1862, shortly after forces under Major General Irvin McDowell seized the town during the Peninsula campaign.

In the summer of 1862, Arthur and representatives of northern governors met with Secretary of State William H. Seward in New York to coordinate the raising of additional troops and spent the next few months enlisting New York's quota of 120,000 men.

While Chester Arthur was recognised as an excellent bureaucrat with a zeal for organisation, his post as quartermaster general was a political appointment.

Despite his undoubted successes, when Governor Horatio Seymour, a Democrat, was elected, Arthur a prominent Republican was relieved of his militia duties in January 1863. Arthur was keen to contribute to the war effort and when the Republicans retook the Governorship of New York in 1864, Arthur petitioned to be reappointed as quarter master general.

However, the new Governor Reuben Fento whilst a Republican was from a different wing of the party to

Arthur and had already committed to appointing another candidate.

A disappointed Arthur finally left the union army having attained the rank of brigadier general in the New York militia to return to his legal practice.

Arthur returned to being a lawyer, and with the help of influential contacts made in the military and the Republican party, he and the firm of Arthur & Gardiner flourished. Even as his professional life improved, however, Arthur and his wife experienced a personal tragedy as their only child, William, died suddenly that year at the age of two.

The couple took their son's death hard, and when they had another son, Chester Alan Jr., in 1864, they lavished attention on him. They also had a daughter, Ellen, in 1871. Both children survived to adulthood.

The election of Arthur's patron ex-Governor Morgan, to the United States Senate also helped his political and business prospects improve. Morgan leaned toward the conservative wing of the New York Republican party, as did the men who collaborated with him in the organization, including Roscoe Conkling (an eloquent Utica Congressman and rising star in the party) who also recognised the political and organisational skills of Chester Arthur.

As Conkling's star rose in the Republican party, he would play a major role in helping Arthur rise on his coat tails.

Arthurs law firm was hired by Thomas Murphy, a Republican politician to represent his interests in Washington. Murphy was a hatter who sold goods to the union army and who profited from the Civil War. The two became close friends within the New York Republican party. In the presidential election of 1864, they worked together raising funds from Republicans in New York. They were rewarded for this effort by both attending the second inauguration of Abraham Lincoln in 1865.

Whilst a prominent member of the New York Republican party, Arthur was recognised more as a man of organisation than ideas. This was not unusual where leaders of the political factions valued loyalty and hard work for the party machine, far more than political ideas that could eclipse their own.

In 1866, Arthur unsuccessfully lobbied for the lucrative patronage post as naval officer at the New York Custom House. Undaunted, he continued his law practice. He also expanded his role in politics, where in 1867. He became a member of the prestigious Century Club a private social, arts, and dining club in New York City, founded in 1847.

Chester Arthur had for many years benefited from the patronage of Ex New York Governor and now US Senator Edwin D Morgan. However, a new power was installed in the New York Republican party when

Roscoe Conkling was elected to the United States Senate in 1867.

Conkling help Arthur become chairman of the New York City Republican executive committee in 1868.

Chester was now devoted to his political career but climbing up the ladder in politics involves sacrifices. Long nights in smoky rooms were beginning to take a toll on his marriage, as his wife started to resent his absence every night from the family home.

New York Republicans led by the Conkling machine, of which Arthur was now a key part, were solidly behind General Ulysses S. Grant's run for the presidency. Arthur threw himself enthusiastically into Grants election campaign.

Despite losing New York State, in part due to the efforts of the Democratic Tammany Hall operation, Grant defeated his opponent former New York Governor Horatio Seymour in the national vote. The new President Grant would not forget the help Arthur had given his campaign.

Arthur began to devote more of his time to politics and less to law, and in 1869 he became counsel to the New York City tax commission. This was a political appointment gifted to him when the Republicans controlled the state legislature.

The role came with a salary of $10,000 and politics was finally starting to pay for Chester Arthur.

He remained in position until the Democrats

regained control in 1870 and Tammany Hall allocated the job to one of their own.

In 1871, President Grant wanted to repay Arthur for his help in his election campaign and offered him the role of commissioner of internal revenue. Arthur though flattered declined the role, he had his eyes on a far more lucrative appointment and he would not have to wait too long for it to come along.

Since Grants election, Senator Conkling had full control over the New York patronage system, including the financially lucrative Custom House at the Port of New York.

The key position was the collectors of taxes role, which was responsible for hiring hundreds of workers to collect the tariffs due at the United States' busiest port. These positions were given to supporters of which-ever political machine was in power at the time. These employees were then required to make political contri-butions (known as "assessments") back to the party machine, which made the job a highly coveted political position.

In 1870, at Rosco Conkling's bidding, President Grant appointed Arthurs old friend and political ally Thomas Murphy as collector of taxes.

Murphy had a reputation as a war profiteer and strangely for a Republican he was closely aligned to the corrupt Democratic Tammany Hall organisation. This made him unacceptable to a large percentage of the

New York Republican party. He also began to act in a highly partisan manner, sacking workers who were loyal to Senator Reuben Fenton's wing of the party and replacing them with supporters of Senator Conklin. Fenton was a sworn enemy of Conkling who now controlled the state party.

The calls for Murphy's removal became louder and louder, so in December 1871, President Grant asked for his resignation. The President then offered the position to two others who both declined, but each recommended Chester Arthur.

For his strong support of the Republican Party as well as Ulysses S. Grant's candidature for president, Chester A. Arthur was eventually rewarded with the position of collector of the Port of New York. The New York Times said of his nomination:

"His name very seldom rises to the surface of metropolitan life and yet moving like a mighty undercurrent this man during the last 10 years has done more to mould the course of the Republican Party in this state than any other one man in the country."

Source: Reeves, Thomas C. (1975). Gentleman Boss: The Life of Chester A. Arthur

The Senate urged on by Conkling, confirmed

Arthur's appointment. As collector Arthur now controlled nearly a thousand jobs and he had the position for which he had waited.

Nominally Arthur's salary as controller was initially $6,500, but senior customs employees were compensated additionally by the "moiety" system, which awarded them a percentage of the cargoes seized and fines levied on importers who attempted to evade the import tariffs.

This meant that his income was in fact nearer to $50,000 which was more than the president's salary! Arthur now had the means to enjoy a fashionable and lavish lifestyle.

However, Arthur was no Thomas Murphy, and his reputation grew rather than become tarnished in the role. It was said that Arthur was one of the fairer collectors in an era of rampant corruption and nepotism.

This was in part, because Arthur had no need to fire many staff as Murphy had already flooded the roles with supporters of Conkling the leader of Arthurs faction in the Republican party.

He was also popular within the Republican party as he efficiently collected campaign donations from the staff and recruited party leaders' friends into jobs as positions became available.

While Arthur had a much better reputation than Murphy, the system was still rotten and many reformers in both parties rightly still criticised the patronage structure and the 'moiety system', as inherently corrupt.

To try and stem a rising tide of reform within the Republican party Arthur renamed the financial deductions from employees as "voluntary contributions" in 1872, but the concept remained, and the party continued to benefit from the funds raised for campaigning and the added benefit of controlling government jobs.

A spirit of reform was sweeping the Republican party and later in 1872, reform-minded Republicans voted against President Grant, but he was re-elected in spite of their opposition.

The drive for reform whilst temporarily halted, was gaining momentum and demands for civil service reform continued to chip away at Conkling's patronage machine.

In 1874, Custom House employees were found to have improperly assessed fines against an importing company as a way to increase their own incomes, and Congress reacted, repealing the 'moiety system' and placing all staff, including Arthur, on set salaries.

This reform meant that Arthurs salary dropped from $50,000 to $12,000 a year, a dramatic drop, but still more than his nominal boss, the Secretary of the Treasury.

Arthur's four-year term as collector expired on December 10th, 1875, and Roscoe Conkling, then among the most powerful politicians in Washington, arranged his protégé's reappointment by President Grant.

In 1876, Senator Conkling was considering a run for the presidency himself, but the selection of reformer Rutherford

B. Hayes by the 1876 Republican national convention ended the presidential dreams of the Republican machine boss and would have dramatic ramifications for Arthur.

Chester and his New York party operation campaigned enthusiastically for Hayes.

The results of the election remain among the most disputed ever. The Democratic candidate Samuel J. Tilden, the governor of New York outpolled Hayes in the popular vote. After a first count of votes, Tilden had won 184 electoral votes to Hayes's 165, with 20 votes from four states unresolved. In Florida, Louisiana, and South Carolina, each party reported that its candidate had won the state, while in Oregon, one elector was replaced after being declared illegal for being an "elected or appointed official". The question of who should have been awarded these electoral votes is the source of the continued controversy.

An informal deal was struck to resolve the dispute, the Compromise of 1877, which awarded all 20 electoral votes to Hayes. In return for the Democrats' acquiescence to Hayes' election, the Republicans agreed to withdraw federal troops from the southern states, ending 'Reconstruction,' which was the hangover from the end of the Civil War.

President Hayes finally took office with a pledge to reform the patronage system.

Conkling's machine in New York was the primary target and a commission was set up under Arthurs old colleague John Jay, to investigate the New York Custom House. Its initial finding was that not unsurprisingly that the Custom House was overstaffed with political appointments, and that 20% of the employees could be sacked. Arthur was ordered to make the reductions. In a stalling tactic and to save face, he appointed a committee of Custom House workers to determine where the cuts were to be made and, after a written protest, carried them out.

Despite this cooperation the Jay Commission issued a second report critical of Arthur and other Custom House employees urging a complete reorganisation from top to bottom. Arthur's position was now under direct attack.

In another reforming act President Hayes issued an executive order that barred federal office holders from: "...taking part in the management of political organizations, caucuses, conventions, or election campaigns." Arthur and his subordinates at the Customs House, naval officer Alonzo B. Cornell and surveyor George H. Sharpe, refused to obey the president's order.

To avoid a scandal and allow Arthur to save face Hayes offered Arthur the consulship in Paris in exchange for his resignation, but Arthur refused.

The die was now cast against Arthur and in September 1877, President Hayes demanded the resignations of all three men, which they refused to give.

With Conkling's support, Arthur was able to resist Hayes for a time, but in July 1878, Hayes took advantage of a Congressional recess to fire him and Cornell, replacing them with the recess appointment of his own nominees Edwin Merritt and Silas Burt.

Hayes cognisant of Arthurs prominent position in the Republican party again offered him the position of consul general in Paris. Again, Arthur refused.

Conkling opposed the confirmation of Merritt and Burt when the Senate reconvened in February 1879, but Merritt was approved by a vote of 31–25, as was Burt by 31–19, giving Hayes the significant civil service reform victory, he craved.

Despite returning to his law firm, politics was Arthurs true passion and he set to work campaigning for the election of Edward Cooper as New York City mayor. In September 1879, Arthur became chairman of the New York State Republican executive committee, a post in which he served until October 1881.

Senator Conkling and Chester Arthur took Hayes' actions against them as a blatant announcement of conflict and war. Arthur and Conkling then decided to reclaim control not only over the port of New York but the Republican party and decided to support the re-election of former President Grant.

They began by working in the 1879 state elections to ensure that their slate of Republican nominees, all people loyal to Conkling would be elected. These would become known as the 'Stalwarts.'

The Stalwart slate was successful partly because of a splintering of the Democratic vote.

Arthur and the Conkling machine had delivered a crushing defeat and sharp rebuke to President Hayes and their Republican party rivals. However, this victory was short lived when Arthurs wife Ellen died suddenly at the age of 42. What made it so devastating for Chester was that he was not with her when she died, he was away overnight in Albany on Republican party business. Arthur was devastated, he would never remarry, guilty at how he had neglected his wife in pursuit of his political career.

President Hayes declined to seek re-election in 1880, true to his earlier pledge to only serve one term.

Conkling and his fellow Stalwarts, including Arthur, wished to follow up their 1879 success at the 1880 Republican national convention by securing the nomination for their ally, ex-President US Grant.

Their opponents in the Republican party, known as 'Half-Breeds,' supported James G. Blaine. The main issue that divided the Stalwarts and the Half-Breeds was political patronage.

Blaine a senator from Maine was like President

Hayes a firm supporter of civil service reform and wanted to end the patronage system.

The convention was deadlocked after thirty-six ballots and neither Blaine nor ex-President Grant could command a majority of delegates. It was time for a compromise candidate and delegates turned to an ex civil war general and Ohio congressman James A Garfield who was not a member of either faction.

Garfield and his supporters knew they would face a difficult election without the support of the New York Stalwarts and decided to offer one of them the vice-presidential nomination.

Levi P. Morton, the first choice of Garfield's supporters, consulted with Conkling, who advised him to decline, which he did.

Garfield then approached Arthur, and Conkling again advised him to also reject the nomination, believing the Republicans would lose the general election. Arthur however thought otherwise and accepted the nomination.

According to a purported eyewitness account by journalist William C. Hudson, Conkling and Arthur argued, with Arthur telling Conkling:

"The office of the Vice-President is a greater honour than I ever dreamed of attaining."

Source: Reeves, Thomas C. (1975). Gentleman
Boss: The Life of Chester A. Arthur.

Arthur was now the preferred vice-presidential candidate to keep the competing interests of the various Republican Party factions from destroying the party. The public, however, responded coldly to Arthur's nomination, viewing the former custom house tax collector as unqualified for the nation's second-highest office.

The election of 1880 was a battle between two civil war generals, James Garfield for the Republicans and Winfield Scott Hancock the Democratic candidate.

It was expected to be a close election, as Hancock was a popular candidate who had avoided taking any definitive positions on many issues, which meant he started out having not offended any of the key electoral segments.

The Republicans as they had done for many years focussed their campaign on warning the country that returning Democrats to the White House would undo the victory of the civil war and reward secessionists.

However, the war was now over 15 years, and with two former union army generals as candidates it was a campaign tactic that was losing traction with the electorate.

The Republicans now concentrated on the economy and claimed that Democrats if successful would lower

Americas protective tariff, which would allow cheaper manufactured goods to be imported from Europe, and thereby put thousands out of work.

This argument resonated in the key swing states of Indiana and New York with many employed in manufacturing. The Democratic candidate, Hancock sealed his fate when he tried to remain neutral on the tariff policy, which made him appear uninformed about the increasing important issue.

In the late 1800's election candidates did not normally personally campaign, instead leaving this to key surrogates. However, Arthur as the New York State Republican chairman played an important role in fund raising. This money proved key in a close election and the Republicans went on to win New York State by 20,000. In comparison they would only win the national vote by just 7,018 votes. The electoral college vote was however more decisive, with Garfield defeating Hancock 214 to 155. James A. Garfield was now president, while Chester A. Arthur, had become the 20th vice president of the United States.

Despite the election victory, close though it was, the Republican party was still split between the pro-reform Half Breed faction now led by President Garfield and the Stalwarts led by Arthurs mentor Senator Roscoe Conkling. As vice president Arthur tried to convince the new president to allocate cabinet and senior positions to his fellow New York Stalwarts. Instead, Garfield appointed James Gillespie Blaine, Conkling's bitter rival as his Secretary of State.

Garfield had never been close to his new vice president, only agreeing to his nomination to balance the ticket and avoid civil war in the party. Now in power, Arthur found himself detached from the centre of decision making. He didn't help himself when shortly before inauguration day, he made an ill-judged speech, in front of reporters suggesting the election in Indiana, a key swing state, may have been won by Republicans through illegal machinations. A strange thing to do and done in a pique of frustration at being frozen out of the administration before even taking office.

President Garfield and his now clearly estranged vice president took office on March 4th, 1881.

Arthurs relationship with Garfield deteriorated further when his mentor Senator Conkling and his fellow New York colleague, Senator Thomas C. Platt, resigned in protest of Garfield's continuing opposition to their Stalwart faction.

With the Senate in recess, Arthur had no duties in Washington and returned to New York.

He accompanied Conkling to Albany , where the former senator was campaigning for a quick return to the Senate, hell bent on defeating the Garfield administration.

While in Albany on July 2nd, Arthur learned that Garfield had been shot by a would-be assassin, while the president still lived his life hung in the balance. Arthurs world was about to change forever.

Just four months into his presidential term James Garfield had been shot by an assassin Charles J. Guiteau.

On the morning of July 2nd, 1881, James A. Garfield arrived at the Baltimore and Potomac train station for a much-needed holiday. His wife had recently contracted a near-fatal case of malaria. With the first lady now on the mend, Garfield was eager to escape the sweltering capital for a summer trip to New England, where he planned to give a speech at his alma mater, Williams College. Along with his two teenage sons and Secretary of State James G. Blaine, he had left the White House and taken a carriage ride to the station entrance near the national mall. Like most presidents up to that point, he was not accompanied by bodyguards or a security detail.

As Garfield's carriage pulled up outside the Baltimore and Potomac station, Charles Guiteau paced the waiting room inside, ready to fulfill what he believed was a mission from God. For weeks, the 39-year-old had stalked the president across Washington, patiently waiting for a chance to gun him down. Family members and acquaintances had long suspected that Guiteau was insane, but he had planned the crime with chilling precision. He had conducted target practice with an ivory-handled .44 calibre pistol which was specially purchased because Guiteau thought it would look nice in a museum one day. Guiteau had even tried to take a tour of the district jail, which he assumed would be his new home after he was arrested. In his pocket Guiteau carried a letter addressed to the White House.

"The president's tragic death was a sad necessity," it read, "but it will unite the Republican Party and save the Republic. Life is a fleeting dream, and it matters little when one goes."

At around 9:20 a.m., President Garfield entered the station alongside Secretary Blaine, who had offered to escort him to his train. As the men strode through the waiting room, Guiteau snuck up behind them and drew his pistol.

Guiteau fired two shots at the president from point blank range. The first bullet only grazed Garfield's right arm, causing him to bellow "My God! What is this?" The second shot was more accurate, striking Garfield in the lower back and knocking him to the floor.

Guiteau proclaimed to onlookers: "I am a Stalwart, and Arthur will be President!"

Within minutes, 10 different doctors had arrived to examine the stricken president and try to locate the second bullet. Though no one knew it at the time, the slug had missed the president's arteries and vital organs and embedded itself near his pancreas. It was a survivable injury, but the army of well-meaning physicians only worsened the damage by using their unsterilized fingers and instruments to probe the wound, introducing germs, and potentially causing an infection.

As the summer dragged on, newspapers printed a steady stream of medical updates on Garfield. The 49-year-old president had rallied in the first few days after the shooting, but his condition worsened after his doctor, D. Willard Bliss, administered heavy doses of quinine, morphine, and alcohol, which brought on bouts of vomiting that left him weak and emaciated. Bliss also conducted repeated medical probes in a futile attempt to locate the second bullet. In August, he even enlisted the help of telephone inventor Alexander Graham Bell, who used a crude metal detector called an "induction balance" to search for the slug. The machine had worked perfectly in tests, but the screening failed due to interference from metal springs on the president's bed. To make matters worse, Bell was only permitted to search the right side of Garfield's body, where Bliss incorrectly believed the bullet was lodged.

While the president was enduring a slow lingering death, the political system was also crippled.

There was confusion over the presidential succession, and no one was now sure who was in charge.

When Conkling resigned from the Senate it had adjourned without electing a president pro tempore, who would normally follow Arthur in the succession.

Arthur was reluctant to be seen acting as president while Garfield lived, and for the next two months there was a void of authority in the executive office, with Garfield too weak to perform his duties, and Arthur reluctant to assume them.

By September, a massive infection (most likely caused by his medical treatment) had left Garfield with a persistent fever and abscesses over his entire body. He was taken to a cottage on the Jersey shore in the hope that the cool sea air would revive him but died on the night of September 19th, 1881. He had been president for just 200 days.

Arthur was at his Lexington home when he learned that James Garfield had finally died.

Judge John R. Brady of the New York Supreme Court administered the presidential oath of office in Arthur's home at 2:15 a.m. on September 20th. Later that day he took a train to Long Branch to pay his respects to Garfield and to leave a card of sympathy for his wife, afterwards returning to New York City.

On September 21st, he returned to Long Branch to take part in Garfield's funeral, and then joined the funeral train to Washington. Before leaving New York, he ensured the presidential line of succession by preparing and mailing to the White House a proclamation calling for a Senate special session. This step ensured that the Senate had legal authority to convene immediately and choose a Senate president pro tempore, who would be able to assume the presidency if Arthur died. This was because until 1967, a vacancy in the vice-presidential office was not filled until the next presidential election.

Arthur was now the 21st president of the United States of America.

As for Guiteau, at his trial he entered a plea of not guilty by reason of insanity, arguing that the assassination had been "God's act and not mine." He even claimed that the true cause of Garfield's death was malpractice at the hands of his doctors. "I deny the killing, if your honour please," he announced at one point. "We admit the shooting."

Guiteau had a point regarding the doctors. Many historians now believe that Garfield would have lived if not for the limitations of 1880s medicine. However, Guiteau's plea of insanity failed to convince the jury, which took less than an hour to return a guilty verdict and he was sentenced to death.

Twenty-nine days before his execution for shooting Garfield, Guiteau composed a lengthy, unpublished poem claiming that Arthur knew the assassination had saved "our land [the United States]". Guiteau's poem also states he had (incorrectly) presumed that Arthur would pardon him for the assassination.

On June 30th, 1882, nearly a year to the day after he shot the president, Guiteau was executed by hanging in Washington, D.C.

From the beginning of his presidency Arthur struggled to combat a negative perception that he was a Stalwart and Senator Conkling's puppet. Arthur set out to show he was his own man.

He was determined to make his mark as president and leave a legacy, this was not just driven by a desire to show his independence of thought and will but due to his health. Early in his presidency Arthur was diagnosed with Bright's disease, a serious health condition that affects the normal working of the kidneys. This led to high blood pressure and heart disease.

Arthur's sister, Mary Arthur McElroy, served as White House hostess for her widowed brother, Arthur became Washington's most eligible bachelor, and his social life became the subject of rumours, though romantically, he remained singularly devoted to the memory of his late wife. His son, Chester Jr., was then a freshman at Princeton University and his daughter, Nell, stayed in New York with a governess until 1882; when she arrived, Arthur shielded her from the intrusive press as much as he could.

Arthur did not expect to live to a ripe old age and while he kept his poor health a secret, he set about creating a presidential legacy immediately.

His first problem was he had inherited Garfield's cabinet which had been predominantly filled with men from the reformist wing of the Republican party and not the Stalwart faction that Arthur belonged to.

To buy himself some time he asked that all cabinet

members remain in office until December, when Congress would reconvene.

However, Treasury Secretary William Windom submitted his resignation in October to enter a Senate race in his home state of Minnesota.

Arthur took the opportunity to appoint his friend and fellow Stalwart Charles J. Folger, as his replacement. He desperately needed a friendly and familiar face around the cabinet table.

Attorney General Wayne MacVeagh was next to resign, believing that, as a reformer, he had no place in an Arthur cabinet.

Arthur pleaded with him to remain, but MacVeagh resigned in December 1881 and Arthur replaced him with Benjamin H. Brewster, a Philadelphia lawyer and machine politician reputed to have reformist leanings.

President Garfield's great friend and ally James G Blaine, who despised the Stalwart faction, remained Secretary of State until Congress reconvened and then departed immediately.

With his departure, Senator Conkling now expected Arthur to appoint him in Blaine's place, but the president chose instead Frederick T. Frelinghuysen of New Jersey, a Stalwart who had been recommended by ex-President Grant.

Arthur was trying at last to show he was his own man. Frelinghuysen advised Arthur not to fill any future vacancies with Stalwarts, but when Postmaster General

James resigned in January 1882, Arthur selected Timothy O. Howe, a Wisconsin Stalwart.

The resignations kept on coming and Navy Secretary William H. Hunt was next to resign, in April 1882, and Arthur attempted a more balanced approach by appointing Half-Breed William E. Chandler to the post, on Blaine's recommendation.

Finally, when Interior Secretary Samuel J. Kirkwood resigned that same month, Arthur appointed Henry M. Teller, a Colorado Stalwart to the office.

This meant that of the Cabinet members Arthur had inherited from Garfield, only Secretary of War Robert Todd Lincoln remained for the entirety of Arthur's term.

Arthur was deeply wounded by the public's perception that he was an accidental president and he wanted to prove that he could rise above expectations.

In 1882, he displayed surprising independence, when he vetoed an $18 million rivers and harbours bill that contained ample funds for projects that could be used for political patronage.

President Arthur made appointments to fill two vacancies on the United States Supreme Court. The first vacancy arose in July 1881 with the death of Associate Justice Nathan Clifford, a Democrat who had been a member of the Court since before the civil war. Arthur nominated Horace Gray, a distinguished jurist from the Massachusetts Supreme Judicial Court to replace him, and the nomination was easily confirmed. Gray would serve on the court for over 20 years until resigning in 1902.

The second vacancy occurred when Associate Justice Ward Hunt retired in January 1882. Arthur first nominated his old political boss, Roscoe Conkling; he doubted that Conkling would accept, but felt obligated to offer a high office to his former patron. The Senate confirmed the nomination but as expected, Conkling declined it, the last time a confirmed nominee declined an appointment.

Senator George Edmunds was Arthur's next choice, but he declined to be considered. Instead, Arthur nominated Samuel Blatchford, who had been a judge on the Second Circuit Court of Appeals for the prior four years. Blatchford accepted, and his nomination was approved by the Senate within two weeks. He would serve on the court until his death in 1893.

Chester had been thought of by many as an east coast privileged conservative, but he surprised everyone with his reforming zeal. He took on the cosy world of the vast and bureaucratic American civil service and on January 16th, 1883, Arthur signed the Pendleton Civil Service Reform Act that mandated federal jobs were awarded on merit and not political affiliation.

The Pendleton Civil Services reform was undoubtedly President A. Chester's greatest achievement. It took a lot of courage for someone so deep in the machinations of New York Stalwart political boss Roscoe

Conkling to break free. Chester A. Arthur did exactly that. And it came in the form of reforms that allowed the meritorious appointment of people into the Civil Service. The interesting thing about those reforms was that Chester Arthur not only had to shrug off Conkling, but he also had to force those reforms through a reluctant Congress.

Positions in the Civil Service could be obtained through objective and competitive examinations. The commission also protected Civil servants from the whims and caprices of politicians in Washington, allowing workers to go about their job in free and fair working environment. This was a great step forward to end the scourge of political patronage that had blighted 19th century America.

Arthur also set about rebuilding the American navy which had declined since the civil war. It had shrunk from nearly 700 vessels to just 52, most of which were obsolete. Funds were made immediately made available for three new steel warships and an armed dispatch-steamer. Arthur would go on to recommended appropriations that would later help to transform the United States Navy into one of the world's great fleets. During Arthur's final year as president, the United States acquired a naval station at Pearl Harbor in the Hawaiian Islands.

In March 1882, President Arthur signed the Edmunds Act that criminalised polygamy. The act also prevented public office holders from engaging in polygamy.

In echoes of a modern American President, immigration was a key plank of his term. In 1882, Arthur signed the Chinese Exclusion Act, which attempted to stop all Chinese immigration into the United States for ten years, with exceptions for diplomats, teachers, students, merchants, and travellers. It was widely evaded.

He also signed in August of that year the Immigration Act of 1882, which levied a 50-cent tax on immigrants to the United States, and excluded from entry the mentally ill, the intellectually disabled, criminals, or any other person potentially dependent upon public assistance.

By the late 1880s the West had been won and the Indian wars were petering out, and public sentiment was shifting toward more favourable treatment of Native Americans. Arthur urged Congress to increase funding for Native American education, which it did in 1884.

Arthur favoured a move to the allotment system, under which individual Native Americans, rather than tribes, would own land. Arthur was unable to convince Congress to adopt the idea during his administration but, in 1887, the Dawes Act changed the law to favour such a system.

While the allotment system was favoured by liberal reformers at the time, it eventually proved detrimental to Native Americans as most of their land was resold at low prices to white speculators.

During Arthur's presidency, settlers and cattle ranchers continued to encroach on Native American territory. Arthur initially resisted their efforts, but after Secretary of the Interior Henry M. Teller, an opponent of allotment, assured him that the lands were not protected, Arthur opened the Crow Creek reservation in the Dakota Territory to settlers by executive order in 1885. Arthur's successor, Democratic President Grover Cleveland, finding that title belonged to the Native Americans, revoked Arthur's order as one of his first acts on becoming president.

With his health failing Chester made little effort to seek re-election in 1884 and retired at the end of his term. The Democrat Grover Cleveland succeeded him.

Journalist Alexander McClure wrote:

"No man ever entered the Presidency so profoundly and widely distrusted as Chester Alan Arthur, and no one ever retired more generally respected, alike by political friend and foe."

He returned to his home in New York City and declined a request by his supporters to run for the US Senate. He re-joined his law firm, but his health was deteriorating rapidly, and he was nothing more than a figurehead.

One of Arthur's most famous quotes is:

"I may be president of the United States, but my private life is nobody's damned business."

This explains why near death on November 16th, 1886, he burned all his personal and official papers.

The next day he suffered a cerebral haemorrhage and never regained consciousness. Chester Arthur died on November the 18th 1886 aged only 57.

On November 22nd, a private funeral was held at the Church of the Heavenly Rest in New York City, attended by President Cleveland and ex-President Hayes. He was laid beside his wife in the Albany rural cemetery in New York.

On his death The New York World summed up Arthur's presidency:

"No duty was neglected in his administration, and no adventurous project alarmed the nation."

Hardly a ringing endorsement and Arthur is ranked as an average president by historians, who often describe him as "the Most Forgotten US president".

CHAPTER 5
MOTHER JONES
THE MOST DANGEROUS WOMAN IN AMERICA

Mary Harris Jones was a teacher, seamstress, labour activist and union organiser.

A champion of the underdog and the working-class Jones was a campaigner for the United Mine Workers Union, founded the Social Democratic Party and helped establish the Industrial Workers of the World. Mary was an inspirational icon for any distressed strikers and used to clad herself in typical black Victorian dresses, which made her look older than she was. She was given the title of Mother Jones by striking miners grateful for the support and leadership she had shown them. Jones in turn referred to the miners as 'my boys.'

During one of her numerous trials for labour activism, a US Attorney once called Jones the 'most dangerous woman in America.'

Mother Jones was revered by many in the working class as a saint while the establishment believed she was the devil disguised as a grey-haired old lady!

Jones was imprisoned many times for her role in the labour movement and for what was perceived as subversive activity. However, imprisonment held no fears for Jones who proclaimed "I can raise more hell in jail than out."

Details of Marys early life are scarce, she was born Mary Harris in county Cork. While her date of birth is subject to debate what is known is that she was baptised on 1st August 1837.

Her parents were Roman Catholic tenant farmers Richard and Ellen Harris.

Like many of their fellow Irish men and women, they faced a stark choice as the famine struck the land in the 1840's, starve or emigrate. The Harris family joined over a million other families who fled the blighted land and the uncaring British authorities to seek a new life across the Atlantic on board the dangerously crammed coffin ships. The Harris family sailed to Canada and settled in Toronto.

In 1847, 38,560 Irish people immigrated to Toronto between May and October, driven there by the famine. At the time only 20,000 people lived in the city.

The Toronto Mirror wrote in July 1847:

"The state of the emigrants daily becomes worse

and worse. This is a horrible traffic in human blood."

Many of the Irish immigrants who came to Toronto in the late 1840s didn't stay in the city. Of those who did settle there, most lived in between the Don River Valley and Bathurst Street.

Over time, the downtown east side, around Parliament and Gerrard Street, became known as "Cabbage town," so called because the poor Irish residents would tear up their lawns to grow cabbages.

By the end of 1847, some 1,186 of the immigrants were buried in the city. 1,100 Irish are buried in a mass grave by St. Paul's Basilica at Queen Street East and Power Street, while others were buried at St. James Cemetery on Parliament Street near the Anglican Cathedral.

Richard Harris tried many professions to help raise his family, starting out as a milk man and ending up as a railway worker.

Mary and her family were victims of the prevailing anti-Catholicism in Toronto that must have made the young Mary, educated in a convent school, seem at times like an outcast.

She left Toronto in August 1859 to start a teaching post at a convent school in Monroe Michigan. Despite it being a well-paid and secure position, Mary would later describe it as a depressing place. She left the convent and accepted work as a seamstress in Chicago with the aim of becoming a professional dressmaker, before accepting another teaching position in Memphis Tennessee.

In 1861, she met and married Robert Jones, an Iron worker and a committed union man active in the iron moulders union. The newlyweds enjoyed relative prosperity and Mary left teaching to raise her young and expanding family. In four years, she gave birth to 3 girls and boy.

Fate has a cruel way of ending happiness and forging your future and in 1867 Mary experienced an unspeakable tragedy that would shape the rest of her life.

In 1867 a yellow fever epidemic swept through Memphis killing her husband Robert and her four young children. At 37 Mary Jones life was devastated, heartbroken she would dress in black for the rest of her life.

The grief-stricken widow moved back to Chicago. She set up as a seamstress and began working for the city's wealthy. However, her marriage to Robert Jones had radicalised her and she bitterly noted the contrast between the "luxury and extravagance" of the few and the misery of the "poor, shivering wretches" she saw on the streets especially the children, who reminded her of her loss.

While she began rebuilding her life, tragedy was to

strike again for Mary Jones, she lost her home, shop, and possessions in the great Chicago Fire of 1871. This huge fire destroyed many homes and shops. Jones, like many others, helped rebuild the city.

After this latest loss, Mary began her work as a labour activist. Mary Jones found in the lives of the downtrodden a new family to nurture and support.

She turned to the Knights of Labour for assistance, attracted by their campaign for improved working conditions and dedicated her life to campaigning for working people.

The Knights of Labour began as a secret society of tailors in Philadelphia in 1869. The organisation grew slowly during the hard years of the 1870s, but worker militancy rose toward the end of the decade, especially after the great railroad strike of 1877, and the Knights' membership grew with it.

Unlike most trade unions of the day, the Knights' unions included all workers in each industry, regardless of trade. The Knights were also unusual in accepting workers of all skill levels and both sexes. African Americans were included after 1883, though in segregated local branches.

Subject to so much grief and tragedy Jones could have hidden from the world and wallowed in self-pity but instead she found a new purpose in life as part of the Knights of Labour.

Mary dedicated her life as a trade union organiser, a

feminist, and a campaigner against child labour in America. Her rallying cry would be:

"Pray for the dead and fight like hell for the living."

She now took up the cause of working people focusing on the rising number of working poor during Americas rapid industrialisation. There was much to fight for, as wages reduced, hours increased, and workers had no insurance for unemployment, health-care or old age.

From 1873-1877, Jones actively supported laborers in achieving their demands. She used to travel to various strike sites and instil more passion into their strikes. She helped the coal miners' strike in Pennsylvania and rail-road workers.

Jones joined strikers in the coal mines of Pennsylvania in 1873. There she witnessed appalling conditions that bordered on slavery and children near starvation. Her own Irish heritage caused her to work passionately on behalf of the mostly Irish workers. It was her kindly, protective concern for the workers in the Pennsylvania coal mines that earned her the nickname "Mother Jones."

Jones went across the east coast of America fighting injustice she travelled so much she commented:

"My address is like my shoes. It travels with me. I abide where there is a fight against wrong."

Source: Autobiography of Mother Jones: Mary
Jones 1925

Mary first displayed her oratorial and organisational skills during the great railroad strike of 1877. America was in the fourth year of a prolonged economic depression after the panic of 1873. The railroad strikes were precipitated by wage cuts announced by the Baltimore and Ohio (B&O) Railroad. This was its second cut in just eight months.

Working on the railroad was already a poorly paid and dangerous occupation and now the railroad companies had taken advantage of the economic downturn to try and break the trade unions that had been formed by the workers before and after the American civil war.

On July 16th, 1877, workers at the B&O station at Martinsburg, West Virginia, responded to the announcement of 10 percent wage cuts by uncoupling the locomotives in the station, confining them in the roundhouse, and declaring that no trains would leave Martinsburg unless the cut was rescinded. West Virginia Governor Henry M. Mathews dispatched the militia when police were unable to break up the supportive crowd that had gathered.

However, the militia proved incapable of freeing the 600 or so trains stranded in Martinsburg (perhaps because many of the militiamen were themselves railroad workers sympathetic to the strike). Mathews then requested and received assistance from federal troops. After their arrival, trains were able to begin leaving Martinsburg on July 20th. Meanwhile, the strike had begun spreading along the mainline of the B&O all the way to Chicago, and on July 19th, it grew to include Pittsburgh and the Pennsylvania railroad. In Pittsburgh, when local police and national guard units were reluctant to act against their fellow townsmen, Pennsylvania Governor John F. Hartranft called in national guardsmen from Philadelphia. On July 21st, after local forces had made only a token effort to clear the tracks of the growing mob, the troops from Philadelphia made a bayonet charge.

A riot then erupted, with guns fired on both sides, and as many as 20 deaths resulted. As anger swelled among the workers, the guardsmen withdrew into a roundhouse while the crowd set fire to the Pennsylvania Railroad's engines, cars, and buildings. Gunfire was exchanged through the next night, with 20 more crowd members being killed, along with five guardsmen. A virtual general strike ensued in the city, with iron and steel workers, miners, and labourers joining the action.

Although the entire national guard of Pennsylvania was summoned, many units were delayed in arriving by the actions of strikers in other towns in the state. In Harrisburg, factories and stores were closed. In

Lebanon, a national guard company mutinied, and in Reading, a mob tore up tracks, derailed cars, and set fires. Nevertheless, by July 29th a fresh contingent of the national guard, supported by federal troops, had brought calm to Pittsburgh and reopened railroad operations.

In 1880 Jones was in Chicago on behalf of workers trying to obtain an eight-hour day.

Everywhere she went, she was now called Mother Jones, for her mother like image. She was around 60 years old by this time and worked vigorously to help male workers achieve their motives and encouraged the women to stay at home to look after the children.

Jones strongly opposed abortion and female suffrage. She believed that women should not take an active role in politics or for that matter work in factories and mines because their primary duty is to look after the children at home.

Jones was ideologically separated from many female activists of the pre-Nineteenth Amendment days due to her views on female suffrage. She was quoted as saying that.

"I have never had a vote, and I have raised hell all over this country. You don't need a vote to raise hell! You need convictions and a voice"!

Source: Autobiography of Mother Jones: Mary Jones 1925

She opposed many of the activists because she believed it was more important to liberate the working class itself.

When some suffragettes accused her of being anti-women's rights, she clearly articulated herself,

"I'm not an anti to anything which brings freedom to my class."

Source: Autobiography of Mother Jones: Mary Jones 1925

A friend of Jones, wrote of her:

"All over the country she had roamed and wherever she went, the flame of protest had leaped up in the hearts of men; her story was a veritable Odyssey of revolt."

This odyssey would next take her to the Haymarket riot in Chicago in 1886.

On May 4th, 1886, a rally at Haymarket Square in Chicago was organised by labour radicals to protest at the killing and wounding of several workers by the

Chicago police during a strike the day before at the McCormick reaper works.

The rally turned into a full-scale riot when a bomb was thrown killing several policemen. In the mayhem, police fired randomly into the demonstrating union workers, killing 11 people and wounding dozens of others.

Despite a lack of evidence against them, over the next few months eight radical labour activists were arrested in connection with the bombing.

In August 1886, eight men labelled as anarchists were convicted in a sensational and controversial trial in which the jury was considered to be biased and no solid evidence was presented linking the defendants to the bombing.

Judge Joseph E. Gary imposed the death sentence on seven of the men, and the eighth was sentenced to 15 years in prison. On November 11th, 1887, four of the men were hanged.

Of the additional three who were sentenced to death, one committed suicide on the eve of his execution and the other two had their death sentences commuted to life in prison by Illinois Governor Richard J. Oglesby. The governor was reacting to widespread public questioning of their guilt, which later led his successor, Governor John P. Altgeld, to pardon the three activists still living in 1893.

One other immediate impact of the Haymarket riot was that the 'Knights of Labour' started to breakdown. Jones wished to continue her labour activism and now became associated with the United Mine Workers.

The union was certainly needed as conditions for mine workers were atrocious.

Men worked in water half-way up to their knees, in gas filled rooms, in unventilated mines where the air was so foul that no man could work long without seriously impairing his health. There was no workmen's compensation law, accidents were frequent. The average daily wage of the miner was from $1.25 to $2.00.

In 1894 Jones joined with Jacob Coxey's Army of 500 unemployed citizens who marched on Washington D.C. to protest at the effects of the crippling economic depression. In 1898 She was one of the founders of the short lived Social Democratic Party which was a predecessor to the Socialist Party of America which was established in 1901.

During the bitter 1989–90 Pittston Coal strike in Virginia, West Virginia and Kentucky, the wives and daughters of striking coal miners, inspired by the still-surviving tales of Jones's legendary work among an earlier generation of the region's coal miners, dubbed themselves the "Daughters of Mother Jones". They played a crucial role on the picket lines and in presenting the miners' case to the press and public.

In 1899 Jones published The New Right in 1899 and a two-volume Letter of Love and Labour in 1900 and 1901.

Now universally known as Mother Jones and in her 60's Mary was not constrained by age and was continuing her travel and work with the United Mine Workers union.

In 1901 workers in Pennsylvania's silk mills went on strike. Mother Jones went to north-east Pennsylvania to encourage unity among the striking workers. She also encouraged the wives of the workers to organise into groups that would wield brooms, beat on tin pans, and shout "join the union!"

She believed that wives had an important role to play in motivating the striking men.

In 1902, at her trial in a West Virginia court for ignoring an order that banned the meetings by striking miners, the Virginian district attorney, Reese Blizzard, addressed her as:

'The most dangerous women in America.' He went on to say:

> "She comes into a state where peace and prosperity reign ... crooks her finger and twenty thousand contented men lay down their tools and walk out."

Mother Jones was appalled at the treatment of children in America she said:

"They began work at 5:30 and quit at 7 at night. Children six years old going home to lie on a straw pallet until time to resume work the next morning! I have seen the hair torn out of their heads by the machinery, their scalps torn off, and yet not a single tear was shed, while the poodle dogs were loved and caressed and carried to the seashore. The employment of children is doing more to fill prisons, insane asylums, alms houses, reformatories, slums, and gin shops than all the efforts of reformers are doing to improve society."

Source: Autobiography of Mother Jones: Mary Jones 1925

In 1903, to protest at the lax enforcement of the child labour laws in the Pennsylvania mines and silk mills, she organized a children's march from Philadelphia to the home of President Theodore Roosevelt in New York.

Permission to see President Roosevelt was denied by his secretary, and it was suggested that Jones address a letter to the president requesting a visit with him. Even though Mother Jones wrote a letter asking for a meeting, she never received a reply.

Though the president refused to meet with the marchers, the incident brought the issue of child labour to the forefront of the public agenda.

In 1905 Jones helped establish the Industrial Workers of the World (IWW) in 1905. This was a labour organisation founded in Chicago by representatives of 43 groups. The IWW opposed the American Federation of Labour's acceptance of capitalism and its refusal to include unskilled workers in craft unions.

Now in her 80s, Mother Jones continued her labour activities.

In 1912 she participated in the Paint Creek–Cabin Creek strike which was a brutal confrontation between striking miners and the mine owners in Kanawha County West Virginia. Jones used her oratory skills to rally the strikers and helped organise them as they faced a shooting war against the private army hired to break the strike.

Such was the violence, that martial law was declared and rescinded twice before Jones was arrested on 13th February 1913 and brought before a military court.

She was accused of conspiring to commit murder among other charges, Jones refused to recognise the legitimacy of her court-martial declaring:

"If they want to hang me, let them. And on the scaffold, I will shout, Freedom for the working class"!

Source: Autobiography of Mother Jones: Mary Jones 1925

During house arrest at Mrs. Carney's Boarding House, she acquired a dangerous case of pneumonia. On her recovery Mother Jones was convicted of conspiracy to commit murder and was sentenced to 20 years in the state penitentiary.

She would later recount that:

"I asked a man in prison once how he happened to be there, and he said he had stolen a pair of shoes. I told him if he had stolen a railroad, he would be a United States Senator."

Source: Autobiography of Mother Jones: Mary Jones 1925

Her supporters could not let their heroine rot in jail, and they campaigned to successfully convince the governor to commute her twenty-year sentence. After 85 days of confinement, her release coincided with Indiana Senator John W. Kern's initiation of a Senate investigation into the conditions in the local coal mines.

Several months later, she helped organise coal miners in Colorado in the 1913-1914 United Mine Workers of America strike against the Rockefeller-owned Colorado Fuel and Iron company, in what is known as the Colorado Coalfield War.

Once again, she was arrested, serving time in prison and inside the San Rafael Hospital. She was escorted from the state in the months prior to the Ludlow Massacre perpetrated by anti-striker militia during the Colorado Coalfield war.

After the massacre, she was invited to meet face-to-face with the owner of the Ludlow mine, John D. Rockefeller Jr. The meeting was partially responsible for Rockefeller's 1915 visit to the Colorado mines and introduction of long sought reforms.

Jones was denounced on the floor of the US Senate as the:

"Grandmother of all agitators".

She replied,

"I hope to live long enough to be the great-grandmother of all agitators."

Source: Autobiography of Mother Jones: Mary Jones 1925

Jones was also a major influence on Irish republican and socialist leader James Connolly who was already aware of Mother Jones before he went to the US where he lived from 1905 until 1910.

Connolly and Jones took a similar path, moving from the Socialist labour Party to the Socialist Party of America and the Industrial Workers of the World so they were often crossing paths.

No correspondence exists between Connolly and Jones, but she certainly cheered the Irish rebellion and joined in hopes for a worker's republic in Ireland and in the US and the world.

In 1925, she published her Autobiography of Mother Jones.

A woman of astonishing vigour, she marched three blocks in a miners' parade at age 83. In her 90s, she returned to Chicago to work at organising dressmakers.

In 1930, she celebrated her self-proclaimed 100th birthday. She was living with her friends Walter and Lillie May Burgess in Adelphi, Maryland and was filmed making a newsreel statement calling for workers to rally to transform an unjust society that had fallen into a great Depression.

She died on November 30th of that year. With the workers to the end, she asked to be buried in the Miners Cemetery in Mount Olive, Illinois alongside miners who died in the 1898 miners' strike Battle of Virden. These were men she had always called my boys.

In 1932, miners decided to place a proper headstone on her grave.

By 1936, the miners had saved up more than $16,000 and were able to purchase "eighty tons of Minnesota pink granite, with bronze statues of two miners flanking a twenty-foot shaft featuring a bas-relief of Mother Jones at its centre.

On 11th October 1936, also known as Miners' Day, an estimated 50,000 people arrived at Mother Jones's grave to see the new gravestone and memorial. Since then, 11th October is not only known as Miners' Day but is also referred to and celebrated in Mount Olive as "Mother Jones's Day.

Mother Jones has a legacy across the world.

A magazine named after her 'Mother Jones' was started in 1970 and became the largest selling underground magazine of the decade.

There is a school named after her in Adelphi, Maryland, where she spent the last few years of her life, 'Mary Harris "Mother" Jones Elementary School.'

Students at Wheeling Jesuit University, Wheeling, West Virginia can apply to reside in Mother Jones House, an off-campus service house. Residents perform at least ten hours of community service each week and participate in community dinners and events.

The imprisonment of "Mother" Jones is commemorated by the state of West Virginia through a historic highway marker.

In 1984, she was inducted into the National Women's Hall of Fame.

Members of the Cork Mother Jones Commemorative Committee unveiled a plaque on 1st August 2012 to mark the 175th anniversary of her birth.

The Cork Mother Jones Commemorative committee was established in 2012 to mark the 175th anniversary of the birth of Mary Harris / Mother Jones in Cork, Ireland. After an extraordinarily successful festival marking that anniversary, it was decided to make the festival an annual event marking the life and legacy of Mother Jones.

A documentary, Mother Jones and her children, was produced by Cork-based Frameworks Films and premiered at the Cork festival in 2014.

In September 2015, Jones was named among the world's top ten revolutionaries by The Guardian alongside Ernesto Ché Guevara, Mahatma Gandhi, and 1916 Easter Rising leader James Connolly.

In 2019, Mother Jones was inducted into the National Mining Hall of Fame.

It is heartening to see that a woman who endured so much suffering and channelled this to work and fight for others is still remembered and respected so long after her death. I will leave you with her own words:

"Someday the workers will take possession of

your city hall, and when we do, no child will be sacrificed on the altar of profit."

Source: Autobiography of Mother Jones: Mary
Jones 1925

No wonder those in power thought she was so dangerous.

James Curley would regale anyone that would listen in his later years, that when he set up the Tammany Club, the poor and needy of the ward would line up around the block waiting to speak to him asking for work or assistance. All in exchange for votes, of course

CHAPTER 6
JAMES CURLEY
MAYOR OF THE BOSTON POOR

J ames Michael Curley will always be remembered as one of the most flamboyant and controversial politicians in American history. Dragged up in the slums of Boston, he was beloved by his fellow Irish emigrants and the working class of all nationalities. So much so, they elected him mayor of Boston 4 times, governor of Massachusetts once and Curley was twice elected to the US House of Representatives.

Curley was so respected by the common people of Boston that he earned the nickname the 'Mayor of the poor.' It is said that very few people who lived in Boston in the first half of the 20th century did not benefit from the social policies implemented by Curley and his supporters. While he reveled in the adoration of the mayor of the poor, he was no saint.

Politics can be a murky profession and many men and women have started out with good intentions and then been seduced by the trappings of power and enriching themselves in the process. James Curley was no innocent corrupted by power, he set out from the start of his political career, with two objectives: make life better for the working class of Boston and his second was to make James Michael Curley rich.

No one has yet estimated the amount of money Curley took from the public purse but despite giving so much back to the people who elected him, he enjoyed a lavish lifestyle. He summed up his philosophy in life when speaking to James Roosevelt the son of President Franklin Delano Roosevelt when he said:

"If you're going to look after the poor people, you have to look after yourself."

Well James Curley not only looked after the poor but himself.

James Curley was born in Boston on November 20th, 1874. His father Michael had left his native Oughterard in County Galway when only 15 to escape grinding poverty. He settled in the Roxbury neighbourhood of Boston, where he met and married a fellow Galway native Sarah Clancy.

Michael Curley worked as a day labourer and sometime political enforcer for local Democratic party boss James "Pea-Jacket" Maguire

An enforcer was code for being hired muscle to encourage people to support the ward boss and to deal with his enemies, usually with his fists. Michael Curley died when James was only 10 years old.

An intelligent child James watched while his father's employer, the ward boss Maguire stood by and did nothing to help alleviate the family's finances, now that his father had passed away.

Even at this early age, James developed an enduring hatred of the old-style political bosses who controlled the slums of Boston and vowed to destroy their stranglehold on the Irish American working class.

His mother Sarah and elder brother John worked cleaning offices and churches all over Boston so that James could stay in school.

His family's sacrifice for his education and the poverty he saw all around him would have a major influence on his future political career, where he would be a champion of the poor and the Irish all his life.

Curley, already contributing to the family income by working as a newsboy and also started jobs at a marketplace and drugstore. He then became a delivery driver, continuing his education by attending night classes twice a week.

After being refused a position as a fireman, ostensibly because he was too young, but in reality, because he did not have a political patron to lobby for him, Curley turned his attention to politics, which in Boston, was an area of growing power for the Irish diaspora and their descendants.

As Curley entered politics, he found the Boston landscape controlled by two factions, the long-standing Yankee protestant establishment which was embodied in the Republican party. They now felt threatened by the rising power of the Irish immigrants in turn controlled by the Democratic party ward bosses, who bestowed patronage and favours for votes in the city's slums.

It was in this environment, that a young James became politically active. He began by involving himself in the local catholic church, a faith instilled in him by his mother, and which would never leave him. He was also a prominent member of the Ancient Order of Hibernians, and he soon gained a name for himself among his fellow Irish immigrants as a man who was willing to help others.

Curley started his political career at the bottom rung, running for a seat on the Boston Common council. He earned his apprenticeship knocking on doors asking for votes and hearing the woes of potential voters. In both 1897 and 1898 he stood and failed to be elected. He blamed his defeats on the corrupt voting system that did not favour the nonaligned candidate who did not have the support of a ward boss, who could for a price guarantee victory. He resolved to find himself a political patron.

He found one in the form of Democratic ward boss Charles Quirk and was duly elected in 1899.

In just two years on the council, he helped 700 of his fellow Irish men and women find jobs in what became known as 'patronage positions'. One local newspaper began to refer to him as the "Mayor of the Poor". A title he enjoyed and one he resolved to make a reality in the years ahead. He first sought the next step on his political journey and in 1901 he won election to the state legislature and began his rise in the Democratic party machine.

While Curley appreciated the help of Boss Quirk, he knew that for him to succeed in his political career he would have to build his own political operation. As he celebrated his electoral success, he also became chair of his local ward 17 in the Boston Democratic organisation.

He also established the Tammany club, which was named in tribute to the infamous Tammany Hall Democratic operation that controlled much of New York City. This was the platform not only for his own political ambitions, but to assist his constituents. He was now a 'Ward Boss,' in his own right.

Curley would regale anyone that would listen in his later years, that when he set up the Tammany Club, the poor and needy of the ward would line up around the block waiting to speak to him asking for work or assistance. All in exchange for votes of course!

James and his operation were not above the law in providing this assistance and he would fall foul of the authorities doing so.

On December 2nd, 1902, Curley and his associate Thomas Curley who was no relation, both sat down to complete a civil service exam. Now as an elected member of the Massachusetts state house of representatives, James was not taking the exam on his own behalf.

What he was doing instead was impersonating one of his constituents who had lobbied him seeking a job as a mail carrier. This role required the applicant to pass the civil service exam.

They both passed but following an investigation started after a disgruntled political enemy complained, James and his accomplice were arrested and charged with fraud on February the 25th 1903.

In April 1903 both men were convicted, and Curley was sentenced to serve 60 days in jail, and began his sentence on November 7th, 1904, after a series of unsuccessful appeals. This could have been a fatal blow to his career, but Curley was determined to succeed and was already planning to run for a seat on the Boston board of Alderman, another step forward politically.

While still in jail James used his political connections and network to win the Democratic primary by a margin of roughly 1,200 votes of more than 3,200 ballots cast.

In the general election, Curley ran with an election

slogan, "he did it for a friend." A clever message designed to combat any criticism of Curley's newly attained criminal record.

His campaign was to prove successful, and he was duly elected to the board of Alderman.

His conviction had made him the Democratic bogeyman for the Yankee protestant Republicans, but among the Boston Irish James Curley was heralded as a hero and a man who would fight for his people. The immigrant working classes of all nationalities resented the civil service exam because it set what many believed were unnecessary high educational requirements for quite menial jobs. They believed it was system designed to exclude immigrants with poor spoken and written English.

In 1906 James married his first wife, Mary E. Herlihy.

Having a criminal record was no obstacle to James Curley, rather than condemn him the Boston Irish applauded him for fighting a system that was stacked against them. They rewarded Curley with their votes and his political future was assured and he would be re-elected as an Alderman until 1910, when he decided his next step in politics was to run for the United States Congress.

Before deciding on a run for Congress Curley had mulled over a campaign for mayor. The Democratic establishment had already selected John "Honey Fitz" Fitzgerald the future maternal grandfather of President

JFK. Curley was not dissuaded from standing just because of establishment deals, he had an organisation of his own and he was unwilling to step out of the race. Eventually a deal was done when Fitzgerald promised not to run for re-election after a single four-year term.

With his focus now on the congressional race, Curley now squared up against incumbent Representative Joseph O'Connell, as well as a former congressman, William McNary in a hotly contested Democratic primary.

Again, the Democratic establishment was against him and his rivals both had larger war chests.

During the primary he discovered that both his opponents had purchased all the advertising bill boards in the area. Undaunted and with typical Curley ingenuity he adorned them with streamers reading, "Elect a Humble Man: James Michael Curley."

Although he came under fire for his personal honesty, especially given his criminal record, Curley vowed not to run a negative campaign against his opponents.

The strategy worked. After winning the primary, Curley was chosen in the general election for a House of Representatives term starting in March 1911. Mr Curley was now off to Washington.

Despite his success on becoming a US congressman, James Curley still craved the position of mayor of Boston despite what the Democratic establishment thought. He was convinced that his deal with Fitzgerald would be upheld. So, from his first moments in Washington, he was planning for his return to Boston as mayor. In November 1913, while still in the House, he announced that he would run for mayor.

The incumbent John F. Fitzgerald, who was actually a friend of Curley, was inclined to honour his pledge to serve only one term. However, the Democratic establishment despised Curley and feared his stranglehold over the working class of Boston, especially his fellow Irish immigrants. More importantly, they could not control Curley.

Fitzgerald on the other hand was one of them and they encouraged him to renege on the agreement. When Curley heard that the deal was off, he was incensed and decided he would take on the Democratic elite and challenge Fitzgerald in the forthcoming primary. Angry with the Democratic leadership he announced he did not want the support of the ward bosses and vowed to end the practice if elected mayor. Curley was a man of the slums who had fought for everything he had, and he was not averse to fighting dirty. In a foretaste of his grandson's future extra marital affairs Fitzgerald had begun a relationship with an entertainer and sometime night club hostess by the name of Elizabeth Ryan, whose nickname was 'Toodles'.

Curley was given this information by Daniel H. Coakley, a lawyer whose specialties included extortion and bribing prosecutors to bury criminal charges against his clients. Curley decided that this was the leverage he needed to remove Fitzgerald from the race.

Faced with public humiliation, scandal and the wrath of Mrs Fitzgerald the mayor withdrew from the race.

The Democratic elite were still not ready to accept Curley and were incensed by Fitzgerald's withdrawal. The Boston city council dominated by their supporters, endorsed city councillor and president of the council Thomas Kenny as their preferred candidate.

The Democratic leadership expected their man to win but they did not reckon on the determination and guile of James Curley. Rather than back off he became even more aggressive.

He relished the battle and became more confrontational during the campaign. When hecklers disrupted one appearance, he denounced them as "second story workers, milk bottle robbers, and doormat thieves." At another rally he asked the audience if anyone wanted to come onstage to "make anything of it."

He had reportedly already laid one heckler flat with a punch before issuing this declaration.

Curley was now taking on the combined might of the Boston council, and he acted accordingly fighting with every tactic he could think of. One election mailing he issued was sent to areas considered strongholds of his opponent, giving them incorrect information on where to find their polling place.

It was during this campaign that Curley is credited with coining the phrase "Vote early and vote often."

On election day Curley defeated Kenny by 43,262 votes to 37,522.

James Curley the Irish man from the slums was now Boston's mayor and he was inaugurated on Monday, February 2nd, 1914.

He would go on to serve four separate terms as mayor, 1914–1918, 1922–1926, 1930–1934 and 1946–1950.

As James Curley took office, he faced many enemies, not least from within his own party who resented a man the working-class slums rising so far. While the Fitzgerald's and other Irish had risen from similar origins, this was now all forgotten in a new genteel middle-class world. His enemies had comfortable lives, which they did not want destroyed by a man who pandered to and represented the poor.

While he faced off his enemies, he found that he had a powerful position and plenty of patronage to dispense. He began by sacking hundreds of office-holders appointed by Fitzgerald and replaced them with his own supporters.

Whilst busy with affairs of the day, the new mayor was well known to personally meet with any citizen who came in asking for a job or favour. All in return for future votes or a kickback.

One of the first actions Curley took in office was to order long handled mops for the cleaning women of City Hall so they wouldn't have to scrub the floors on their hands and knees, in memory of his mother who had toiled so he could prosper. He sought to connect those looking to work with jobs that would benefit the city, including raking leaves, shovelling snow, reseeding the grass at cemeteries, and cataloguing books at the library.

With his trademark energy and enthusiasm Curley began numerous public improvements, a practice he continued in his later terms as mayor.

These projects included the development of recreational facilities in the poorer parts of the city, an expansion of public transit, and an enlargement of Boston City Hospital.

He did all this with scant regard for how to pay for it. The poor needed it and he would provide it.

He was not averse to raising property taxes and securing loans from city banks, sometimes by threatening city inspectional actions against bank facilities.

This was an affront to the protestant yankee establishment Republican's and the middle-class Democratic elite. They genuinely feared this man from the slums with a criminal past. They were embarrassed that what they perceived as a criminal from a poor background, could become the leader of their beautiful city.

This fear and embarrassment led to a Republican

and Democratic coalition on the council passing legislation to keep his power in check. The most important law passed by the Republicans was that any mayor of the city could not serve more than four successive terms.

While Curley did much for the poor, we must not forget his conversation with James Roosevelt when he said:

> "If you're going to look after the poor people,
> you have to look after yourself."

Well, the poor were getting looked after it was now time for Curley to look after himself.

In 1915, work began on what would become a luxurious mansion for Curley and his family in Jamaica Plain.

Curley's home in Jamaica Plain still stands today and can be identified by its distinctive shamrock-shaped cutouts in the second-floor window shutters.

The sheer scale of the project was obviously well beyond the means of a mere civil servant. The house was allegedly built at a minimal charge and in some cases no charge at all by a series of building contractors who wanted favours from Mayor Curley.

All this did not go unnoticed by his enemies and his finances were regularly investigated by the Boston Finance Commission, a body dominated by hostile protestant Republicans.

Aided by his ruthless lawyer Daniel H. Coakley, he managed to avoid any charges of corruption. He also dealt harshly with the press ending any investigations by threatening libel charges against any offending media. He even went as far as to physically assault the publisher of the Boston Telegraph for publishing unflattering articles about his financial dealings.

Curley had the establishment spooked, the Republicans thought he was a crook from the wrong side of the tracks and his fellow Democrats feared he would destroy their comfortable status quo. His attacks on the ward boss system to consolidate power in his own hands had now created a powerful coalition against him.

They put their considerable support behind Curley's opponent in the 1917 election Andrew Peters who was the Assistant Secretary of the Treasury in President Woodrow Wilson's administration.

Curleys bid for re-election was further hampered by his long-time enemy, Martin Lomasney, the boss of Boston's west end. Lomasney arranged for Congressman Peter Francis Tague to enter the race. Tague also an Irish American siphoned enough votes away from Curley to hand victory to the Republican Andrew Peters.

Even though he was defeated, the elite still feared Curley. The Boston state legislature worried that Curley would seek a return and passed a law in 1918 barring

Boston mayors from running for re-election. Now while they would be able to compete in future elections, they could only serve one term at a time. This legislation would stand for 20 years.

Curleys opponents had been too clever by half, scared by his powerful constituency of the poor and appalled at his flagrant corruption their law to prohibit mayors serving consecutive terms would limit his future power but it also meant that a competent and popular mayor Andrew Peters could not now stand in the 1921 election.

This gave Curley an opportunity to return to power. He had spent his time since leaving office preparing and ensuring his political machine was ready for the election. This was despite facing personal tragedy when his infant twin sons sadly passed away.

Undaunted, James Curley narrowly defeated John R. Murphy, former Commissioner of the Boston Fire Department.

The election of 1921 was also the first municipal election in which women could vote, following the ratification of the Nineteenth Amendment, which granted female suffrage in 1920.

James Curley was inaugurated into his 2nd term as mayor on Monday 6th 1922, because of the one term restriction while he was mayor, he could not run for re-election in 1925.

Continuing the reforming agenda of his first term Curley got to work helping the poor.

He paved the way for a 48-hour working week for city employees, at a time when a 60 hour or 72-hour week was common in the private sector.

Curley had witnessed the unhealthy slums of his youth and wanted to improve the health and surroundings of his constituents. The L Street Bath House brought hot-water hygiene to South Boston neighbourhoods that had only cold-water installed.

He began a series of parks and recreation facilities such as the three-mile strand way to Castle Island which gave Bostonian's access to exercise and fresh air. He also began work on 12 new parks, health care relief stations, and hospital improvements.

He also ordered the modernisation of the Boston fire department which cut response times in half.

Ever the champion of the poor and keen to wind up his enemies in the upper-class, Curley sought to make residential properties in Boston more affordable by keeping their assessments low while raising assessments on downtown properties.

Naturally, the tactic of taxing wealthier neighbourhoods to help poorer ones put the mayor at odds with the business community.

He did not care as they never supported him, and the dislike was mutual.

While Curley may have had noble intentions, this

strategy may have helped accelerate the degradation of Boston's downtown. Looking to escape Curley's onerous tax assessments, businesses fled to the suburbs and left empty storefronts in their wake. This urban blight would not be remedied for many decades.

James Curley was immensely popular during his 2nd term but knowing he could not run at the next election, he sought to capitalise on this popularity and gain more power, so he decided in 1924 to enter the race to become the governor of Massachusetts.

Curley confident of victory dangerously overestimated his popularity. While he enjoyed the support of the poor and working class in Boston, he had less support in the rest of the state.

In the election Curley was heavily defeated by his Republican opponent the Lieutenant Governor Alvan T. Fuller.

Curley was disappointed to lose in a year when other Democrats fared well nationally.

His campaign had eventually descended into farce when Curley was involved in a physical altercation with his old friend, the publisher Frederick Enwright.

Curley had helped Enwright launch the Boston Telegram, a tabloid newspaper in 1921.

A grateful Enwright returned the favour by having the paper endorse Curley in the 1924 election, the only one of Boston's six daily newspapers to do so.

But the relationship soured as each man accused the

other of owing money, and the newspaper's coverage of Curley quickly turned negative.

Curley had been incensed for some time at attacks on him published in The Telegram. On Oct. 4th, 1926, the two men engaged in a public brawl in front of the old State House in Boston. After the encounter, each charged the other with having started the fight.

An enraged Enwright ran an editorial with a cartoon portraying a man resembling Mr. Curley in a prison cell wearing a striped convict's uniform and a ball and chain.

Curley promptly filed a libel suit, and the jury ruled in his favour and Enwright served five months and four days of an eight month prison sentence.

In 1929, Curley won a third non-consecutive term as mayor with 54.1% of the vote.

Despite his triumph, he would soon suffer tragedy again when his wife Mary Emelda, died of cancer. In her memory he built the new Our Lady of Lourdes church in Jamaica Plain and arranged for the main alter to be dedicated to her memory and the side alters were dedicated to those children who had predeceased him. One of whom was his namesake James Jr., a Harvard Law student groomed as Curley's political successor, who died in 1931 at age 23 following an operation to remove a gallstone. A Daughter Dorothea died of pneumonia as a teenager.

Curley built the Charles Street Station In 1932, on

what is now the Red Line so Bostonians could have better access to Massachusetts General Hospital.

In 1932, Curley was denied a place in the Massachusetts delegation to the 1932 Democratic National Convention by Governor Joseph B. Ely.

Never a man to take a slight lying down Curley engineered a bizarre situation to attend the convention in Chicago.

Using his political connections, he arranged for his selection as a delegate from Puerto Rico under the alias of Alcalde (which is Spanish for mayor) Jamie Curleo!

Despite being a long-time ally of Al Smith, he switched his support to Franklin D. Roosevelt (FDR) who secured the nomination. This was a surprise as Smith a former New York governor and the Democratic candidate in 1928, was the preferred choice of most of the city's sizable Catholic population.

While he campaigned enthusiastically for FDR during the 1932 election, he would soon turn against the new president when he refused to appoint him as the new ambassador to Ireland. Instead, the newly elected president offered him the less appealing role of ambassador to Poland. A disappointed Curley rejected the offer with a quote from Shakespeare's Henry VIII, pointedly charging that FDR "left me naked to mine enemies."

James Curley wanted to be governor of Massachusetts. He had lost heavily in 1924 but in 1934 the landscape was more positive for Democrats and Curley ran for governor again.

In the election he defeated Republican Lieutenant Governor Gaspar Bacon, an opponent of Roosevelt's New Deal, by more than 100,000 votes.

As governor of Massachusetts, Curley oversaw FDR's New Deal programs and bolstered them with his own state relief programs. He focused on infrastructure, spending large sums to improve roads and bridges. However, a later analysis suggested that he may have unnecessarily delayed New Deal programs in the state by squabbling with federal authorities over who would control the funding.

Being mayor of a major city like Boston brings scrutiny but as governor of Massachusetts he was under a more intensive microscope and Curley's single term as governor was described by one commentator as:

"Ludicrous part of the time, shocking most of the time, and tawdry all of the time."

Source: Frances Russell Last of the Bosses 1959

Under attack for his financial irregularities as mayor Curley used the bully pulpit of the governor's mansion to attack and undermine the Boston finance commission.

This was forensically scrutinising his time as mayor

and Curley was in no mood to stand meekly by and be exposed for his financial laxity. Curley continually attacked committee members accusing individuals of failing to do their job. He even went as far as to impeach the investigators who were fired.

Curley was eventually able to install a more pliant commission and turned its attention to his political opponents. His popularity began to plummet due to negative press reporting of his actions against the finance commission. Despite authorising the construction of the Quabbin Reservoir, he did little to address widespread unemployment.

The press also insinuated Curley had benefited financially from the contracts secured to build the reservoir.

In 1935, in a tweak at the state's WASP elite, Curley appeared at Harvard's commencement which was a traditional ceremonial function of the governor, wearing silk stockings, knee britches, a powdered wig, and a three-cornered hat with flowing plume. When university marshals objected, the story goes, Curley whipped out a copy of the 'Statutes of the Massachusetts Bay Colony,' which prescribed proper dress for the occasion and claimed that he was the only person at the ceremony properly dressed, thereby endearing him to many working- and middle-class attendees.

In 1936, instead of seeking re-election, Curley ran for the United States Senate. He lost against a moderate

Republican, Henry Cabot Lodge Jr., despite a national landslide in favour of Democrats.

After leaving the office of governor, Curley squandered a substantial sum of his money in unsuccessful investments in Nevada gold mines; then he lost a civil suit brought by the Suffolk County prosecutor that forced him to forfeit to the city of Boston the $40,000 he received from General Equipment Company for "fixing" a damage claim settlement.

In 1937 James remarried, his new wife was Gertrude Casey the widowed mother of two young sons George and Richard.

In 1938, he made another try for the governorship, defeating incumbent Democrat Charles F. Hurley in a close primary. He lost the general election to Republican Leverett Saltonstall.

Curley was twice defeated, in November 1937 and November 1941, for the Boston mayoralty by one of his former political confidants, Maurice J. Tobin. Curley took his revenge against Tobin later, supporting Republican Robert F. Bradford for governor against Tobin in 1946.

There is one thing I have learned about James Curley and that is you could not keep him down and in 1942 he used his populist roots to unseat the Incumbent Democratic US congress man Thomas Elliot.

Curley led a campaign that accused Elliot of being part of the Yankee establishment to stir up working class anger. This proved phenomenally successful, and Curley was back in power when he secured victory. Mr Curley was off to Washington again.

He would be re-elected in 1944 but he would only serve one year of his second term when in 1945 Joseph P Kennedy the father of a young ambitious would-be politician John F Kennedy encouraged Curly to run for mayor of Boston and vacate the Congressional seat for his son who would run for Congress in 1946.

Despite the enmity between the Kennedys and Curley, who had effectively ended the political career of John 'Honey' Fitzgerald, Joseph Kennedy agreed to pay off Curleys debts and bank roll his campaign for mayor.

Curley agreed and in 1945, he stepped aside vacated his Congress seat and began his campaign for what would be his fourth non-consecutive term as Boston mayor.

James Curleys 1945 campaign should have been a triumphant return to his Boston power base, but this was overshadowed accusations of fraud. However, his popularity with the Boston Irish was so high that despite the charges, he was re-elected on the slogan "Curley Gets Things Done." It was a landslide count of 111,824 votes. This was more than both of his opponents combined and Curley was mayor of Boston again, but for how long as Curley was now under federal indictment at the time. His trial had even been postponed allowing him to run for office.

During his 4 years in congress numerous investigations had been conducted against Curley's political machine and he now faced felony indictments for bribery brought by federal prosecutors.

This was related to his participation in the company Engineers Group Inc. This was to prove a fraudulent front organisation that misrepresented its resources to win war contracts for clients.

Curley would claim that his role in the scheme had been minimal. He protested that he had simply let the company use his name on their letterhead. His defence was that he was the:

"Victim of a professional confidence man whose professions of honesty deceived me and others."

Source: James Curley, I'd do it again 1957.

This may have been the case, but the fact he still received

$60,000 in government funds by attaching his name to the group was a damning piece of evidence. The scheme was uncovered during then Senator Harry S. Truman's investigation into the US national defence program.

In February 1946, just a month into his fourth term as mayor, Curley was convicted of 10 counts of mail fraud. Also convicted were Donald Wakefield Smith, a former member of the National Relations Board, and James G. Fuller, who had acted as the vice president of Engineers Group Inc.

Curley continued to serve as mayor as his case went through the appeals process. He finally ran out of options when the Supreme Court opted not to consider his arguments.

Curley, determined to avoid jail, disregarded his doctor's orders and travelled to Washington to personally request that the sentence be suspended.

A federal judge refused, and In June 1947, he was sentenced to serve six to 18 months at the federal correctional institution in Danbury, Connecticut.

In normal circumstances and with any other politician a criminal conviction is typically enough to get a politician to resign their office, Curley refused to step down. City clerk John B. Hynes served as acting mayor during Curley's imprisonment.

Hynes, at Curley's direction, collected the mayor's salary but donated it to charity. It is unclear just how much influence Curley continued to have from his out-of-state jail cell. During Curley's six months in Danbury correctional facility in 1947, temporary mayor John B. Hynes only acted upon necessary matters that could not wait until Curley was released from prison.

Upon Curley's release from jail, over forty-million dollars' worth of contracts were awaiting his approval and signature. At one half of the customary rate of ten percent, the illegal cut for Curley, the take would be a staggering two million dollars.

Curley was still immensely popular in Boston and crowds demonstrated in the streets demanding the 'mayor of the poor' be released and more than 172,000 people (about a quarter of the city's population) signed a petition demanding clemency "because of his health and other extenuating circumstances."

This was also taken up by the Massachusetts congressional delegation who put pressure on President Truman to commute his sentence due to poor health. There was one notable exception, John Fitzgerald Kennedy, who had succeeded Curley as a congressman and would go on to be elected president in 1960. The action was widely seen as a rebuke to Curley for how he had treated Kennedy's grandfather John 'Honey' Fitzgerald.

President Truman agreed, and after serving only five months James Curley was now a free man and, on his way, back to Boston. Miraculously despite having been granted freedom due to his ill health, he was now fit and eager to return to work.

Thousands of his constituents lined the streets on his triumphant return to Boston, bands played hail to the chief and hail glorious St Patrick. Curley seemed to be at the height of his powers, but his pride made him make a fateful mistake on his first day back in office, in front of the gathered Boston press he said:

"I have accomplished more in one day than has been done in the five months of my absence."

Source: James Curley, I'd do it again 1957.

This was taken as a massive slight and insult by John Hynes who now decided that he would challenge James Curley in the 1949 election.

In his last year in office in 1949 Curley went back to his old ways. Curley's moneyman, Peter Allen, a graduate of Princeton University, who had been appointed by Curley to the position of Chairman of the Board of Assessors, would arrive at Curleys mansion with pillowcases full of money from grateful petitioners. All records at that time were kept in pencil. The entire process was extremely secretive. Curley also granted exorbitant city contracts to his close associates. However, politics was changing, and the era of the old corrupt party bosses was over, and John Hynes had not forgotten or forgiven Curleys harsh words on his return to power.

Hynes decided to stand against Curley in the forthcoming election. The restriction on running for re-election had been lifted, so Curley was trying to hold on to the mayor's office for the first time since 1917. He denounced Hynes as a candidate who would favour Boston's businesses over its people. Hynes fired back that Curley was out of touch and a relic of a past of city bosses that Boston should move on from.

Despite his popularity politics was changing, the era of the corrupt ward boss was over and in the Democratic primary John Hynes was victorious.

Curley would not give up and stood in the general election but lost out narrowly to Hynes who was elected as mayor.

Soon after this defeat, a dual tragedy struck the Curley household. On February 11th, 1950, his 41-year-old daughter Mary suddenly died of a cerebral haemorrhage while talking to her 34-year-old brother Leo on the phone. Later in the same day, Leo collapsed and died of the same ailment after learning of his sister's death.

On April 14th, 1950, Truman issued Curley a pardon for both his 1903 fraud conviction and his more recent incarceration. It was a favour, a way of offering Curley a clean slate; the charges hadn't included any lasting sanctions, since he could still vote and hold office under Massachusetts law.

Curley launched two more mayoral bids in 1951 and 1955, both unsuccessful.

A renowned orator Curley was always in demand as an entertaining and controversial speaker at functions. Curley began lecturing at the Stanley school of the spoken word and in 1952 he travelled to the Speech Arts studio in New York to record some of his most memorable and entertaining speeches. Ever the salesman these sold well, and he would ensure a supply was available at all his speaking arrangements.

In 1956 with his finances fading and no political office to milk, something turned up for Curley. Edwin O'Connor had written a best-selling novel called 'The Last hurrah.' The book was so popular it was later made into a movie directed by John Ford and starring Spencer Tracy.

It was so obvious the main character of both the book and the film, Frank Skeffington, was based on the life and campaigns of James Curley, that Curley threatened to sue, but settled out of court, for a sum of $46,000.

In 1957, the new Massachusetts governor Foster Furcolo appointed Curley to the state Labour Relations Commission. The post came with a yearly salary of $7,500, not bad when you consider that the average salary in the state was just $4,900.

That year he published his memoir I'd do It again; it was to prove extremely popular read by friend and foe and would have 6 reprints.

The mayor of the poor was not only still popular, but his memoir and the last hurrah had brought him to a new audience and not just in Boston. He was interviewed by Edward

R. Murrow on his nationwide television program

"Person to Person" and proceeded, book in hand, to talk about his life and autobiography "I'd do It again."

James Michael Curley died on November the 12th 1958 just months after the release of the Film Last Hurrah which was so obviously based on his life.

James Curley was waked in the hall of flags in the Massachusetts State House and over a million people paid their respects.

When his funeral cortege drove through Boston, hundreds of thousands paused and paid respects to the 'mayor of the poor.'

Whatever you think of James Curley, he will be remembered as one of the most flamboyant politicians ever to have lived. His progressive policies did so much for the poor and working class of Boston especially his native Irish.

He did however ensure that as his constituents' lives improved, he also prospered and while he undeniably helped the poor, he also helped himself to millions.

We will never see his like again, or will we?

66

Shortly after his election to the presidency, JFK renamed the presidential yacht the 'Honey Fitz' in honour of his maternal grandfather, John 'Honey Fitz' Fitzgerald, the founder of a political dynasty and the man who influenced his political career

CHAPTER 7
JOHN FRANCIS 'HONEY' FITZGERALD
FOUNDER OF A POLITICAL DYNASTY

John Francis Fitzgerald was the first American born; Irish American Roman Catholic elected as mayor of Boston. He was also a state senator, US congressman and made several unsuccessful runs for governor of Massachusetts. Fitzgerald maintained a high profile in the city whether in or out of office, and his theatrical style of campaigning and charisma earned him the nickname "Honey Fitz".

However, his greatest claim to fame, was that he mentored and began the political career of his grandson John Fitzgerald Kennedy, the 35th president of the United States of America.

John Francis Fitzgerald was born in Boston on 11th February 1863, the fourth child of Irish businessman and politician Thomas Fitzgerald who was from county Limerick and his mother Rosanne from Cavan.

His parents lived on Ferry Street in the north end area of Boston it was no longer the fashionable enclave it had been in Paul Revere's Day; it had become a ghetto for impoverished immigrants fleeing famine in Ireland. Fitzgerald's parents had settled there in the late 1840s. His father's grocery and liquor store supported the large family.

His parents would go onto have 12 children, but tragedy was no stranger to the Fitzgerald family, as only 3 survived childhood. One of those Joseph, was severely brain damaged because of a bout of malaria and his mother Rosanne herself, died when John was just 16.

Thomas wanted John to be a doctor to help prevent others suffering the misfortunes that had befallen his family.

His early friends knew him as "Johnnie Fitz" or "Fitzie" and he was a competitive and entrepreneurial child.

He distinguished himself early on as a bright lad with an extraordinary work ethic, tremendous determination, confidence, and gregariousness. He was among the first Irish Catholic students to win a place at the prestigious Boston Latin school, where he excelled as a scholar, athlete, and student journalist.

After graduating, John Fitzgerald with little enthusiasm enrolled at Harvard medical school. He did not want to be a doctor and left Harvard the following year when his father died in 1885, so that he could support his younger siblings.

In 1886, he took a civil service exam and landed a job as a clerk in the Boston customs house. He was such an efficient worker that his boss, collector of the port, Leverett Saltonstall, made him a customs inspector.

Politics was his passion and while he worked as a clerk in the customs house, he began to make his mark in the local Democratic party. The Boston ward system wielded immense power in the city and Fitzgerald soon became the protégé of powerful 8th ward boss Martin Lomansney.

An avid reader, with a fine memory, he could dazzle audiences with his informed opinions, presented in a blaze of eloquent oratory and with a touch of what one reporter called "his consummate Irish charm." One newspaper printed a poem that began, "Honey Fitz can talk you blind on any subject you can find."

John was a natural politician, with an impish sense of humour and liable to burst into song at political meetings or while out campaigning. This warmth of character earned him the nickname he would be known by for the rest of his life, 'Honey Fitz.'

By September 1889, "Honey-Fitz" had earned enough money to start his own insurance company and to marry his second-cousin, Mary Josephine "Josie" Hannon. They would have six children: Rose Elizabeth (1890-1995), Agnes (1892-1936), Thomas

Acton (1895-1968), John Francis Jr. (1897-1979), Eunice (1900-1923), and Frederick Hannon (1904-1935). His daughter Rose later married Joseph P. Kennedy, whom she had first met as a teen during family vacations in Maine, according to the JFK Library. She would give birth to the Fitzgerald/Kennedy political dynasty.

In 1890, Fitzgerald founded the Jefferson Club, a political organisation founded to galvanise the Irish Catholic voters of south Boston. It was modelled on earlier clubs like Tammany Hall in New York and his mentor Martin Lomasney's Hendricks Club in the west end of Boston. He worked his way up the ranks in the ward system winning a seat on the Boston Common council in 1891.

He set up his campaign offices and encouraged anyone with a problem to stop by for help. With immense energy, he placed constituents in jobs, delivered holiday food baskets to the needy, sent gifts to every newly married couple in the neighbourhood, and never missed a North End wake. When he was campaigning, he made as many as ten speeches in a night, denouncing his opponents as anti-Catholic, anti-Irish, and anti-immigrant.

By 1893, Fitzgerald had been elected to the state senate. He increased his support among Italian immigrants by sponsoring a bill to make Columbus Day a state holiday. With this expanded power base, he decided to run for a congressional seat in the US House of Representatives.

In the congressional primary held in September 1894, Fitzgerald beat sitting Congressman Joseph H. O'Neill, a popular Democrat who had held the seat since 1889. In the final election, Fitzgerald beat Republican challenger, Boston Alderman Jesse Morse Gove, winning by 1,916 votes.

He was now Congressman John Fitzgerald for the 9th district and the only Democratic representative elected to the 54th Congress from New England.

As a congressman, Fitzgerald authored legislation to fund construction of Boston's subway system and the Cape Cod canal. He opposed anti-liquor laws as "paternalistic" (although he himself was a non-drinker) and fought for immigrants and working people. He constantly fought anti-immigrant sentiment, even within his state's own delegation.

"Honey-Fitz" also became known as a champion of Italian, Jewish, and African American peoples, and his most celebrated moment as a congressman came when he opposed an anti-immigration bill supported by Republican Senator Henry Cabot Lodge. Amongst other clauses, the bill would have required new immigrants to be able to read the constitution.

After Congress approved the bill, "Honey-Fitz" visited President Grover Cleveland and persuaded him to veto the bill, keeping immigration unrestricted for the next twenty-five years. Cabot Lodge was incandescent with rage and Fitzgerald later claimed the two political adversaries had the following exchange after he gave a speech rebuking the Republican senator:

"You are an impudent young man," Lodge reportedly said, after running into Fitzgerald in the halls of the Capitol. "Do you think the Jews and Italians have any right in this country?"

"As much as your father or mine," Fitzgerald, the son of immigrants, replied. "It was only a difference of a few ships."

Source: Boston.com 2017

All this made John F. Fitzgerald a national figure and many people predicted that after running for a fourth congressional term in 1900, he would seek the mayoralty of Boston in 1901. This frightened other Boston political bosses like Patrick J. "P.J." Kennedy and Martin "the Mahatma" Lomasney, who feared that Fitzgerald was gaining too much power. They successfully blocked his congressional nomination in 1900, and in 1901, "Honey-Fitz" was now out of a job.

Undeterred, Fitzgerald bought a failing Boston newspaper called "The Republic" described on the masthead as "an Irish-American Family journal," Over the next few years he turned it into a thriving enterprise.

Using his growing political machine, he master-minded the election of his brother Henry S. Fitzgerald to the Massachusetts state Senate. His fellow Bostonians began referring to the Fitzgerald's as an "Imperial Dynasty" or "Boston's Royal Family".

"Honey-Fitz" reinforced this impression by buying a palatial Victorian mansion at 39 Welles Avenue in Dorchester in 1903, where he would entertain friends, celebrities, and common folk alike in a lavish fashion.

Fitzgerald was still determined to run for mayor of Boston and get his revenge on the old-style ward bosses who had ended his congressional career.

He was able to use his newspaper "The Republic" as a political mouthpiece and over the next four years he grew his political connections and constituency.

In 1905, Fitzgerald began his campaign for election. He ran a populist campaign, He toured the wards in a large red car, an extraordinary sight at the time, proclaiming his slogan "Bigger, Better, Busier Boston!"

He also condemned the city's ward system, which had ironically helped him rise in politics. This led to a split with the Democratic establishment, and he narrowly secured the nomination.

He went on to win the 1906 mayoral election and heralded his victory as the start of a political dynasty. Fitzgerald was now the first American-born Irish Catholic to be elected mayor.

In his inaugural address as mayor, he gave special

attention, among other things, to the financial burdens of the city, the escape of much personal property from taxation, the reorganisation of the street department, the erection of a new city hall, a hospital for consumptives, the adoption of a pension system, and a largely increased installation of water meters.

In the campaign to become mayor Fitzgerald had condemned the ward boss system and vowed to clean up politics. But despite wanting to develop the Boston Infrastructure, his tenure descended into little more than a jobs for votes program, where patronage was handed out for promises of future support.

His victory had come at a price, he had now made enemies of his old mentor the Democratic ward boss Martin Lomasney. Whilst he was not an immediate threat, as his term progressed the lack of support from the traditional Democratic machine would prove pivotal in his re-election prospects.

Despite this, the young mayor Fitzgerald and his family were ecstatic at his success. His eight-year-old son, Johnny, proudly predicted that his daddy would go on to be governor of Massachusetts and then president of the United States. While previous Irish mayors had sought to placate the 'Yankee' protestant ruling class of Boston, "Honey-Fitz" clung proudly to his Irish heritage and stood up for the working man.

Once, on a visit to a Boston bank, "Honey-Fitz" noticed that there were no Irish people in the higher echelons of the bank. He confronted the bank president who told him that many of the tellers were Irish. "Yes, and I suppose the charwomen are too!", Fitzgerald angrily responded. He made it a primary mission to advance the Irish in Boston society, finding them good jobs and founding the City Club, where wealthy Yankees and Irish could mingle.

His daughter, Rose the future mother of the Kennedy clan, founded the 'Ace of Clubs,' a society for wealthy young Irish girls, as a counterpart to such Yankee ladies' establishments as the Junior League and the Vincent Club.

As mayor, Fitzgerald built a citywide political machine. He continued his work on behalf of the city's neediest residents; he also continued to tolerate, even promote, a political culture of graft and corruption. He created such unlikely new jobs as "rubber boot repairers," "tea warmers," and "watchmen to watch the watchmen" and gave them to his supporters, cronies, and relatives.

Despite his support from the native Irish and the working class, "Honey-Fitz's" term as mayor quickly became well known for its corruption and graft. The Boston financial commission decided to investigate allegations of pay offs and deals with building contractors as well as embezzlement from city funds. Fitzgerald welcomed the investigation. He had friends on the commission and was confident that he would be given a clean bill of health. Instead, the commission recommended a trial of the Fitzgerald administration, which became one of the most sensational courtroom cases of its day.

In the end, the Prosecutor was unable to causally link Fitzgerald with any illegal activity, but a close friend of the Fitzgerald family went to prison and the judge openly stated that he believed that "Honey-Fitz" was not exactly an innocent individual.

As Fitzgerald began to campaign for a second term as mayor, the Boston newspapers were full of stories of his incompetence, overspending and alleged corruption. This combined with a lack of support from Democratic ward bosses led to his defeat in the 1907 election.

He failed to win re-election as his Republican opponent, George A Hibbard, promised to clean up the mess Fitzgerald had created.

The Republicans took advantage of their unexpected victory to revise the city charter to curb the power of the Irish Democratic ward bosses like Fitzgerald and Lomasney. They eliminated the large common council, replaced the board of aldermen with a nine-seat city council, extended the mayor's term to four years, and made all offices formally non-partisan, removing the advantage of party recognition in the predominantly Democratic city.

In 1910 Fitzgerald sought to become mayor again.

His re-election bid was marred by a bribery scandal relating to alleged kickbacks received in his first term.

He also faced opposition from younger Boston Democrats, led by the charismatic James Curley. A rising star in the Democratic party and a powerful ward boss.

The famous Fitzgerald charm defused the bribery charges and he escaped prosecution. Fitzgerald however made a long-term enemy in Daniel H. Coakley, an Irish lawyer who had defended one of the key figures in the case. As for Curley, he was offered a Congress seat and a promise that Fitzgerald would only serve one more term as mayor.

With Curley out of the race Fitzgerald won a narrow victory over Republican candidate, James Jackson Storrow.

The Storrow-Fitzgerald campaign was a bitter one, during which "Honey-Fitz" fought hard for vindication, accused his opponent of being a tool of wealthy interests, and employed campaign posters with pictures of City Hall and the slogan:

"NOT FOR SALE, MR. $TORROW!"

It was also during this election that he sang for the first time, "Sweet Adeline", a song that would become his signature tune. So much so that when he left office he said: "Mayors may come and mayors may go, but the municipal anthem remains!" and sang the song.

Early in his first term as Boston's mayor, Fitzgerald had formulated a plan to revitalize the commercial importance of the city under the banner of "a Bigger, Busier and Better Boston." This plan was not pursued by Hibbard but gained traction after Fitzgerald's return to office. Fitzgerald was able to persuade businesses and the Massachusetts legislature to invest $9 million for improvements to the Boston port by 1912. Within a year, the investments began to pay off in the form of new and increased commercial traffic in the port to and from Europe.

During his second term as mayor (the first four-year term a Boston mayor ever had), "Honey-Fitz" reached the zenith of his popularity, both locally and nationally, and achieved a great deal, becoming the first Boston mayor to fly in an airplane, giving Boston a zoo, and an aquarium.

Fitzgerald drew massive investment into Boston and helped establish Fenway Park home of the Boston Red Sox. He threw the inaugural ceremonial first pitch in 1912.

100 years later, his great granddaughter Caroline Kennedy, threw out the first pitch for Fenway Park's 100th anniversary.

He also established the tradition of "Banned in Boston", by banning such popular dances as the "Turkey Trot" and the "Tango" and banning plays like Oscar Wilde's "Salome." Once, after attending a concert at symphony hall, Fitzgerald could not see over the large feathers on the hats of women in the aisle in front of him. He issued a city ordinance prohibiting women from wearing hats in any public place! During his time as mayor, "Honey-Fitz" earned praise from the likes of Presidents Theodore Roosevelt and William Howard Taft and Kaiser Wilhelm II of Germany (for whom he sang "Sweet Adeline" in Berlin).

In 1912, he decided to seek the Democratic nomination for vice-president. It looked like a sure thing, but curiously, he withdrew from the race at the last moment. The reason for this would not become apparent until 1913 when he announced his intention to run for another term as mayor. James Curley enraged by what he perceived as a betrayal, used his mob connections and Fitzgerald's old enemy Daniel Coakley to blackmail Fitzgerald into leaving the race. Curley threatened to expose an affair Fitzgerald was allegedly conducting with a cigarette girl in a mob run club. Curley announced that he would present a series of "educational" lectures with titles such as "Graft in Ancient and Modern Times" and "Great Lovers from Cleopatra to Tootles" this was a blatant reference to the blond cigarette girl Tootles Ryan, who was rumoured to be Fitzgerald's mistress.

Curley then sent Mrs. Fitzgerald a letter informing her that her husband was again allegedly seeing a 23-year-old showgirl named "Tootles". Curley threatened to expose the affair if Fitzgerald did not drop out of the race. "Honey-Fitz" told his wife that it was a lie and that he must challenge it, but "Josie" Fitzgerald was afraid of a scandal and insisted upon her husband's immediate withdrawal.

Fitzgerald withdrew and Curley would go on to serve 4 terms as mayor.

Not long after leaving office, Fitzgerald's daughter, Rose married Joseph P. Kennedy, the son of "Honey-Fitz's" rival, "P.J." Kennedy. Some say that "Honey-Fitz" did not approve of the marriage as he considered the Kennedys socially beneath the Fitzgerald's and he had hoped that Rose would marry a wealthy Irishman or even a rich Yankee!

After withdrawing from the 1914 mayoral campaign, Fitzgerald turned his attention to business and family.

Politics was still in his blood in 1916 he challenged his old political rival Henry Cabot lodge for the Senate but lost. He ran for mayor in 1917, but lost yet again to Andrew James Peters, but in doing so he denied James Curley re-election by siphoning off the Irish vote.

Undaunted Fitzgerald ran for congress in 1918 and won his seat by the slimmest of margins, 238 votes. His defeated opponent Peter F. Tague contested the result. The subsequent investigation of the election revealed systematic fraud. Numerous votes came from falsely registered voters who resided elsewhere, or were serving overseas, or were dead. Thugs were hired to intimidate voters who supported Fitzgerald's opponent. Fitzgerald served from March 4 to October 23rd, 1919, when the House voted unanimously that Fitzgerald had not won and announced that Tague was now elected. Ironically, the man who helped Tague contest the election results and unseat "Honey-Fitz" was Joe Kane, a legendary Boston political operative who was Joe Kennedy's cousin and would later run campaigns for Fitzgerald and John F. Kennedy.

After his congressional debacle, Honey Fitz spent a lot of time with his two eldest grandsons, Joseph Jr., and John. Despite his earlier misgivings about the union, Fitzgerald loved his grandchildren dearly.

Fitzgerald was upset that the couple's firstborn son, Joe Kennedy Jr., was not named after him. Nevertheless, according to Doris Kearns Goodwin's book The Fitzgerald's and the Kennedys, he proudly informed the local press that his grandson would go on to become the first Irish-Catholic president of the United States.

As it turned out, it was his second grandson, born two years later, who would receive both his name and follow through on that prophecy.

His namesake, John Fitzgerald Kennedy was a particular favourite of his. He also helped save the future president's life.

At the age of 2 in February 1920, John Kennedy nearly died from a bout of scarlet fever. And since the family lived in Brookline, he wasn't allowed to be admitted to the area's best hospital, Boston City Hospital, which was only available to city residents at the time. However, Fitzgerald was able to "pull some strings" and persuaded the hospital to admit his grandson.

Though he remained popular, Fitzgerald's public service career was on the decline. In 1922, Fitzgerald unsuccessfully challenged the incumbent governor of Massachusetts Channing Cox. In 1932, he campaigned for Franklin Delano Roosevelt for president. James Michael Curley and P.J. Kennedy joined him. Fitzgerald unsuccessfully tried to recruit Martin Lomasney to the cause as well.

After Roosevelt won the election, Fitzgerald's son-in-law Joseph was appointed chairman of the new US Maritime Commission. Joseph would later serve as chairman of the new US Securities and Exchange Commission and as US Ambassador to Great Britain.

"Honey-Fitz" spent his last years as the commissioner of the Boston Port authority, where he tried to turn Boston's seaport into one that would rival New York. The public largely forgot about his supposed mistakes, and he was viewed as a lovable, old, living legend. His fame was still so widespread around the world that when President Franklin D. Roosevelt visited Argentina in the '30's, a band played "Sweet Adeline", remembering a Fitzgerald visit to their country and thinking that it was the US national anthem. From then on, Roosevelt referred to "Honey-Fitz" as "La Dulce Adelina".

The ex-mayor ran unsuccessfully for governor of Massachusetts, twice. Fitzgerald ran for office again, in 1942, as a candidate for United States Senate, merely to act as a spoiler to block the election of one of his son-in-law's Democratic party rivals.

He was defeated by the Republican, Henry Cabot Lodge Jr.

Despite his own mixed campaign record, Honey Fitz was instrumental in launching his 28-year-old grandson's start in politics.

John F. Cahill, the chair of the state Democratic Party at the time, later said in a 1967 interview, that Fitzgerald lived near the party's offices in Boston and consistently nagged the party chair about putting his grandson in an advantageous position to run.

"He'd come in every day, as sure as another morning would come, and want to know if I'd done anything for young John," Cahill said.

After a few meetings with Kennedy and some local political jockeying, it was decided JFK would run for Congress in the crowded 1946 Democratic primary field for the open 11th district seat. Fitzgerald campaigned with his grandson John for the latter's first election, the old city boss shaking hands beside the ambitious, photogenic youngster.

Fitzgerald was also said to be involved with the

Kennedy campaign's alleged ballot shenanigans. Faced with a popular city councillor, Joseph Russo, a "proven vote-getter" who was also running for the House seat, the campaign sought out another Joseph Russo. Eventually, they found a 27-year-old janitor from the West End and put him on the ballot in hopes of confusing the electorate and splitting the Italian vote. According to one Kennedy autobiography, Russo, the janitor, was given "an undisclosed amount" to run.

Not that it mattered much. Kennedy went on to win the election with 22,183 votes, compared to 5,661 for Russo and 799 for the other Russo.

In a 1964 interview, Russo said the same tactic was later used to defeat him in his city council race, when his opponents ran two other Joseph Russos against him: "I had to advertise myself as the "Middle Russo".

The young Kennedy had won the seat in the House of Representatives that his grandfather had first held fifty years earlier.

At the victory party, Fitzgerald danced an Irish jig, sang 'Sweet Adeline,' and announced to everyone in the room that his grandson would someday be president. Sadly, he would not live to see this.

On Fitzgerald's eighty-fifth birthday, Mayor James Curley declared an all-day city celebration in honour of his old friend and sometime rival, "Honey-Fitz".

Two of "Honey's" sons tried, unsuccessfully to follow in his political footsteps. Thomas would become

Boston's street commissioner, while John F. Jr. was elected to a minor position.

Agnes Fitzgerald had once predicted that her brother, Fred would someday be president, but these hopes were dashed when Fred became an alcoholic and died of liver problems at the age of 31.

On October 2nd, 1950, John "Honey-Fitz" Fitzgerald died in Boston at the age of eighty-seven. His funeral was one of the largest in the city's history. President Harry S. Truman sent his sympathies and "Honey-Fitz's" pallbearers included US Senator Henry Cabot Lodge Jr. (who would be defeated in a re-election bid by JFK two years later),

U.S. Senator Leverett Saltonstall (the grandson of the man who had given "Honey-Fitz" his first job), US Speaker of the House John McCormick, Massachusetts Speaker of the House Thomas P. "Tip" O'Neill, and former Boston mayor and Massachusetts governor James Michael Curley.

As "Honey-Fitz" was carried to his final rest from Holy Cross Cathedral to St. Joseph's Cemetery in West Roxbury, MA, a crowd of thousands who had gathered along the streets sang "Sweet Adeline".

Shortly after his death, state officials named the newly constructed central artery in Boston the John F. Fitzgerald expressway.

Fitzgerald never got to see the height of his grandson's career. Kennedy was elected to the Senate in 1952 (defeating Lodge's son, the incumbent), before winning the 1960 presidential election.

However, his grandson would not forget him and shortly after his election to the presidency, JFK renamed the presidential yacht the 'Honey Fitz,' in honour of his maternal grandfather, John 'Honey Fitz' Fitzgerald, the founder of a political dynasty.

News of Citizen Kane now reached Hearst and he didn't like what he was hearing. It is easy to believe that Hearst was enraged by the veiled attack on his life, but his real anger towards the movie was not vanity but his love for Marion Davis

CHAPTER 8
WILLIAM RANDOLPH HEARST
THE REAL CITIZEN KANE

William Randolph Hearst is best remembered as one of America's richest businessmen, a media mogul and the main inspiration for Charles Foster Kane, the lead character in Orson Welles's 1941 film Citizen Kane. He would build up the nation's largest newspaper chain and his methods profoundly influenced American journalism and not always positively.

However, like many rich and powerful men he also believed he should be president and he also had a controversial political life.

William Randolph Hearst was born in San Francisco on the 29th of April 1863. He was the only child of the wealthy and influential couple George Hearst and his much younger wife Phoebe Apperson Hearst.

George Hearst married Phoebe Apperson in June

1862, he was 41 and she was 19. Phoebe became pregnant during their move to San Francisco.

The Hearst's were of Ulster protestant decent. Williams paternal great grandfather John Hearst had left Ballybay county Monaghan with his wife and six children in 1766, as part of the 'Cahans Exodus', which was the emigration of a group of 100 families, strict Presbyterians, who settled in South Carolina.

Williams mother Phoebe also had Irish ancestry, as her family came from county Galway.

George Hearst, despite being an older father, was a major influence on his son. He was born into humble origins, in Franklin County, Missouri, in 1820. But he used his sharp wits to improve his own position within the world that was accessible to him, in his case, mining.

Graduating at the age of 18 from the Franklin County mining school. He weathered a few setbacks, but eventually made a series of investments in some of the most successful mines in the country including the Homestake gold mine in the Black Hills of South Dakota

He also bought ranches in California, including the land that his son later used for his famous home, San Simeon, between San Jose and Los Angeles.

Having spent some of his self-made millions funding other aspiring political candidates' campaigns, George decided he could do a better job himself.

In 1865, just three years after moving to San Francisco, he was elected to the state assembly as a Democrat but failed to get re-elected after he voted against the 13th Amendment (outlawing slavery).

In 1882 he decided to run for governor but was defeated. Four years later he was appointed by Congress to fill a Californian Senate seat left open when its former occupant died.

George was elected in his own right in 1887 as a Democratic senator, but died before his first term was up, in 1891.

Williams mother Phoebe Elizabeth Apperson Hearst was a prominent feminist and campaigner for a women's right to vote. She was appointed as the first woman regent of University of California, Berkeley, donated funds to establish libraries at several universities, funded many anthropological expeditions, and founded the Phoebe A. Hearst Museum of anthropology.

William Hearst enjoyed a privileged upbringing spoiled by his adoring mother and elderly father. While loved he had a lot to prove. He had a highly educated mother with equally lofty standards, and a father who had worked his way from modest beginnings from Missouri mining school to mine owner, rancher, senator, and multi-millionaire.

Hearst received the finest education money could buy, first private tutors, then two grand tours of Europe before he was 16, followed by prep school at St. Paul's School in Concord, New Hampshire.

The young Hearst loved to read and to understand machinery. He used his parents' wealth to impress his peers and had a mischievous side, where he pulled pranks involving setting small animals loose at inopportune moments and inappropriate situations such as his parents dining room when entertaining.

He enrolled in Harvard in 1885. William seemed to enjoy his first year, but he was soon distracted. He was famous for his parties, enthusiastically participated in various clubs, wrote for humorous student paper the Lampoon, and took part in political campaigns. However, he was suspended for his outrageous antics, which included sponsoring wild beer parties in support of Grover Cleveland's successful presidential bid.

The suspension was initially temporary, but William Randolph lost any remaining good will among the faculty when he sent the professors who had voted to suspend him chamber pots with their own pictures and names printed at the bottom.

Upon leaving Harvard, William was determined to show his parents he could be a success and in 1886 he started working for Joseph Pulitzer's newspaper, the New York World as a reporter. His lengthy career in newspapers had begun and he immersed himself into studying how a newspaper operates and what made a good story.

In 1887, Hearst wrote to his father and told him: "I want the San Francisco Examiner."

This was a publication his father had obtained in a circuitous route when it was offered to him as repayment for a gambling debt.

Despite not being involved in the newspaper business, the shrewd elder Hearst realised its potential to promote his burgeoning political career.

George wanted his son to follow him into mining or ranching, which he felt would be more lucrative. However, in a bid to mature his son and heir he agreed to his sons request and in 1887 William Randolph Hearst was given control of the San Francisco Examiner and a legend in the newspaper business was born.

William Randolph showed a remarkable aptitude for regenerating the struggling newspaper, borrowing (or stealing) tricks he'd learned from his time at the New York World. Hearst would go on to spend more than $8 million of his family's money making the San Francisco paper a success. He used this wealth to attract some of the best writers of the day to his new project, such as Mark Twain, Jack London and political cartoonist Homer Davenport.

Under his stewardship the Examiner focused on scandals and crimes, knowing these were irresistible to readers looking for entertainment over information. If the facts of a story weren't interesting enough, he ordered his team of writers to embellish them.

He realised that working class readers (his core

market) desired easy-to-understand, attention-grabbing headlines accompanied by graphic illustrations.

The Daily Examiner became young Hearst's laboratory, where he gained a talent for making fake news and faking real news in such a way as to create maximum public interest and sales.

In just a few years the Examiner dominated the San Francisco market and was showing a profit.

Turning around the fortunes of the San Francisco Examiner was just the beginning for Hearst, whose vision was to create a national media empire.

In 1891 George Hearst died, he left his vast wealth to his wife who in turn gave William a monthly allowance of ten thousand dollars, equivalent in today's terms of $291,000 certainly enough to get by on. William used this wisely investing in a wide variety of stocks and shares whilst enjoying a lavish lifestyle

To make his vision a reality, Hearst knew that the east coast was the bastion of journalism and that for him to create his empire he would have to conquer New York.

In 1895, he turned his attention east, purchasing the sinking New York Morning Journal for $150,000 (about $4.8 million today.)

The Journal had been founded in 1882 by Albert Pulitzer, the younger brother of the legendary newspaperman Joseph Pulitzer who himself had founded the New York World in 1883. The Journal was a gossipy light-hearted publication that sold for a penny and was failing miserably. The challenge of reviving the Journal and taking on the older Pulitzer's reputation as a brilliant newspaperman, excited Hearst and he immediately resolved to challenge the Pulitzers dominant position in New York. A circulation war was about to break out.

To prepare for this, Hearst first imported his best managers from the San Francisco Examiner. He then used his financial muscle to hire the best newspaper men in town and even poached some of Pulitzer's most talented staff, including Morrill Goddard, managing editor of the World's Sunday edition, cartoonist Richard F. Outcault and a young Arthur Brisbane, who became managing editor of the Hearst newspaper empire, and a legendary columnist.

While he undoubtedly had the financial resources to entice these men away from Pulitzer, they were not just attracted by the salaries available. Each man would later explain they had become disillusioned with life at the New York World and had grown tired of Pulitzers temperamental and domineering managerial style.

For a paper aimed at the working man, Richard Outcault was an important appointment, he was famous for drawing an extremely popular comic strip for the World called Hogan's Alley which had a character called the Yellow Kid.

When he left the World to join the Journal, Pulitzer

was determined to carry on his prize asset and immediately hired another cartoonist to draw a different Yellow Kid.

This led New Yorkers to describe the bitter circulation war as 'yellow journalism.'

Pulitzer's World had pushed the boundaries of mass appeal for newspapers through bold headlines, aggressive news gathering, generous use of cartoons and illustrations, populist politics, progressive crusades, an exuberant public spirit, and dramatic crime and human-interest stories.

Hearst's Journal used the same recipe for success, selling papers by printing giant headlines over lurid stories featuring crime, corruption, sex, and innuendo.

The rising popularity of the Journal driven by sensationalism and its price of just a penny soon saw its circulation double.

This forced Pulitzer to drop the price of the World from two cents to a penny. Soon the two papers were locked in a fierce, often spiteful competition for readers in which both papers spent large sums of money and saw huge gains in circulation.

Hearst was also using the Journal to further his political ambitions. Under his stewardship it was a stalwart of the populist or left wing of the Democratic Party. It was the only major publication in the east coast to support William Jennings Bryan in his failed 1896 presidential campaign.

As the circulation war with the World continued, 1898 saw both papers demand the United States declare war on Spain. An event which was later recreated in a memorable scene from Citizen Kane.

The story goes, that when an illustrator Hearst had dispatched to Cuba to cover a simmering rebellion against Spanish rule wrote back that there was no sign of war in 1898, Hearst cabled him a reply that read: "You furnish the pictures, I'll furnish the war."

However, Hearst denied this and there's no evidence that the message ever existed. But the legend lives on.

Historians today point out that the US and Spain had been getting closer and closer to war over the latter's harsh colonial rule in Cuba for most of the 19th century. Hearst's and Pulitzer's inflammatory reporting during the 1890s played into these existing resentments.

However, both men's newspapers were quick to blame Spain without any evidence, for an explosion that sank the U.S.S. Maine in the Havana harbour on February 15th, 1898. Although official reports did not directly implicate Spain, public sentiment that was partly driven by Hearst and Pulitzer saw the US officially declare war on Spain that April. Ironically, the costs of the Journal's and World's sensational coverage of the Spanish-American War nearly bankrupted both papers.

The two papers finally declared a truce in late 1898, after both lost vast amounts of money covering the

Spanish American War. Hearst lost several million dollars in his first three years as publisher of the Journal, but the paper began turning a profit after it ended its circulation and editorial war with the World.

William Randolph Hearst was building his media empire for two reasons. Firstly, he wanted to create a truly nationwide media conglomerate and dominate the US market. Secondly, he wanted to follow in his late father's footsteps and enter political life.

To aid his political ambitions he began to open papers in Boston, Chicago and Los Angeles.

Hearst was asked by the Democratic party to expand his growing empire into Chicago and in 1900 he set up the Chicago American, an evening paper. He wired his mother who sent him the funds needed for the venture.

Hearst's newspapers papers were aimed at the urban white working class, many of whom were recent immigrants.

Each of his publications were pro union, supported progressive taxation, and municipal ownership of utilities.

They all had a simple formula, featured abundant pictures, agony aunts for the lovesick and lonely, controversial columns, and sentimental stories.

These sentimental stories were aimed at the large Irish and German readership.

Hearst also used his newspapers to condemn the British empire and an unsavoury element was a tendency to spread fears about the 'yellow peril' of Asian immigration. The groundwork done; it was time for William Randolph Hearst to stand for election. Hearst was on the left wing of the progressive movement, speaking out for the working class, who bought his papers in droves. He was the enemy of the rich and powerful who were often the focus of his controversial editorials.

In 1902, with the support of the powerful and corrupt Democratic ward boss network of Tammany Hall, he successfully stood for election to the house of representatives as a congressman for New York. He would go on to be re-elected in 1904. However, running his ever-expanding media empire gave him little time to be in Washington.

In 1903, the day before his fortieth birthday, Hearst married Millicent Veronica Willson, a 21-year-old chorus girl, in New York City. He had just ended his relationship with Tessie Powers, a former waitress he had supported as his lover since his Harvard days.

The Hearst's had five boys. George Randolph Hearst, born on April 23rd, 1904; William Randolph Hearst Jr., born on January 27th, 1908; John Randolph Hearst, born in 1910; and twins Randolph Apperson Hearst and David Whitmire Hearst, born on December 2nd, 1915.

In 1904, Hearst made an unsuccessful run for the Democratic nomination for president eventually spending $2 million in the process.

The Democratic party now controlled by the conservative wing did not wish to endorse Hearst's populism and instead choose Alton B Parker who would go on to lose the presidential election to the incumbent Theodore Roosevelt.

Undaunted Hearst ran for New York mayor in 1905. Despite the ringing endorsements of his newspaper empire, he was narrowly defeated by New Yorkers angered at his poor congressional voting and attendance record.

Hearst also failed to be elected governor of New York in 1906.

In 1907 Hearst broke with Tammany Hall who controlled the Democratic party in New York. And decided to run for mayor again under a third-party banner of his own creation, the Municipal Ownership League. Tammany Hall had the power to make or break a political career and in 1909 they broke William Randolph Hearst who came 3rd in the election.

Hearst's political failures despite his vast wealth and influence earned him the nickname 'Also-Randolph' Hearst.

In 1915, three major events happened in Heart's life. Firstly, he founded the International Film Service, an animation studio designed to exploit the popularity of the comic strips his newspapers controlled. Secondly, his twin sons Randolph and David were born and finally he first saw the woman that he would leave his wife and children for.

Hearst first noticed the chorus girl and actress Marion Davies one of the Ziegfeld Follies, when he watched her perform in a Broadway show.

As a devout Roman Catholic, Hearst was staunchly opposed to divorce, but not too adultery.

Two years later in 1917, the now 54-year-old Hearst began an affair with the 20-year-old Davies that would eventually end his marriage and last until his death.

Hearst would cofound the movie studio Cosmopolitan Pictures, casting Davies in many of its projects and later naming her company president.

Away from the romance, his business life was booming and his political views changing.

Hearst's and his newspapers had been vocally against America entering the first world war but after the horrors of the conflict, his once left-wing radical views gradually changed, and Hearst began adopting more conservative positions.

He and his media empire proposed an isolationist foreign policy to avoid any more entanglement in what he regarded as corrupt European affairs which could only lead to another war.

He was now a militant nationalist, a fiercely anti-communist after the Russian Revolution, and deeply suspicious of the League of Nations and of the British, French, Japanese, and Russians.

In April 1919, William Randolph Hearst's mother Phoebe died, and he inherited the wealth his father had built up through his mining endeavours. As the New Yorker reports, before this, Randolph was only rich on paper. The media empire he'd always dreamed of had put him into debt.

Now financially secure, he took up permanent residence on his father's 168,000-acre ranch in southern California.

Hearst used his inheritance to build an elaborate estate, which he called 'La Cuesta Encantada' (the Enchanted Hill), but which would later be known as Hearst Castle.

With money no object he hired the San Francisco-based architect Julia Morgan to create his vision of an enormous, elaborate palace with multiple guest houses that would fill with many famous visitors over the years.

He spent $37 million on a private castle, put $50 million into New York City real estate, and put another $50 million into his art collection, the largest ever assembled by a single individual.

He furnished the mansion with art, antiques, rare manuscripts and entire historic rooms purchased and brought from the great houses of Europe. He established an Arabian horse breeding operation on the grounds. He also collected exotic animals which became part of the private zoo he established on the estate.

Hearst's last bid for office came in 1922, when he ran for the US Senate nomination in New York, only to be vetoed by fellow Irish American politician Al Smith the New York governor who would go on to seek the presidency (*See chapter 9*).

Hearst had made peace with the still powerful Tammany Hall, and they now backed his bid for the Senate. However, Al smith was now the most powerful man in the Democratic party, and he feared Hearst's populism and ensured he did not secure the nomination.

Hearst never forgave Smith for this slight and took his revenge not once but twice. In 1928 Al Smith was the Democratic candidate for president, the first Roman Catholic nominee for any major party. Despite him being a fellow Irish American and sharing Hearst's anti Prohibition views, William threw the weight of his media empire behind the Republican candidate Herbert Hoover, who swept aside Smith in the General election.

Smith would try for the presidency again in 1932 but Hearst swung his support behind Franklin D. Roosevelt at the 1932 Democratic National Convention, via his allies William Gibbs McAdoo and John Nance Garner.

I can't help but wonder if Al Smith had not stood in Hearst's way in 1922, America would have had its first Irish American Roman Catholic president much sooner than 1960.

With his political career now all but over, Hearst concentrated on his business empire and love life.

By the mid-1920s, one in every four Americans read a Hearst owned newspaper.

Hearst owned twenty daily and eleven Sunday papers in thirteen cities, among them the Los Angeles Examiner, the Boston American, the Atlanta Georgian, the Chicago Examiner, the Detroit Times, the Seattle Post-Intelligencer, the Washington Times, the Washington Herald, and his flagship, the San Francisco Examiner.

His empire also included King Features syndication service which placed featured articles or comics in multiple papers at once, the International News Service, the American Weekly a syndicated Sunday supplement, International Newsreel, and six magazines, including Cosmopolitan, Good Housekeeping, Town and Country, and Harper's Bazaar.

He also ventured into motion pictures with a newsreel and a film company. His wealth was also boosted by his art collection, two million acres of land and shares in a mine. William Randolph Hearst and his empire were at their zenith.

It was now time to make his love for Marion Davis public. The couple began to openly live together in California from 1924 onwards.

His wife Millicent could tolerate a rival in the background but not in public and she officially separated from Hearst. The couple remained legally married until Hearst's death. Millicent went on to build a life independent of Hearst and lived in New York becoming a noted philanthropist. She would outlive William by 23 years dying aged 92 in 1974.

In 1925, after seeing photographs in Country Life magazine, Hearst decided to buy and renovate St. Donat's Castle in Vale of Glamorgan, Wales. William besotted with Davies wanted to create a romantic base for them in Europe.

True to his extravagant nature Hearts spent astronomical sums on restoring the castle. In scenes reminiscent of a Hollywood movie, entire rooms from other great houses and castle across Europe were purchased, moved and rebuilt in St Donat's. Hearst built 34 green and white marble bathrooms, for the many guest suites in the castle and completed a series of terraced gardens, which survive intact today.

Hearst and Davies spent much of their time entertaining and held several lavish parties, the guests at which included Charlie Chaplin, Douglas Fairbanks, Winston Churchill, and a young John F. Kennedy.

When Hearst died, the castle was bought by Atlantic College, an international boarding school, which still uses it.

Hearst and Davies spent their time between America and Europe and the lavish parties continued at their fabulous home in San Simeon.

Perhaps because of the negative portrayal of a character based on her in Citizen Kane people now think of Marion Davis as a beautiful but dizzy blonde. A man with the power and wealth of William Randolph Hearst could get a beautiful woman anywhere, what kept him with Davis, was not only her beauty but her warm and funny personality. This is reinforced by one of the guests at their many lavish parties Winston Churchill, who after staying with the couple wrote to his wife Clementine:

> "Were all charmed by her. She is not strikingly beautiful nor impressive in any way. But her personality is most attractive... She asked us to use her house as if it was our own."

There were dinner parties every weekend the couple was in town, as well as Christmas and birthday parties and themed masked balls. While they were a lot of fun, Hearst had rules. Davies struggled with alcoholism, and Hearst controlled how much alcohol guests could drink. You were allowed two pre-dinner cocktails, followed by wine at dinner, but not too much.

After the meal, Hearst would show a movie, a habit that was quickly picked up by other Hollywood hosts.

Life seemed charmed for Hearst, 1929 started well when he became one of the sponsors of the first round-the-world voyage in an airship, the LZ 127 Graf Zeppelin from Germany.

Ever the show man his sponsorship was conditional on the trip starting at Lakehurst Naval Air Station, New Jersey.

The ship's captain, Dr. Hugo Eckener, first flew the Graf Zeppelin across the Atlantic from Germany to pick up Hearst's photographer and at least three Hearst correspondents.

One of them was Grace Marguerite, Lady Hay Drummond-Hay, who by that flight became the first woman to travel around the world by air.

In October 1929, the stock market crash and resulting economic depression hit his media empire hard, especially the newspapers, many of whom were unprofitable.

It is unlikely that the newspapers ever paid their own way; mining, ranching and forestry provided whatever dividends the Hearst Corporation paid out.

Hearst had to shut down his film company and several of his publications.

During this time, his editorials became more isolationist and nationalistic. He turned against President Roosevelt, while most of his working-class readership supported FDR and his New Deal policies.

Hearst's reputation was tarnished when, in 1934, after despite checking with Jewish leaders to ensure a visit would be to their benefit, he visited Berlin and interviewed Adolph Hitler, helping to legitimise the Nazi regime in Germany.

Hearst's papers ran columns without rebuttal by Nazi leader Hermann Goering and Hitler himself, as well as Mussolini and other dictators in Europe and Latin America.

Hearst's crusade against Roosevelt and the New Deal, combined with union strikes and boycotts of his properties, undermined the financial strength of his empire. Circulation of his major publications declined in the mid-1930s, while rivals such as the New York Daily News were flourishing.

He refused to take effective cost-cutting measures, and instead increased his expensive art purchases. His friend Joseph P. Kennedy offered to buy the magazines, but Hearst jealously guarded his empire and refused. Instead, he sold some of his heavily mortgaged real estate. San Simeon itself was mortgaged to Los Angeles Times owner Harry Chandler in 1933 for $600,000.

However, Hearst's funds and the empire suddenly ran out. In 1937 the two corporations that controlled the empire found themselves $126 million in debt. Hearst had to turn them over to a seven-member committee whose purpose was to save what they could. They managed to hold off economic failure only by selling off much of Hearst's private fortune and all his public powers as a newspaper owner. From that point, Hearst was reduced to being an employee, subject to the directives of an outside manager.

Hearst reluctantly sold many of his antiques and vast art collection to pay creditors. The first year he sold items for a total of $11 million.

Legally Hearst avoided bankruptcy, although the public saw it as such, as appraisers went through the tapestries, paintings, furniture, silver, pottery, buildings, autographs, jewellery, and other collectibles. Items in the thousands were gathered from a five-story warehouse in New York, warehouses near San Simeon containing copious amounts of Greek sculpture and ceramics, and the contents of St. Donat's.

His collections were sold off in a series of auctions and private sales in 1938–39. John D. Rockefeller, Junior, bought

$100,000 of antique silver for his new museum at Colonial Williamsburg.

The market for art and antiques had not recovered from the depression, so Hearst made an overall loss of hundreds of thousands of dollars.

While World War II restored circulation and advertising revenues, his great days were over.

The Hearst Corporation continues to this day as a large, privately held media conglomerate based in New York City. Ironically, one reason William Randolph Hearst has remained alive in the public imagination is because he was immortalised in Citizen Kane. The debut feature of young director Orson Welles, who also wrote and starred in the 1941 movie.

The film told the tale of the life of a genius media mogul-turned-megalomaniac, who dies power-crazed, hated, and isolated in his huge Florida estate.

Wells was aware that the film could draw parallels to Hearst and to avoid any backlash he limited access to dailies and intensively managed the film's publicity.

A December 1940 feature story in Stage magazine compared the film's narrative to Faust and made no mention of Hearst.

The film was scheduled to premiere at RKO's flagship theatre Radio City Music Hall on February 14th, but in early January 1941 Welles was not finished with post-production work and told RKO that it still needed its musical score.

To ensure maximum publicity for launch in the national press RKO without Wells approval, arranged for a rough cut of the movie to be previewed for selected journalists on 3rd January 1941.

Gossip columnist Hedda Hopper (an arch-rival of Louella Parsons, the Hollywood correspondent for Hearst papers) showed up to the screening uninvited. Most of the critics at the preview said that they liked the film and gave it good, advanced reviews. Hopper wrote negatively about it, calling the film a "vicious and irresponsible attack on a great man" and criticising its corny writing and old-fashioned photography.

Wells and his script collaborator, screenwriter Herman J. Mankiewicz, argued that they created Kane as a composite character, who was brought to life using elements from among others such as Harold McCormick, Samuel Insull and Howard Hughes.

News of Citizen Kane now reached Hearst and he didn't like what he was hearing.

It is easy to believe that Hearst was enraged by the veiled attack on his life, but his real anger towards the movie was not vanity but his love for Marion Davis. He was upset at the portrayal of the character Susan Alexander Kane, Kane's mistress and second wife, played by Dorothy Comingore. Hearst believed this character who was portrayed as a talentless alcoholic actress and virtual prisoner in a vast lavish castle represented his partner, Marion Davies.

The assumption that the character of Susan Alexander Kane was based on Marion Davies was a major reason Hearst now resolved to destroy Citizen Kane.

Hearst's career in newspapers had taught him that attacking the movie would only bring it more attention. Instead, he banned his chain of papers from covering or advertising it. He had help from powerful friends, including gossip columnist Louella Parsons and MGM head Louis B. Meyer, who sent a representative/enforcer to offer George Schaefer the president of RKO, which owned Citizen Kane, $800,000 to destroy all the negatives.

Welles and the studio RKO Pictures resisted the pressure, but Hearst and his Hollywood friends succeeded in pressuring theatre chains to limit showings of Citizen Kane, resulting in only moderate box-office numbers and seriously impairing Welles's future career prospects.

After the disastrous financial losses of the 1930s, the Hearst Company returned to profitability during the Second World War, when advertising revenues skyrocketed.

Hearst, after spending much of the war at his estate of Wyntoon, returned to San Simeon full-time in 1945 and resumed building works. He also continued collecting, on a reduced scale. He threw himself into philanthropy by donating a great many works to the Los Angeles County Museum.

Construction ended in 1947 when Hearst became too ill to travel there from his main home in Beverly Hills. He died four years later, on August 14th, 1951, at the age of 88.

He was interred in the Hearst family mausoleum at the Cypress Lawn Cemetery in Colma, California, which his parents had established.

The real Citizen Kane was now dead.

The Founding Fathers sign the Declaration of Independence

Richard Crocker (right), boss of Tammany Hall (depicted above), and owner of Epsom Derby winner (see Chapter 2)

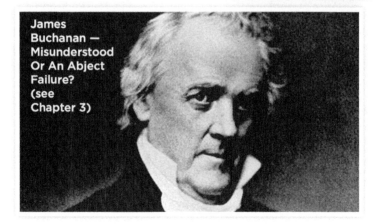

James Buchanan — Misunderstood Or An Abject Failure? (see Chapter 3)

A depiction of the assassination of President James Garfield

Chester Arthur — The
Accidental President
(see Chapter 4)

James Curley (left) was
known as the Mayor of the
Poor (see Chapter 6)

Mother Jones and a large group of children marching from Philadelphia to New York.

Mother Jones's 100th birthday. See 'Mother Jones — The Most Dangerous Woman In America' (Chapter 5)

John Francis 'Honey' Fitzgerald — Founder of a Political Dynasty (see Chapter 7)

William Randolph Hearst — The Real Citizen Kane (see Chapter 8)

William Randolph Hearst with three of his sons

Al Smith finally secured the Democratic presidential nomination in 1928 (below). See 'Al Smith: The Man Who Wanted To Be President But Helped Build The Empire State Building Instead' (Chapter 9)

James Farley the Post Master General with First Lady Eleanor Roosevelt inspecting Mother's Day stamps. See 'James Farley: The Power Behind FDR's Presidency' (Chapter 10)

Mayor Daley — The Man Who Handed The Presidency To JFK
(see Chapter 11)

Jane Byrne — The Woman Who Smashed The Glass Ceiling
In The Windy City (see Chapter 12)

Daniel Patrick Moynihan
— The Democrat Who
Worked For Nixon
(see Chapter 13)

Eugene McCarthy — The
Great Liberal Who Backed
Reagan (see Chapter 14)

Joseph McCarthy — The Anti-Communist
Senator Or Opportunist? (see Chapter 15)

JFK, the first Roman Catholic President of the United States

With the election of President Joe Biden,
the Irish are back in power

In 1904 Al Smith was first elected to the New York State Assembly where he would serve for 11 years. Smith built on his working-class beginnings, identifying himself with immigrants and campaigning as the champion of the working man. His political journey was long but faltered just before the White House

CHAPTER 9
AL SMITH

THE MAN WHO WANTED TO BE PRESIDENT BUT HELPED BUILD THE EMPIRE STATE BUILDING INSTEAD

Al Smith was the dominant force in New York State politics for over 20 years. He was the first politician of national stature to rise from the ranks of urban Irish American Roman Catholic immigrants, in his case, the Irish American immigrants of downtown Manhattan. He served 4 terms as New York State governor. He ran unsuccessfully as the Democratic candidate for president in 1928 as the first Roman Catholic candidate nominated by a major party. After his career in politics ended, he became the president of Empire State, Inc., the corporation that built and operated the Empire State building.

Alfred Emanuel Smith was born on December 30th, 1873, to Joseph Alfred and Catherine Smith.

His father was of German and Italian descent and was a civil war veteran who had fought with the 11th

New York Infantry regiment, a fighting force raised by Colonel Elmer E. Ellsworth, a personal friend of US President Abraham Lincoln. Drawn from the ranks of the city's many volunteer fire companies, the unit was known alternately as the Ellsworth Zouaves.

Catherine Smiths parents were Maria Marsh and Thomas Mulvihill, who were immigrants from County Westmeath.

The young Alfred (known as Al) was brought up on the lower east side of Manhattan close to the new Brooklyn bridge an area he would live in all his life. He often said at stump speeches "The Brooklyn bridge and I grew up together".

While Al Smith was from a mixed cultural background, he identified most with the Irish American community. He would go on to be one of its most committed advocates and campaigners.

His father, who owned a small trucking firm, died when Alfred was just 13. The young boy who was then studying at St. James school dropped out to support his family.

Those few years in the public school system would be his only formal educational experience.

He served as an altar boy and was strongly influenced by the Catholic priests he worked with. His faith would have a lasting impact on his political beliefs.

Smith found work at the local Fulton fish market

where he worked for $12 per week, to help support his family.

While he would never attend high school or college, he would later claim he learned more about life and politics by watching people at the Fulton fish market than any college course could teach him.

On May 6th, 1900, aged just 17, Al Smith married his childhood sweetheart, Catherine Ann Dunn, with whom he would have five children, Two daughters and three sons. Smith remained deeply in love with Catherine all his life.

He developed a love of amateur dramatics and was recognised as a fine actor. He would soon put his smooth oratorical style to effective use as he entered politics.

At the outset, Smith saw himself as a defender of the working man and especially of the Irish emigrants. He became a protege of the Democratic party ward boss 'Silent' Charles Murphy, who was a leading figure in the infamously corrupt Tammany Hall organisation which effectively controlled Democratic politics in New York.

Murphy also known as Boss Murphy was responsible for the election of three mayors of New York and three governors of New York State.

While never personally accused of corruption, Murphy and Tammany Hall made Smiths first political appointment, when in 1895, Smith was appointed as an investigator in the office of the commissioner of jurors.

In 1904 Smith was first elected to the New York State assembly, where he would serve for 11 years. Smith built on his working-class beginnings, identifying himself with immigrants and campaigning as the champion of the working man all his life.

This was to prove a great education in political manoeuvring and leadership. His lively intelligence, dedication to the voters of his district, and genial manner won him powerful offices. In 1911, the Democrats obtained a majority of seats in the state assembly, and Smith became majority leader and chairman of the committee on ways and means. The following year, after the loss of the Democratic majority, he became the minority leader. When the Democrats reclaimed the majority after the next election, he was elected Speaker for the 1913 session. He became minority leader again in 1914 and 1915.

He became known as an eloquent speaker and a great champion of workers' rights campaigning against dangerous and unhealthy workplace conditions bringing legislation such as fire regulations, toilet facilities for workers, and limiting the number of hours worked by women and children. Perhaps his greatest achievement at this stage was as vice chairman of the commission set up to investigate the tremendous tragedy of the Triangle Shirtwaist factory fire.

On the evening of the 25th of March 1911 in a cramped New York sweat shop on the eighth floor of the

Asch Building, 23–29 Washington Place, just east of Washington Square Park a discarded cigarette sparked a deadly conflagration among scattered cloth, which would be known as the Triangle Shirtwaist factory fire.

The flames, fed by the large piles of cotton and paper waste cast aside from the machinists, quickly spread upward to the top two floors of the building.

The Triangle factory, owned by Max Blanck and Isaac Harris, was a sweatshop in every sense of the word, a cramped space lined with workstations and packed with poor immigrant workers, mostly teenaged women who did not speak English.

At the time of the fire, there were four elevators with access to the factory floors, but just one was fully operational and it could hold only 12 people at a time. There were two stairways down to the street, but one was locked from the outside to prevent theft by the workers and the other only opened inward. The fire escape, as all would come to see, was shoddily constructed, and could not support the weight of more than a few people at a time.

Despite the quick reaction of the New York fire services the fire truck ladders were only able to reach six stories, and the building's overloaded fire escape collapsed. Many workers, trapped by doors that had been locked to prevent theft and people taking a break, leapt from windows to their deaths.

The 129 women and 17 men who perished in the 18-

minute conflagration were mostly young European immigrants, some of whom were Irish.

It took several days for family members to identify the victims, with many burned beyond recognition.

Six of the victims, all interred under a monument in a New York City cemetery, were not identified until 2011 through research conducted by an amateur genealogist. A citywide outpouring of grief culminated on April 5th, 1911, in a 100,000-strong procession behind the hearses that carried the dead along Fifth Avenue; thousands more observed the memorial gathering.

Though the owners of the factory were indicted later that month on charges of manslaughter, they were acquitted in December 1911.

To make matters worse for survivors and the families of those that perished, the owners ultimately profited from inflated insurance claims that they submitted after the tragedy. However, the uproar generated by the disaster led to the creation of the Factory Investigating Commission by the New York state legislature in June 1912.

Smith was approached by activist Frances Perkins who made him aware of the city's atrocious factory conditions. The commission, chaired by State Senator Robert F. Wagner, held a series of widely publicised investigations around the state, interviewing 222 witnesses and taking 3500 pages of testimony. They hired field agents to do on-site inspections of factories.

Starting with the issue of fire safety, they studied broader factors of the risks of injury in the factory environment. Over the following year and a half, members of the commission visited factories, interviewed workers, and held public hearings across New York State.

One witness John Kenlon New York City's Fire Chief told the investigators that his department had identified more than 200 factories where conditions resulted in risk of a fire like that at the Triangle Factory.

As vice chairman of the commission, Smith worked with Frances Perkins who was then secretary for the committee on safety of the city of New York. She would later become the US Secretary of Labour from 1933 to 1945, the longest serving person in that position. In addition, she also made history as the first woman and first known LGBT person to serve in the US cabinet.

Perkins had a personal interest in the commission, as just one year earlier she had worked with the women at Shirtwaists to campaign and eventually win a 54-hour work week and other benefits that Perkins had agitated for. She knew many of the women who died.

Frances Perkins encouraged Smith to meet with the families of those that had perished in the tragedy.

Meeting the families of the deceased Triangle factory workers left a strong impression on Smith.

Working closely with Perkins, Smith crusaded against dangerous and unhealthy workplace conditions and championed corrective legislation. Smith was determined the commission would improve the conditions of factory workers and not just be a show of concern in response to public anger.

The commission's findings would eventually result in thirty-eight new laws regulating labour in New York State and gave both Smith and Perkins reputations as leading progressive reformers working on behalf of the working class.

The raft of new laws mandated better building access and egress, fireproofing requirements, the availability of fire extinguishers, the installation of alarm systems and automatic sprinklers, better eating and toilet facilities for workers, and limited the number of hours that women and children could work.

In the years from 1911 to 1913, sixty of the sixty-four new laws recommended by the commission were legislated for, with the support of the then New York Governor William Sulzer.

In November 1915, Smith again with the help of Tammany Hall was elected Sheriff of New York County. This was a role with large scope for patronage appointments which would provide loyal followers for his future political ambitions. Al Smith was now recognisesd as the leader of the progressive movement in New York City and State. The progressive movement had a focus on cleaning up the murky aspects of politics, modernisation of all aspects of life, a focus on family and education, prohibition, and women's suffrage. It was ironic that Smith had been propelled to power by Tammany Hall, one of the most corrupt organisations in American history and also that Smith was no fan of prohibition.

In 1917, he was elected president of the board of aldermen of the city of New York.

Al Smith had served his political apprenticeship. Now a seasoned player with a solid support base and strong campaign network, it was time for him to run for governor of New York State.

In 1918, Smith was encouraged to run for New York governor by Boss Murphy and the Democratic Tammany Hall operation. He was also helped by the support of the rising star of the Democratic Party and political strategist James Farley (*see chapter 10*).

In a close fought election, Smith defeated his Republican opponent Charles S. Whitman 47.36% to 46.66% with the Socialist candidate Charles W. Ervin a distant 3rd with 5.7% of the vote.

Smith's victory was down to both his personal popularity and the organisation skills of James Farley, who helped deliver the vote of upstate New York, usually a Republican stronghold.

In 1919, Smith gave the famous "A man as low and mean as I can picture" speech at the Carnegie Hall where he made a dramatic break with the publisher and fellow progressive Democrat, William Randolph Hearst (*see chapter 8*).

Hearst, known for his notoriously sensationalist and largely left-wing position in the state Democratic Party, was now the leader of its populist wing in New York. He had allied with Tammany Hall in electing the local administration and had attacked Smith while governor for starving children by not reducing the cost of milk.

In his speech Smith denounced William R. Hearst as an assassin of character, an enemy of the people, and an apostle of discord, and his newspapers were called a pestilence that walks in the dark.

This was a brave thing to do considering the power of the press and the Tammany Hall operation.

In 1920 it was no surprise then that Al Smith lost his bid for re-election when he was defeated by Nathan L Miller as Republican candidates swept the board across the USA on the coat tails of Warren G. Harding's landslide victory in the US presidential election, held on the same day as the race for governor.

Al Smith had more work to do for New York and he and Farley immediately began planning for another run. This would prove to be more successful and in 1922 he secured the second of what would go on to be his four terms as New York governor, when he defeated his old rival Nathan Miller with over 55% of the popular vote.

In his 1922 re-election campaign encouraged by fellow prohibition 'Wet' James Farley, he embraced his position as an anti-prohibitionist. Smith brazenly offered alcohol to guests at the executive mansion in Albany, and repeated the New York prohibition enforcement statute, the 'Mullan-Gage' law.

As governor again, Smith became known nationally as a progressive who sought to make government more efficient and more effective in meeting social needs.

He fought for adequate housing, improved factory laws, proper care of the mentally ill, child welfare, and the expansion of state parks.

Smith's young assistant Robert Moses built the nation's first state park system and reformed the civil service, later gaining appointment as Secretary of State of New York.

During Smith's time in office, New York strengthened laws governing workers' compensation, women's pensions and children and women's labour rights, again with the help of his old friend Frances Perkins, who would eventually be the future President Franklin D. Roosevelt's labour secretary.

As governor, he also effected a reorganization of the state government on a consolidated, business-like basis and repeatedly demonstrated his leadership by forcing Republican legislatures to accept his recommendations.

With this high profile he not only stood for re-election as governor in 1924 but decided to seek a national platform for his reforming agenda as the Democratic candidate for president at the Democratic convention held in Madison Square Gardens in New York from June 24th to July 9th, 1924.

This was to prove a legendary example in compromise politics, as delegates took 103 ballots to nominate a presidential candidate, which was sadly not to be Al smith. The newspapers called the convention a "Klanbake," as pro-Klan and anti-Klan delegates fought bitterly over the party's future platform.

Smith's leading opponent was former Wilson cabinet member William G. McAdoo, who was supported by the Ku Klux Klan.

The Klan was a major source of power within the Democratic party, and McAdoo did not repudiate its endorsement.

The convention opened on a Monday and by Thursday night, after 61 ballots, the convention was deadlocked.

Al Smith now represented the party's anti-Klan, anti-prohibition wing. McAdoo also backed prohibition, which was then the law of the land.

Smith and his supporters failed by a slim margin to pass a platform position condemning the Klan. The convention also had no African American delegates.

To celebrate this defeat, tens of thousands of hooded Klansmen rallied in a field in New Jersey, across the river from New York City. This event, known subsequently as the "Klanbake," was also attended by hundreds of Klan delegates to the convention, who burned crosses, urged violence and intimidation against

African Americans and Roman Catholics, and attacked effigies of Smith.

The convention was also notable for the return to the political stage of Franklin D. Roosevelt, who nominated Al Smith. His excellent speech in which he dubbed Smith the 'Happy Warrior" and praised his socially progressive platform and history, was his first major political appearance since contracting polio in 1921.

As a two-thirds vote was needed to win the nomination, McAdoo and Smith cancelled each other out. There were also scores of vanity candidates each wanting a moment of fame, but with no chance of success. This crowded field prevented either man from collecting even a simple majority of votes and the nomination.

A total of 19 candidates got votes on the first ballot. By the time the process concluded, 60 different candidates had received a delegate's vote.

The famous reporter and political columnist H.L. Mencken, who covered the rowdy, sweltering, never-ending convention for the Baltimore Evening Sun, wrote:

"There may not be enough kluxers in the convention to nominate McAdoo, but there are probably enough to beat any anti-Klan candidate so far heard of, and they are all on their tiptoes today, their hands clutching their artillery nervously and their eyes a pop for dynamite bombs and Jesuit spies."

The conference descended at times into chaos, with

numerous rowdy floor demonstrations between ballots, with the chants for "Mac! Mac! McAdoo!" countered by Smith's forces who cried out, "Ku, Ku, McAdoo,"

McAdoo came to the convention fully expecting to be the nominee and led through the 77th ballot. Smith now knew he could not prevail and that his sole purpose, was primarily to block McAdoo.

While he failed in securing the nomination, he ensured that the Klan backed McAdoo would also fail and not secure the nomination and potentially the presidency.

On the 103rd ballot McAdoo finally faced reality and withdrew along with Smith. The nomination was then finally awarded to corporate lawyer and the US ambassador to the United Kingdom, John W. Davis. He would go on to lose the general election to the Republican candidate Calvin Coolidge.

Disappointed but buoyed by his blocking of McAdoo, Al Smith concentrated on securing his fourth term as governor of New York. Again, aided by James Farley's wise council and strategic skills he went on to narrowly defeat Theodore Roosevelt, Jr. the eldest son of former President, Theodore Roosevelt.

Roosevelt would later go on to win the US Medal of Honour in WW2 for directing American troops at Utah Beach during the Normandy landings.

Smith was now recognised as the foremost urban leader of what became to be known as the Efficiency

Movement in the United States which was noted for achieving a wide range of social and business reforms.

In 1926, Al Smith stood for and won his fourth and final term as New York State governor easily beating his Republican challenger. Ogden Livingston Mills.

Mills would later be a great asset to the Democrats as his incompetent handling of the US economy as Secretary of the Treasury in President Herbert Hoover's cabinet deepened the economic crisis in the early 30s and helped FDR win the White House.

Whilst he continued his reforming agenda in New York, Smith still yearned for the national stage and in he again sought the Democratic nomination for the presidency.

Four years after his withdrawal from the 1924 convention and with 4 terms as New York State governor, Smith was now viewed as the front runner for the nomination and the most credible candidate the Democrats could field in the general election.

His old rival William McAdoo decided not to run against Smith. He concluded that Smiths nomination was a foregone conclusion, and his standing would be a futile gesture. The Democratic convention was held in the Sam Houston Hall in Houston Texas over 3 days June 26th to the 28th The convention was broadcast via radio, allowing Smith to follow it from Albany New York.

Despite the inevitability of Smiths nomination, his

rivals who disliked his Roman Catholicism and Wet views on prohibition, made a final attempt to encourage delegates to reject him.

The leader of the Texas delegation, Governor Dan Moody spoke out against his anti-prohibition sentiment by fighting for a "dry", prohibitionist platform. A compromise pro prohibition Roman Catholic candidate was even suggested, Thomas J. Walsh. However, this attempt was quickly snuffed out. The Smith campaign countered by pledging that despite Smiths own personal views, he would always ensure "honest enforcement of the constitution".

In marked contrast to the chaotic scenes of 4 years earlier, which took 103 ballots to secure a winner Al Smith was selected as the Democratic candidate for the Election after the first ballot. The boy from Brooklyn had now become the man who was the first Roman Catholic candidate for any major political party in American history. The choice for vice president was also straight forward. At the convention, the party leadership selected Senator Joseph Robinson from Arkansas to balance the tickets regional profile.

As Smith basked in the glory of his nomination, storm clouds were already on the horizon.

Firstly, Franklin D. Roosevelt who had acted as Smith floor manager at the convention delivered his nomination speech. This was received with rapturous applause and even as Smith had secured his lifelong dream of the Democratic nomination, many delegates wondered if they had done the right thing nominating a Roman Catholic. Was it possible Roosevelt was the better candidate? After all he was a Protestant and a bearer of the Roosevelt name (Theodore Roosevelt was still immensely popular) would FDR fare better than Smith in the general election?

Secondly, under New York election laws, no individual could be on the ballot for both president and governor in the same election cycle, so Smith could not run for re-election as governor of New York.

Smith knew that to secure the presidency he would have to win his home state of New York, which had the most electoral college votes of any state.

Smith now believed that Roosevelt was the only individual capable of defeating Albert Ottinger, the popular Republican Party nominee for governor. Smith believed that Roosevelt would be capable of drawing 200,000 more votes than any other prospective Democrat. Smith also thought that Roosevelt running for governor would boost voter turnout among Protestant Democrats in upstate New York, without which Smith might lose his home state (and its crucial 45 electoral votes).

In September, Smith formally approached Roosevelt about running for governor. However, he failed to convince Roosevelt to commit to enter the race.

Since at least the early 1920s, Roosevelt had planned

to seek the governorship, viewing it as a stepping-stone to the presidency. Roosevelt's long term strategic plan was focused on a gubernatorial campaign in 1932 as a springboard for a presidential candidacy in 1936.

Roosevelts reluctance was based on his belief that was going to be a poor year for Democratic candidates across the board. This was due to the popularity of Republican President Calvin Coolidge and a prosperous economy which would benefit Republicans across the board.

Still unsure of whether to run or not Roosevelt decided to go on holiday and place himself out of reach of the Democratic state leadership who along with Smith were trying to convince him to run.

As the New York Democratic party was preparing to convene in Rochester, Roosevelt was now enjoying his vacation.

However, Smith was determined to convince Roosevelt to run and try and secure the New York electoral votes in the general election. He managed to reach Roosevelt by telephone and after a lengthy conversation he eventually convinced him to seek the nomination.

Despite FDR being on holiday, Jimmy Walker the mayor of New York who was a close friend of Roosevelt and a political ally placed FDRs name into the nomination at the convention. Once this was done, his victory was a formality.

Smith believed he had secured a political victory, but

it came at a high price. James A Farley now left his campaign and went to work for FDR. Farley would go on to help Roosevelt secure the governorship and his strategic guidance and political expertise would be sorely missed by Smith in the presidential election.

While governor of New York planning his bid to securing the Democratic nomination Smith thought he would be running against the incumbent Republican President Calvin Coolidge, but in 1927 Coolidge announced he would not stand for re-election.

In his memoirs, Coolidge explained his decision not to run:

"The Presidential office takes a heavy toll of those who occupy it and those who are dear to them. While we should not refuse to spend and be spent in the service of our country, it is hazardous to attempt what we feel is beyond our strength to accomplish."

Smith would now be up against the Republican candidate Herbert Hoover the US commerce secretary.

Interestingly Coolidge had declined to endorse Hoovers nomination, once saying of him:

"For six years that man has given me unsolicited advice—all of it bad."

Ever the politician, Coolidge had no desire to split the party by publicly opposing the nomination of the hugely popular commerce secretary, so the battle was now set for a contest between Al Smith and Herbert Hoover.

Smith threw himself into the campaign, but he was not a particularly good campaigner. His campaign theme song, "The Sidewalks of New York", had little appeal among rural voters, and they found that his 'city' accent, when heard on radio, seemed slightly foreign, dare I say even like an Irish Catholic.

Smith was always up against it in the election campaign, the Republican Party was still benefiting from an economic boom, as well as a failure to reapportion Congress and the electoral college following the 1920 census, which had registered a 15 percent increase in the urban population. This favoured Hoover, whose Republican party was biased toward small-town and rural areas.

Despite Smiths efforts and even those of Roosevelt in the latter stages of the campaign, it was not yet time for religious prejudice to be set aside and Smith lost to his Republican opponent Herbert Hoover.

The buoyant US economy and no American involvement in a war combined with a distrust of a Roman Catholic candidate who many Protestants believed would be dictated to by the Pope in Rome, led to a Republican landslide.

The fatal blow was that Smith narrowly lost New York State.

Smith was an articulate proponent of good government and efficiency, as was Hoover. Smith swept almost the entire Irish American vote, which had been split in

1920 and 1924 between the parties. He also attracted millions of other Catholics, generally ethnic whites, to the polls for the first time, especially women, who were first allowed to vote in 1920. He lost important Democratic constituencies in the rural north as well as in southern cities and suburbs. However, he successfully won votes in the deep south, thanks in part to the appeal of his running mate, Senator Joseph Robinson from Arkansas, but he lost five southern states to Hoover.

Smith carried the ten most populous cities in the United States, an indication of the rising power of the urban areas and their changing demographics.

Reporter Frederick William Wile made the oft-repeated observation that Smith was defeated by "the three P's: Prohibition, Prejudice and Prosperity".

On prohibition Smith was a committed "wet", which was a term used for opponents of prohibition; as New York governor, he had repealed the state's prohibition law. As a "wet", Smith attracted voters who wanted beer, wine and liquor and did not like dealing with criminal bootleggers, along with voters who were outraged that new criminal gangs had taken over the streets in most large and medium-sized cities.

The Democratic Party split north and south on the issue, with the more rural south continuing to favour prohibition. During the campaign, Smith tried to duck the issue with non-committal statements.

The election was the first-time electors had the choice of as Roman Catholic with a chance of the presidency. It led to the mobilisation of both Catholic and anti-Catholic forces.

Anti-Catholic prejudice was nothing new in America, it had been transported across the seas in immigrant ships from Europe. Protestant domination of the political and economic system in America allowed myths and superstitions regarding Catholicism to be nurtured and become embedded in large parts of American society.

The earlier Protestant settlers descendants now viewed the influx of Catholic immigrants from Ireland, Italy and Eastern Europe since the mid-19th century with suspicion and feared the progress of their descendants of which Al Smith was now the personification and standard bearer.

Smith was connected to the hopes and aspirations of immigrants, especially Catholics and Jews from eastern and southern Europe. Smith was a devout Catholic, but his struggles against religious bigotry were often misinterpreted when he fought the religiously inspired Protestant morality imposed by prohibitionists.

Many Protestants carried old fears, and others believed that Smith would answer to the Pope rather than the United States constitution and the American people.

The Ku Klux Klan held cross burnings across the

country in protest to his nomination and this was a major factor in Smith losing 5 southern states which were traditionally Democratic strongholds. He also became the first Democratic candidate since Reconstruction to lose more than one southern state.

Smith failed to develop a successful strategy to combat arguments that targeted his faith, once again highlighting how much he missed the support and sage advice of James Farley who ironically helped FDR win the New York governor's race, while Smith lost his home state and with it the chance of the presidency.

Herbert Hoover benefited incredibly from the perception of Republican-led economic prosperity, which, less than a year later, would be proven to have been an illusion with the stock market crash and the beginning of the Great Depression.

As president, Hoover dealt with the financial crisis of 1929 by reversing the low-tax policies of Calvin Coolidge, which turned a short, sharp fiscal crisis into a long, painful depression for the first time in US history.

Some political scientists believe that the election started a voter realignment that helped develop Roosevelt's New Deal coalition. One political scientist said, "...not until , with the nomination of Al Smith, a north-eastern reformer, did Democrats make gains among the urban, blue-collar and Catholic voters who were later to become core components of the New Deal coalition and break the pattern of minimal class polarization that had characterized the Fourth Party System."

Political scientist Samuel Lubell wrote, "Before the Roosevelt Revolution, there was an Al Smith revolution."

However, despite the anti-Catholic prejudice every presidential candidate since 1960 has honoured Smith by going to the Alfred E. Smith Memorial Foundation Dinner and in 1960 John F. Kennedy the first Catholic president said "When this happens then the bitter memory of will begin to fade, and all that will remain will be the figure of Al Smith, large against the horizon, true, courageous, and honest, who in the words of the cardinal, served his country well, and having served his country well, nobly served his God".

A defeated Al Smith had seen his presidential hopes crushed and with FDR now in the governor's mansion with his eyes firmly set on the presidency in 1932 it was time for Smith to reflect on his future.

After the election, Smith moved into business becoming the president of the Empire State corporation. He even arranged for construction to begin on St Patricks day 1930. Just 13 months later, the world's tallest skyscraper at the time opened on May 1st, 1931, which was a record for such a large project.

Smith sought the 1932 Democratic nomination but was defeated by Franklin D. Roosevelt, his close friend and successor as governor of New York. This led to a rift that some say was never healed.

Smith saw the evil of Hitler and was an early opponent of the Nazi regime in Germany. He spoke at a mass rally against Nazism in Madison Square Gardens in March 1933. In 1934 Smith became the Honorary night zookeeper of the newly renovated Central Park Zoo. Despite this being a purely ceremonial title, Smith was given the keys to the Zoo and often took his grandchildren and other guest to see the animals at night.

In 1939 Smith was appointed a Papal Chamberlain of the Sword and Cape, one of the highest honours which the Papacy can award a layman.

Al Smith died on October 4, 1944, of a heart attack, at the age of 70.

Al Smith who FDR referred to as the 'Happy warrior' was the trail brazier for future Irish American presidential candidates. His groundwork would eventually reap rewards for JFK and more recently Joseph Biden.

CHAPTER 10
JAMES FARLEY
THE POWER BEHIND FDR'S PRESIDENCY

I n 1850 a young couple left their home in Castletown Kilpatrick, in the townland of Balli-naskerry, County Meath, which was still suffering the ravages of 'An Ghort a Mhor', the great famine. In a desperate bid for survival, they had decided in common with many of their fellow Irish men and women to seek a new life across the Atlantic Ocean in America.

John Farrelly and his wife Margaret bid a final farewell to their families as they knew this would be a one-way journey with no guarantees of a safe arrival in America aboard the harsh conditions of the cramped coffin ships.

The couple walked the 15 miles to Drogheda where they began their journey by first sailing to Liverpool, where they would soon embark on their arduous passage to the USA, cramped in the steerage section of one of the many steamers that moved across and back the Atlantic carrying new citizens for the young America.

The Farrelly's were among the lucky ones who survived the perilous conditions, and they finally arrived for processing on Ellis Island New York. The immigration officials told them that from then on, their name would be changed from Farrelly to Farley.

John Farrelly, or as he was now Farley, was 30 years of age when he disembarked on Ellis Island, while his wife Margaret was 8 years younger. They settled in Verplank's Point, Westchester, New York State, working hard to secure a better future for their children.

Years of arduous work was rewarded when one of their grandchildren became one of the most influential and powerful men in American politics, James Aloysius Farley. He would go onto be Post-Master General of the US and National Chairman of the Democratic party, which at the time was the highest position a Roman Catholic politician had reached.

He was also a business executive with Coca Cola, a Knight of Malta and a political kingmaker who was President Franklin Delano Roosevelt's (FDR) campaign manager for most of his major elections, including his presidential victories in 1932 and 1936.

James Aloysius Farley was born on May 30th, 1888,

one of five sons born to Irish catholic immigrant parents James and his wife Ellen (nee Goldrick). He was born in Grissy Point in Rockland County in upstate New York.

His father, James senior was a brick maker whose business acumen helped him acquire a part ownership of three small brick carrying schooners. He was also extremely interested in politics and a staunch supporter of the Democratic party.

His mother Ellen was a home maker and devoted to her five boys.

As the family's fortunes prospered, tragedy struck when James was 10 in 1897, his father was fatally injured when the family horse accidentally kicked him in the ribs.

He left a small life insurance policy worth around $3000 and his share of the schooners to his widow Eileen, but this was not enough to support the family.

James Farley and his brothers would spend the next few summers working as labourers in brickyards.

They used this income to support themselves and help their mother eventually purchase a small grocery and bar saloon. James and his brothers would spend what spare time they had left working in the combination shop and bar alongside their mother.

James attended the public school system, completing high school and, in his own words, "did enough studying to get by."

After graduating from high school, he attended Packard business college in New York City in August of 1905 to study bookkeeping and other business skills.

In the spring of 1906, Farley obtained a job with the Merlin Keiholtz paper company.

From 1911 to 1926 he was employed as bookkeeper and sales manager for the Universal Gysum Company.

While working for Universal Gypsum Farley began to follow his late father's interest in politics.

In his 1938 Autobiography 'Behind the ballots', Farley stated he always had his heart set on a political career.

Farley moved to Stony Point in upstate New York not far from his hometown and at just 23 in 1912 James began his political career when he was elected as a Democratic candidate for the position of town clerk. He would go on to serve 3 terms in this unpaid role, despite the Republican leanings of the local area. This was down to the nature of the man that James Farley was becoming.

He was a renowned campaigner for social and civil rights earning a reputation as a progressive thinker and supreme organiser. He was also well liked by both Democrats and Republicans. This was due to an affable manner, dedication to extra service, for instance he refused his share of license fees and saved prospective brides the embarrassment of an office visit by bringing the marriage license to their homes. He also had a phenomenal memory for names and faces, which made him one of Rockland County's best-liked citizens.

These personality traits never left him, and when coupled with an uncanny capacity for political predictions would earn him his reputation as a political seer.

In 1918 he was elected Chairman of the Rockland County Democratic Committee, a post he would hold until 1929. Part of Farley's famed political insight was spotting a winner and he used his newfound power to lobby the Democratic Tammany Hall Boss Charles F. Murphy and convinced him that his fellow Roman Catholic Alfred E. Smith, would be the best choice for governor of New York State.

Smith would go on to win the 1919 election after Farley's organisational skill and personal popularity helped deliver votes north of the Bronx line which was considered Republican territory.

After Smith's victory, he rewarded Farley with the post of New York Port Warden, a post which was abolished a year later when the New York Port Authority was established.

James married Elizabeth A. Finnegan on April 28th, 1920; they would go onto have 3 children. Two daughters and one son, Elizabeth, Ann and James Aloysius Farley, Jr. Farley ran for the New York State Assembly in 1922 and won in Rockland County, normally a solid Republican stronghold. He sat in the 146th New York state legislature in 1923, but he lost it at the next election for having voted for the repeal of the Mullan–Gage act, the state law that enforced prohibition.

His position was so powerful in Democratic New York state politics that he was appointed as the campaign manager for Al Smiths bid to regain the state governorship in the 1922 election.

Farley master minded Smith's campaign, it was such as success that the entire Democratic ticket was elected, and Smith easily defeated the incumbent Republican Governor Nathan Lewis Miller.

A delighted and grateful Smith looked to reward James Farley and their fellow Irish State Senator Jimmy Walker, who would go onto become New York mayor suggested Farley would be ideal as the chairman of the New York State Athletic Commission.

Farley accepted and became a great advocate of civil rights for African American athletes. So much so, that in 1926 he threatened to resign his post as Athletic Commissioner if boxing champion Jack Dempsey did not fight the mandatory challenger, African American fighter Harry Wills.

Farley even banned Dempsey from fighting white challenger Gene Tunney and publicly threatened to revoke boxing promoter Tex Rickard's Madison Square Garden license if he ignored the ruling of the commission.

While Willis never did fight Dempsey, Farley's

public stand for civil rights proved to be a valuable asset to the Democratic party for generations, and it would sow the seeds of the African American support for the Democratic party New Deal.

Because of his time as Athletic Commissioner Farley is well remembered in sporting circles.

The James A. Farley Award is the Boxing Writers Associations highest honour, awarded to those who exhibit honesty and integrity in the sport of boxing.

Farley's Box is the name given to a group of front row seats along Baseballs Yankee Stadium's first base line, which was frequented by Farley and many famous VIPs and guests. In later years, Farley would donate those tickets to boys clubs in New York City and the surrounding areas.

As for Willis, well he retired from boxing in 1932, and ran a successful real estate business in Harlem, New York.

He was known for his yearly fast, in which, once a year, he would subsist on water for a month. Wills admitted that his biggest regret in life was never getting the opportunity to fight Dempsey for the title. Wills was confident that he would have won such a match.

James Farley was now one of the most powerful men in New York state politics and it was now time for him to enter the national stage.

Farley was an ardent supporter of Governor Al

Smith's re-election bids, but he also felt a great admiration for another New York politician Franklin Delano Roosevelt (FDR).

In 1924, James served as a delegate to the Democratic National Convention in Madison Square Garden New York City, where he formed a lifelong friendship with FDR.

The 1924 convention is famous for 2 things. The first is that it was the longest continuously running convention in US electoral history. It ran from June 24th until July 9th, 1924, and it took 103 ballots to eventually nominate a presidential candidate.

Secondly, it marked the re-entry of FDR into mainstream politics following his recovery from polio, when he nominated Al Smith for the presidency, proclaiming him "the Happy Warrior."

The success of this speech and his other convention efforts in support of Smith signalled that he was still a viable figure in politics, something that did not pass the attention of James Farley.

The 1924 convention ended when Al Smith and the other front runner, conservative William Gibbs McAdoo (President Woodrow Wilson's Secretary of the Treasury and son-in-law) accepted that they could not break the deadlocked convention.

Both stepped aside to urge the delegates to nominate a compromise candidate.

This was John William Davis, a veteran diplomat and lawyer, who would eventually lose to Republican incumbent President Calvin Coolidge.

FDR used the springboard of the 1924 convention as a platform to renter politics and impressed by the organisational skills of James Farley, FDR asked him to become his campaign manager and run his campaign for the New York governorship.

1928 was a momentous year for Farley as his great friend Al Smith finally secured the Democratic nomination for President with FDR again making a rousing speech in his favour at the convention in Sam Houston Hall in Houston, Texas.

Smith was the first Roman Catholic nominee of a major party, he opposed prohibition, and he enjoyed broad appeal among women, who had won the right of suffrage in 1920.

James Farley now threw himself enthusiastically into campaigning for FDR while hoping his other great friend Al Smith would win without him, Smith for president and FDR for governor. He also began a close working relationship with Eleanor Roosevelt that would last a lifetime. Farley was extremely impressed with her organisational and political talents.

FRD narrowly won the governorship by just 25,000 votes while Al Smith was heavily defeated by the Republican candidate Herbert Hoover, who benefited from an economic boom and the fact that anti Catholic sentiment was still rife in American politics.

Sadly, for Al Smith the land of the free was still not ready to accept a Roman Catholic president.

As a reward for steering FDR to victory Farley was named secretary of the New York State Democratic committee and plotted FDR's re-election in 1930.

He set about rebuilding the Democratic party organisation in New York State ward by ward. This hard work was rewarded by Roosevelt's landslide re-election in 1930 by over 700,000 votes.

After the election, a grateful FDR ensured Farley was named chairman of the New York State Democratic committee, which he held until his resignation, in 1944.

It was at this stage that political seer in Farley would surface again when he predicted to anyone that would listen, that the newly elected FDR, governor of New York would be the Democratic nominee for president in 1932.

Acting as a king maker, Farley introduced FDR to the newspaper tycoon William Randolph Hearst who put his media empire behind electing Roosevelt as president in 1932.

As chairman of the New York state assembly committee, Farley launched the pre-nomination campaign for Franklin D. Roosevelt and was largely responsible for his adoption at the 1932 Democratic convention.

Farley, and a few other faithful workers created over the next two years what for the time was an astonishing organisational effort based on personal meetings, letter writing, and telephoning.

Building up county by county in New York State, the organisation was expanded into other states with a whirlwind national trip undertaken by Farley in mid-1931 covering 18 states in 19 days.

At the Chicago convention of 1932, Roosevelt was one of nine candidates, but under Farley's astute guidance and management, his organisation and delegate management strategy overwhelmed his opponents.

It was also a bittersweet moment for Farley, as the two favourites where his old friend Al Smith and his preferred candidate FDR.

Farley was determined to put sentiment aside and ensure that FDR secured the nomination. As the convention seemed split between FDR and Smith, Farley used his influence with William Randolph Hearst, who hated Al Smith, to lobby John Nance Garner III, the speaker of the house. Garner also known as "Cactus Jack" controlled the Texas delegates who could secure the nomination for FDR. Once the Texas and then Californian delegation backed Roosevelt, the convention realised Roosevelt had reached the required 770 delegates to win the nomination.

Roosevelt received 945 votes on the fourth ballot to Smith's 190. Garner was then nominated for vice-president by acclamation from the convention floor. This was his agreed reward for the deal on providing his delegates for FDR.

This was a master stroke by Farley who at 44 years old was now a national figure and one of the most powerful people in the Democratic party, with one overriding ambition to elect FDR as President.

Farley now used all the political skills he had learned throughout life, his memory, personable qualities, party loyalty, organisational ability, and tireless energy.

All this was used to maximum effect in the 1932 campaign, and the result was victory for FDR.

Farley again the political seer had predicted Roosevelt would defeat Hoover by 7.5 million votes and came within a few hundred thousand of his estimate, James Farley was now on the national stage.

Farley was appointed Postmaster General, which is the usual reward given to the new president's campaign manager or an influential member of his campaign. This made him the first Catholic cabinet member in the 20th century. James was also made the chairman of the Democratic National Committee. These appointments made James Farley the first Irish American Roman Catholic to achieve national success with either of the main American political parties. Farley was constantly criticized by Roosevelt's opponents for insisting on keeping both posts simultaneously.

As Postmaster General, Farley exercised the traditional patronage dispensing function with masterful skill, rewarding loyalty; cementing regional, ethnic, and occupational alliances; and providing the president with bargaining chips for congressional dealings.

Farley worked hard to ensure the post office survived the great depression. His expert stewardship made the once-unprofitable post office department begin to turn a profit. Farley was instrumental in revolutionising transcontinental airmail service and reorganised the post office's airmail carriers. Farley worked closely with the Pan American World Airways' (Pan Am) president, Juan Trippe, to ensure that the mail was delivered safely and cost-effectively. That was after a brief period of the army carrying the mail, with servicemen killed flying in bad weather.

His time as Postmaster General is celebrated by stamp collectors for the many souvenir sheets, he issued to commemorate great American events and also the Farley's Follies, 20 stamps ungummed and never issued which have become much prized amongst stamp collectors.

The "Farley's Follies," were preprints, mostly imperforated and ungummed, of stamps of the period. Farley bought them at face value, out of his own pocket, and gave them to Roosevelt and Interior Secretary Harold Ickes, both stamp collectors, and to members of his family and special friends of the administration. (Farley himself did not collect stamps.) Unfortunately, some of them reached the market, offered at the soaring prices commanded by rarities. When ordinary stamp collectors learned of that, they lodged strenuous protests, newspaper editorials levelled charges of corruption and a heated Congressional investigation ensued.

Finally, in 1935 many more versions of the unfinished stamps were produced and made generally available to collectors at their face value.

Today, the souvenir sheets and the single cut-out reprints are not scarce. The original sheets were autographed to distinguish them from the reprints, and 15 were displayed in an exhibit at the Smithsonian's National Postal Museum in June 2009.

Farley controlled federal patronage in the new administration and was very influential within Roosevelt's inner circle and the Democratic party throughout the United States. James Farley was an immense networker and was famous for never forgetting the names of anyone he met.

He was the gate keeper of the Roosevelt administration and controlled the allocation of all presidential appointments.

Whilst FDR is known for his New Deal which revitalised the US economy during the great depression it was Farley that put together the coalition of Catholics, labour unions, business leaders, African Americans and farmers, that helped make the deal work.

Farley also used his control of the patronage to see

that Roosevelt's first 100 days of New Deal legislation was passed. The wily Farley used the patronage machine to cajole waivers with offers of government jobs and prestige positions to line up support for the New Deal's liberal social and infrastructure programs. He managed most mid-level and lower-level appointments, in consultation with state and local Democratic organisations.

Farley is also known for his eponymous device, the 'Farley file,' which was the reason FDR appeared to never forget a name. Farley kept a file on every single person he or President Roosevelt met.

Whenever people were scheduled to meet again with Roosevelt, Farley would review their files. That allowed Roosevelt to meet them again while knowing their spouse, their children's names and ages, and anything else that had come out of earlier meetings or any other intelligence that Farley had added to the file. The effect was powerful and intimate. A keen reader Farley got the idea from ancient Rome's Nomenclator, which was a slave who attended his master during canvassing and on similar occasions, for the purpose of telling him the names of those he met in the street.

Not surprising these documents now referred to as 'Farley files' are still used by other politicians and businesspeople.

He also helped bring an end to prohibition and to

develop closer ties between America and the Roman Catholic Church. In 1933 he travelled to Rome where he had an audience with Pope Pius XI and Cardinal Pacelli who was to later become Pope Pius the XII.

Farley was asked by FDR many times to run for the governor of New York, but James always refused.

Farley would go on to mastermind President Franklin

D. Roosevelt's successful campaign for re-election in 1936, against Republican challenger Alf Landon, the governor of Kansas.

Again, the political Seer, Farley wrote him a note before the election in which he predicted:

"I am still definitely of the opinion that you will carry every state but two, Maine and Vermont."

The election panned out as Farley predicted and Roosevelt went on have a landslide election victory.

Roosevelt and his inner circle had predicted a loss of 171 electoral votes for the campaign. Farley's correct estimate of a mere eight vote loss, and his ability to correctly pick the very states, marked James Farley out as not only one of the most powerful men in Washington but as one of America's most brilliant and insightful political strategists. Political scientists now refer to Farley's Law which is that it is by mid-October that voters will decide the presidential candidate they are most likely to vote for.

Also, in 1936, James Farley revisited his Irish roots with a trip to his ancestral home at Ballinaskerry, which is situated half a mile from the village of Castletown. All that remained of the old homestead was a mound surrounded by sunken terrain. He met his cousins, Mr and Mrs Peter McDonnell and other members of the Farrelly family.

He also met the local school children and was photographed accepting a copy of the Meath Chronicle from one of the pupils.

With the winds of war blowing in Europe, the astute Farley used his close ties with Irish American congressmen to defeat the Ludlow Amendment, a 1939 attempt by Congress to limit the foreign affairs powers of the president.

This was a proposed amendment to the constitution of the United States which called for a national referendum on any declaration of war by Congress, except in cases when the United States had been attacked first.

Farley faced an issue in the Congress where many Irish American congressmen were minded to refuse aid to Great Britain because of anti-English sentiment stemming from the famine era.

By persuasively swaying the votes of the Irish Catholic legislators in the Congress, Farley was able to defeat the amendment. If this had passed it would have prevented the president from sending military aid to

Britain perhaps altering forever the history of western Europe.

In 1938 Farley wrote the first of what would be two autobiographies 'Jim Farley's Story'.

Despite Farley's admiration and close relationship with FDR, he broke with the president in 1940.

There is a quote from an American Congressman William Lacy "Bill" Clay, Sr that sums up the emotional side of politics:

"This is quite a game, politics. There are no permanent enemies, and no permanent friends, only permanent interests."

This was highlighted for Farley when his close relationship with FDR deteriorated in 1940, as Farley opposed FDR's pursuit of a third term and because FDR believed that Farley had presidential ambitions of his own.

Farley lost Roosevelt's confidence and therefore his effectiveness as a political fixer.

He refused to join FDRs re-election committee and resigned from the administration. Farley began seeking support for a presidential bid of his own after Roosevelt refused to publicly seek a third term but indicated that he could not decline the nomination if his supporters drafted him at the 1940 convention to be held in Chicago.

While never speaking out publicly, he privately made it known he vehemently opposed Roosevelts 3rd term and allowed his name to go forward for nomination for president at the Democratic convention.

For much of the time leading up to the convention Roosevelt had played it cool as to whether he was planning to break the two-term tradition established by Washington and run again. A week before the convention he made it known that the worsening war in Europe (France had just been invaded and surrendered to the Germans), made him feel that he should run again.

Roosevelt, did not attend the convention himself, instead sending his wife Eleanor as his representative.

As the convention began on July 15th, 1940, two candidates had declared, Farley and Vice President John Nance Garner.

Roosevelt still did not want to declare openly for re-nomination, so his backers arranged for a clever stunt. The president dictated a message on the phone to Kentucky Senator Alben Barkley, who read it out during the first day's proceedings of the convention. The message was:

"The President has never had, and has not
today, any desire or purpose to continue in the
office of President, to be a candidate for that
office, or to be nominated by the convention for
that office. He wishes in earnestness and
sincerity to make it clear that all of the delegates

in this convention are free to vote for any candidate."

Source: Gunther, John (1950). Roosevelt in Retrospect. Harper & Brothers. pp. 308–309.

As if by magic, a seemingly spontaneous demonstration of support for the president began. A cry began "We want Roosevelt! We want Roosevelt!" The leading voice was Thomas D. Garry, superintendent of Chicago's department of sanitation (the sewers department), a trusted henchman of Chicago Mayor Ed Kelly. Garry was stationed in a basement room with a microphone, waiting for that moment. Kelly had posted hundreds of Chicago city workers and precinct captains around the hall.

Meanwhile, other Democratic bosses had brought followers from their home territories. All of them joined in Garry's chant. Within a minute, hundreds of delegates joined in. Many poured into the aisles, carrying state delegation standards for impromptu demonstrations. Whenever the chant began to die down, state chairmen, who also had microphones connected to the speakers, added their own endorsements: "New Jersey wants Roosevelt! Arizona wants Roosevelt! Iowa wants Roosevelt."

The president's nomination and Farley's defeat were now inevitable, and James gained just 72 votes to

Roosevelt's 946. While this gave him some personal satisfaction, it further alienated him from the president.

Roosevelt accepted his party's nomination after the convention had closed. Shortly after midnight eastern time on July 19, 1940, Roosevelt delivered his acceptance speech from the White House in front of news radio microphones and newsreel cameras.

Later that morning, the American Pathé sent footage of his speech to New York City, where it was developed and had a portion aired on television at 3:30 eastern time, making Roosevelt the first incumbent president to be shown on television accepting his party's nomination.

FDR did not want to lose the considerable skills of Farley and Eleanor Roosevelt tried to repair the relationship after the votes had been cast.

This was to no avail, and while Farley would always remain close to Eleanor and her eldest son James, he felt betrayed by FDR and refused to join FDR's 1940 campaign team. He also resigned from the cabinet as Postmaster General and as chairman of the Democratic National Committee.

Farley was much in demand in the business community, and he was soon named chairman of the board of the Coca-Cola export corporation, a position that was created exclusively for his talents and relationships. Farley held this post until his retirement in 1973.

During World War 2, Farley ensured Coca Cola was included in food parcels for US soldiers.

These were used to boost the morale and it was claimed energy levels of the US fighting men. Shipped with food and ammunition as a "war priority item," the deal spread Coke's market worldwide at government expense.

After the war ended, Farley's ingenuity grew bolder. At his biding, the US government built 59 coca cola plants all over Europe as part of the Marshall plan to rebuild Europe!

Farley once again became an important national political force when his old friend, Harry Truman, became president on the death of President Roosevelt in April 1945.

The following year in April 1946, Farley returned to his native land where University College Dublin gave him a special presentation on behalf of the people of Ireland on the occasion of his visit.

President Truman recalled James into political life, and he was instrumental in the development and ratification of the 22nd amendment which limited American presidential terms. The very cause of his estrangement from Roosevelt and political exile. Sweet revenge perhaps. The amendment was ratified on February 6th, 1947.

Farley was also the first guest on NBC's Meet the

Press, the longest-running show in television history, on November the 6th 1947.

In 1948 Farley decided to write another autobiography to cover the last few turbulent years in politics. This was called "Jim Farley's story; the Roosevelt years," published by McGraw-Hill Publishers.

Farley attempted to outline what he perceived as his achievements and legacy in the Roosevelt administration. Given what had happened, it is no surprise that his opinion of the president was not glowing as he outlined why he should have been allowed a crack at the presidency.

Roosevelts allies did not take this lying down. A year later the late president's former secretary Grace Tully, was scathing in her opinion of Farley, when she published her book F.D.R: My Boss, published in 1949 by Scribner's Sons. In this she said:

"...aside from his role as a party leader, inside the cabinet, he contributed little or nothing to the shaping of Administration policies."

She went on to attack Farley's book as "a hymn of hate against Roosevelt." Tully then ridiculed Farley's perceived popularity in the Democratic party:

"Jim made the mistake of thinking that the

applause which greeted him at new post offices was an applause for him personally."

James again went home to Ireland and was entertained by the Meath GAA in Navan when he visited Meath in May 1952. The function was held in return for the kindness of Mr. Farley who looked after the interests of the Meath team and officials when they visited New York in 1951.

In 1962, Farley received the Hundred Year Association of New York's Gold Medal Award, in recognition of outstanding contributions to the city of New York.

In the summer of 1971 James Farley and his granddaughters holidayed throughout Europe which culminated in an audience with Pope Paul VI, and a visit to ex-King Umberto who lived in Estoril Portugal. He had first met Umberto in Italy in 1946 when Umberto was still on the Italian throne. In 1974, he was awarded the Laetare medal by the University of Notre Dame, the oldest and most prestigious award for American Roman Catholics.

After a full and exciting life both politically and commercially, James Aloysius Farley died in New York on 9th June 1976 at the age of 88.

In 1982, the General Post Office in New York City was renamed the James Farley Post Office, in recognition of his work as Postmaster General.

In 2007 the Roman Catholic Archdiocese of New

York named Farley as one of its "Bicentennial People/Innovators" in commemoration of its 200-year anniversary in 2007.

James Farley was a giant of US politics and commerce. One of the first Roman Catholics to rise to national political prominence, the king maker who launched FDR to the presidency and the man who brought coca cola to Europe. Not a bad legacy for a boy whose ancestors left Ballinaskerry, County Meath to escape hunger.

His stranglehold over the city was so secure he was now referred to as 'Boss Daley', a throwback to the old ward bosses of the early Democratic party of the 1920s and 30s. Daley enjoyed the attention, but said: "I'm not the last of the old bosses. I'm the first of the new leaders."

CHAPTER 11
MAYOR DALEY

THE MAN WHO HANDED THE PRESIDENCY TO JFK

When JFK won the 1960 presidential election, Republicans claimed electoral fraud in both Texas, the home state of Vice President elect Lyndon Johnson and in Illinois, the fiefdom of Richard Joseph Daley who was major of Chicago from 1955 until his death in 1976. While no evidence of corruption was ever found, one thing was sure, Mayor Daley was more than capable of arranging it.

Daley played a significant role in the history of the United States Democratic party, especially with his support of John F. Kennedy in 1960 and of Hubert Humphrey in 1968. He would be the longest-serving mayor in Chicago history until his record was broken by his own son Richard M. Daley in 2011.

Richard J. Daley is said by many to have created the modern city of Chicago.

Since its formation by its first settler Jean Baptiste Point du Sable, a free African American, who built a farm at the mouth of the Chicago River in the 1780s, the area and in future the new city have always opened its arms to immigration. From 1890 to 1914, migrations increased, attracting to the new city hundreds of thousands of mostly unskilled Catholic and Jewish immigrants from southern and eastern Europe, including Italians, Greeks, Czechs, Poles, Lithuanians, Ukrainians, Hungarians, and Slovaks.

Chicago was fast becoming the industrial capital of the Midwest, a tough town dominated by factories that spewed forth the black smoke of the industrial revolution.

It was a town in which the cramped slum tenements sprung up almost daily to house the displaced farmhands and struggling immigrants.

Poverty was rife and crime a growth industry. Block after block of "disorderly houses" did a brisk business corrupting hordes of guileless young innocents, who arrived daily from small towns or across the Atlantic in hope of building a better life.

The writer Rudyard Kipling visited the city in 1889 and wrote:

"Having seen it, I urgently desire never to see it again. It is inhabited by savages."

Perhaps he was influenced by the fact it was Chicago saloonkeepers who invented the 'Mickey Finn,' a chloral hydrate-laced drink slipped to solitary patrons so they could be easily robbed!

Thousands of Irish fled the famine and crossed the Great Plains to reach Chicago and find work in the growing meat packaging industry.

One such Irish couple were Michael and Lillian Dunne Daley, whose only child Richard J. Daley was born on the 2nd of May 1902. Michael and Lillian's parents had immigrated to America from Dungarvan county Waterford during the great famine.

Daly was born in Bridgeport, a working-class area of Chicago that had provided many Democratic politicians. In later years Daley would say that his poor but happy upbringing had provided him with his great foundations in life. Religion, family, neighbourhood and his beloved Democratic party.

Richard Daley was politicised at an early age by his parents. His father Michael was a sheet-metal worker and labour activist, but his main mentor was his mother. Lillian Daley who was an intelligent and outspoken individual and a prominent suffragette in the city, who often took him along on marches.

His mother had high hopes for Richard and wanted

more than a manual job for her son. Just before she died, Richard Daley had been nominated as the Democratic candidate for Cook County sheriff. Lillian Daley wanted more than this for her son, telling a friend, "I didn't raise my son to be a policeman." She would never live to see him rise to the very top of Chicago politics.

After leaving elementary school Daley attended the De La Salle Institute and took night classes four nights a week at DePaul University College of law. He undertook his law degree while juggling work and political responsibilities. It would take Daley more than a decade to achieve his degree. A fellow student said of him:

"Daley was a nice fellow, very quiet, a hard worker, and always neatly dressed,"

Another who Daley would later make a judge recalled: "He never missed a class and always got there on time. But there was nothing about him that would make him stand out, as far as becoming something special in life."

Daley was focused on achieving his legal degree while his friends went out dancing, Daley would go home to study his law books.

Daley had several jobs to pay for his studies, these included selling newspapers and making deliveries for a door-to-door peddler. He also worked in Chicago's Union stock yards like many fellow Irish Americans.

Richard J. Daley's passion was politics and his rise in the Democratic party was down to four things. His hard work and dedication to each of the roles he assumed, unfailing loyalty to the party, a series of mentors and finally and quite bizarrely an extraordinary series of well-timed deaths.

His first role in Democratic politics was because of his involvement in the Hamburg Athletic Club, a Bridgeport club active in Chicago election politics. At age 22, he was elected president of the club and served in that office until 1939.

Club sponsor, alderman and ward committeeman Joseph McDonough, chose Daley to be his personal ward secretary and a precinct captain in the politically active eleventh ward, where his home and the club were located. As precinct captain he was the main link between the voters in the area and the Democratic party machine.

After the 1923 election of Mayor William Dever, Daley began work as a clerk in the Chicago City Council. In 1930, McDonough became Cook County treasurer and Daley became his deputy, shouldering the day-to-day activities of the office. As county treasurer, McDonough was even less conscientious than he had been as an alderman. While his boss frequented racetracks and speakeasies, Daley applied the skills he had acquired in the De La Salle counting rooms to the county finances.

In 1930 Daley had met his future wife Eleanor Guilfoyle, known as Sis. She came from a large Irish-Catholic family in the neighbouring southwest side community of Canaryville. She had graduated from Saint Mary high school and was working as a secretary at a paint company and caring for an invalid mother when Daley asked her out on their first date, to a White Sox game.

"We had a very happy courtship," Sis once recalled. "I used to meet him after law school and go to the opera."

Source: Cohen, Adam; Elizabeth Taylor (2000).
American Pharaoh: Mayor Richard J. Daley: His
Battle for Chicago and the Nation

She would later say that:

"Of course, I knew Dick was bound to succeed — even when I first met him. Anyone who would work in the stockyards all day long, then go to school at night was determined to get ahead."

Source: Cohen, Adam; Elizabeth Taylor (2000).
American Pharaoh: Mayor Richard J. Daley: His
Battle for Chicago and the Nation

In 1933 Daley finally obtained a law degree from DePaul university.

After McDonough's death, Daley continued to work

under Cook County treasurers Thomas D. Nash, Robert
M. Sweitzer, and Joseph L. Gill.

Following the death of 20-year veteran Michael J.
O'Connor in 1936, Daley's knowledge of county
finances led to his appointment as chief deputy comptroller for the county. He would hold this post until
1949.

In his new job, Daley learned the intricacies of local
government law and municipal finance, and how to
work a budget. And he saw at first-hand how a government office operates when it is inextricably tied to a
political machine. He learned how the machine farmed
the county treasurer's office with patronage appointees,
who were hired for their political work. And he saw
how it ensured that county funds were deposited with
bankers who contributed to the campaigns of machine
candidates.

After a six-year courtship, Richard and Eleanor
married on June 17th, 1936, when Daley was thirty-four
and his new wife was twenty-eight. It was three years
after his graduation, and the same year that he established a law partnership with an old friend, William
Lynch, the politically minded son of a Bridgeport
precinct captain.

They would go on to have 3 daughters and 4 sons.
Richard, their eldest son, was elected mayor of Chicago
in 1989 and served until his retirement in 2011. His
youngest son Michael was US Secretary of Commerce

under President Bill Clinton and for a time chief of staff for President Barrack Obama.

In November 1936, despite being a lifelong Democrat, Daley's first elective office was in the Illinois House of Representatives, as a Republican, to which he was elected for the 9th district on November 3rd , 1936.

This was political opportunism at its best. Daley took the place of the recently deceased Republican candidate on the ballot and went on to defeat his opponent. This was due to the peculiar setup for legislative elections in Illinois at the time, which allowed Daley to take the place on the ballot of the recently deceased Republican candidate David Shanahan. Daley's name was not printed on the ballot due to the closeness of Shanahan's death to the election, but he was able to defeat Shanahan's friend, Robert E. Rodgers

Though elected as a Republican, he quickly crossed the aisle and returned to the Democratic party. Daley supported progressive legislation, such as a school lunch program and a fairer state sales tax.

In 1938 Daley would be elected to the Illinois state Senate, After the death of incumbent Democratic Senator Patrick J. Carroll.

In 1939, Illinois State Senator William "Botchy" Connors said of Daley:

"You couldn't give that guy a nickel, that's how honest he is."

*Source: Kennedy, Eugene (1978). Himself! The Life
and Times of Mayor Richard J. Daley*

In 1939 Daly moved his wife and growing young family into a seven-bedroom bungalow at 3536 South Lowe in Bridgeport.

Daley would go on to serve as minority Leader of the Illinois Senate from 1941 through to 1949. He would be the youngest party leader in Illinois Senate history.

In 1946 Daley lost a bid to become Cook County sheriff. He unsuccessfully challenged Republican candidate Elmer Walsh in the election, this defeat was his only electoral defeat in a long political career.

Throughout the 1940s, Daley was a major player in Democratic national politics and Daley moved into the Chicago Democratic machine's hierarchy in 1947, with his election as ward committeeman of the southwest side's eleventh ward.

In 1948, Daley was appointed Governor Adlai Stevenson's state director of revenue. Working out of the State of Illinois building in downtown Chicago, he was an advocate for fiscal and tax reform. While there Daley expanded his grasp of budgets and public finance, which later served him well as mayor.

Working behind the scenes, he engineered the removal of Jacob M. Arvey as Democratic chairman following Republican victories in the 1950 elections.

After the death of the current Cook County clerk,

Daley was appointed to fill out the rest of the unexpired term. He was successfully elected to a full term in 1950 and re-elected in 1954. As county clerk, Daley was responsible for vital records such as business and notary records and for birth, death, and marriage certificates. Daley instituted several innovations, such as the first county court calendar of law, and he streamlined marriage license procedures.

In late 1953 Daley made his move to become chairman of the central committee of the Cook County Democratic party. This would make him the undisputed political boss of Chicago.

When the current chairman of the Cook County Democratic party resigned, Daley made his move unleashing a bitter fight between party factions.

Daley was thwarted by an alderman by the name of Clarence Wagner, but just a few months later Wagner died in a car crash on a fishing trip in Minnesota and Daley succeeded him.

As the chairman of the Democratic central committee, Daley was now in a powerful position to pursue his long-cherished dream of becoming mayor of Chicago.

Daley made his move in 1955, when he ran against the current mayor Martin Kennelly and former state Representative Benjamin Adamowski in a bitterly contested primary election.

He would now face Republican alderman Robert Merriam in the general election.

Merriam hoped that the bitterly fought Democratic primary would result in the Democratic machine splintering and allow a Republican victory through the back door. His campaign was endorsed by the city's three largest newspapers, the Chicago Tribune, Chicago Sun-Times, and Chicago Daily News.

A confident Merriam expected to win, but he underestimated the organisational skills of Daley and his now complete control over the Democratic machine. One other factor was to play a key role in Daley's triumph, this was the support of Chicago's African American residents, whose votes would prove pivotal.

In the General election Merriam received 581,461 votes, while this was the largest Republican vote since 1943 it was not enough to defeat Daley who was victorious with 54.93% of the vote. Aided in large by dedicated support from the African American community who made up 20% of the electorate.

Daley's win was the narrowest victory in a Chicago mayoral race in over a decade.

Richard J. Daley at the age of 53 had finally achieved his aim in politics and was now Chicago's third consecutive mayor from the working-class, heavily Irish American South Side neighbourhood of Bridgeport, succeeding Edward J. Kelly and of course Martin Kennelly whom he had defeated in the Democratic primary.

As we will see the voters of Chicago would go on to

re-elect Daley in 1959, 1963, 1967, 1971, and 1975. He served a total of five full terms and one partial term in office, the longest serving mayor up to that time.

In a new tradition, he was sworn into office by childhood friend, Judge Abraham Lincoln Marovitz, instead of the outgoing mayor.

Daley was now in a unique position as mayor, traditionally the real power in Chicago lay with the city council. However, Daley was not only the mayor but the head of the local Democratic party, this allowed Daley to now wielded enormous local, state, and eventually national political influence.

Daley would use this power to transform Chicago which was then a tired and decaying city into a modern metropolis. Chicago could easily have suffered the fate of many of the rust belt cities such as Detroit, Buffalo and Cleveland that were also in decline.

Instead through sheer force of political will and with the aid of 21 years in office Daley created a powerhouse of skyscrapers, freeways and a vibrant and prosperous downtown. Daley focused on municipal services and the development of the city centre, contributing to the oft-cited image of Chicago as "the city that works." During his first term, the city added new garbage trucks, sewers, street and alley lighting, downtown parking facilities and more police and fire personnel.

Daley was a passionate builder as mayor. Major projects during his term of office included O'Hare

International Airport, the Sears Tower, the University of Illinois, numerous expressways and major subway construction projects. Shortly after his first election, Daley recruited new policy professionals to his administration and consolidated his power over the city council. He transferred city budget responsibility from the council to his comptroller's and budget director's offices, shifted the approval and issue of city contracts to the city's purchasing agent, centralised many ward services, and limited the ability of council members to grant such potentially lucrative favours as issuing driveway permits.

Throughout his tenure, except for a small number of independents and northwest side Republicans, he faced limited opposition from the aldermen, never losing a vote in the city council.

Daley was determined that Chicago would be recognised as a great city by national and foreign dignitaries, but he didn't forget his Irish roots. Just after his election the annual Southtown parade in honour of St. Patrick's Day was moved downtown, and the Chicago Journeymen Plumbers union began a tradition of dyeing the Chicago River green in celebration. Venetian Nights also attracted crowds to the riverfront.

In 1959, an international trade fair celebrating the opening of the St. Lawrence Seaway was attended by Queen Elizabeth and Prince Phillip. The city sponsored downtown parades for the crews of Apollo 10, 11, and

13 space missions and hosted visits by the Taoiseach of Ireland Sean F. Lemass, Eleanor Roosevelt, Levi Eshkol, Premier of Israel, King Frederik IX and Queen Ingrid of Denmark, numerous politicians, and celebrities such as Frank Sinatra, Danny Thomas, and Jack Benny.

In 1959 Daley was re-elected for a 2nd term after defeating Lar Daly in the primary and Republican Timothy Sheehan in the general election.

His stranglehold over the city was so secure he was now referred to as 'Boss Daley,' a throwback to the old ward bosses of the early Democratic party of the 1920s and 30s. Daley enjoyed the attention but said:

> "I'm not the last of the old bosses. I'm the first of
> the new leaders."

In 1960, Senator John F Kennedy won Illinois by just 8,858 votes out of 4.8 million cast, amid loud charges that Boss Daley, had stolen the election. Allegations of fraud weren't just a Chicago problem.

In Texas, JFK won by 46,257 out of 2.3 million after 100,000 Kennedy voters seemed to appear magically in future Vice President Lyndon B. Johnson's state.

Nixon is reported to have said:

> "In our campaigns, no matter how hard-fought
> they may be, no matter how close the election

may turn out to be, those who lose accept the verdict and support those who win."

Source: New York Post 10/11/2000

The man later known as "Tricky Dick" also reportedly convinced the now-defunct, Republican-leaning New York Herald Tribune to kill a planned 12-part series on election fraud.

Nixon is said to have told Tribune reporter Earl Mazo:

"Our country can't afford the agony of a constitutional crisis–and I damn well will not be a party to creating one, just to become president or anything else."

While much has been made of Richard J. Daley's efforts to ensure that Senator John F. Kennedy prevailed at the polls on November 8th, 1960, a pivotal, though largely forgotten element of that effort was the purchase of half an hour of prime time on the NBC television network by the Democratic party of Cook County. This allowed the nation to watch J.F.K. addressing a wildly enthusiastic crowd at the Chicago stadium on the Friday before the 1960 election. It is normal for local political parties to purchase time locally to promote candidates. But for a local organisation to purchase national television time was a rarity indeed.

What viewers from coast-to-cast saw the night of February 4th, 1960, was Senator John F. Kennedy at his best, thanks to a local party organisation at its most powerful.

Viewers within range of WNBQ-TV (Chicago's NBC owned-and-operated station now known as WMAQ-TV) saw an additional half-hour that preceded the Kennedy speech.

Richard J. Daley's purchase of the 8-8:30 half hour on Channel 5 had the added benefit of locking the Republican national organization out of the Chicago market during prime time that night. In all other markets, the Republicans purchased this slot on NBC for an address by President Dwight D. Eisenhower on behalf of presidential candidate Richard M. Nixon. Since the Cook County Democrats had already bought this time slot, the Republicans had to settle for a tape-delayed broadcast of the Eisenhower speech at 10:15. This was well after prime-time following WNBQ's late evening news.

Both half-hours are remarkable examples of stagecraft and scripting and of Richard J. Daley's ability to target demographic groups that were essential to the victories of his party. Present-day political gurus would do well to study this video.

Also, in 1960 Daley faced a trouble closer to home, when what would become known as the 'Summerdale

Scandal', threatened to destroy the people of Chicago's faith in law and order.

It was an innocuous series of events that began in June 1958 when a young serial burglar by the name of Richard Morrison was approached by a Chicago cop by the name of Frank Faraci.

Faraci told Morrison that he wanted a cut of his haul.

During subsequent police interviews Morrison claimed that Faraci told him:

"You know, we like nice things too."

He went on to allude to Morrison that one of his partners an officer by the name of Allan Brinn wanted a set of golf clubs.

On the 31st of July 1958, while out at night looking for a set of golf clubs in the Evanston area Morrison unwittingly walked into a sting operation. After being shot at by police officers and abandoning his car Morrison managed to evade capture, however, the next morning Morrison was arrested at his apartment located at 4332 N. Sacramento Avenue.

Rather than face trial Morrison said:

"It was after that I figured I might as well go in with them since I was in trouble again anyway."

So began a burglary spree that would span the next 12 months.

Morrison committed his burglaries with the help of eight Chicago police officers working in the Summerdale district on the North Side. The officers not only covered for him during the break-ins, but also helped haul away the loot in their squad cars.

Morrison would case the joints. The police officers would act as lookouts and then swoop in to help cart away the loot in their squad cars. They would then meet up at one of their homes to divvy up the goods. Morrison got the cash and jewellery; the cops got the other contraband.

Morrison found it useful having the cops on your side when you're a crook. In one case, at a tyre store, Morrison was spotted, and an alarm was sounded. His police buddies showed up first, told him to lie flat on the roof and they then convinced the other police officers that they had it under control. Morrison and his associates then completed the job. When Morrison was burgling a music store, he again was noticed, and police were called. But one of his protectors raced to the scene first so Morrison could run out the back while the honest cops were coming in the front.

If a job wasn't lucrative enough, they kept going. The gang once hit three businesses in one night.

Almost 1 year to the day from the criminal conspiracy's inception Richard Morrison was finally arrested by the police.

He was taken to a police station in Cooks County and soon became what the Chicago press would dub him the 'babbling burglar.'

The eight police officers from Summerdale were convicted in August 1961. Five were sentenced to terms ranging from one to five years. Two were just fined $500 each. The eighth officer, whose home was free of stolen goods, spent six months in jail and faced a $1,000 fine.

As for the 'babbling burglar' himself, he survived an assassination attempt outside the Cook County courthouse and moved to Florida after charges against him were dropped in exchange for his help as a state witness.

The public outcry was so intense that Daley was forced to sack the Chicago Police Commissioner Timothy O'Connor. He appointed Orlando Wilson as his replacement who instigated wide ranging reforms to professionalise the police force.

In 1963 Daley was again re-elected. Given his stranglehold hold on the Democratic party it was no surprise he was unopposed in the primary and easily defeated Republican challenger Benjamin Adamowski.

Under Daley, new building projects dramatically changed the physical character of Chicago.

The construction of the massive McCormick Place Convention Centre on the lakefront and the enlargement of O'Hare International Airport brought travellers and business to the city.

President John F. Kennedy attended the O'Hare dedication.

In 1966 a new civic centre was dedicated in downtown Chicago and in 1967 it was graced by the gift of an outdoor sculpture commissioned from artist Pablo Picasso.

Daley's tenure was not without controversy, however. He was mayor at a contentious time when urban centres were confronted with dramatic socioeconomic change, issues of racial segregation in schools and housing, and affirmative action in fire and police forces. These issues, along with perceptions of concentration on infrastructure and services for the downtown area at the expense of neighbourhoods, especially in the racially segregated South and West Sides, eroded Daley's initial strong support among African American voters.

Ticket fixing, bribes, inflated contracts, and other corruption scandals brought investigations and led to prison terms for some public officials, including city council floor leader Thomas Keane.

His administrations also set a rapid pace for urban renewal, the demolition of blighted areas, and the building of additional public housing. As with all his enterprises he mixed politics and business, and for the scoffers, Daley repeated over and again:

"Good politics makes for good government."

Source: Cohen, Adam; Elizabeth Taylor (2000).
American Pharaoh: Mayor Richard J. Daley: His
Battle for Chicago and the Nation

When taunted about the evils of the "party machine," Daley snapped back to reporters: "Organisation, not machine. Get that, organisation not machine." Although evidence of corruption occasionally tainted Daley's cronies, the mayor himself appeared to remain free of corruption. One notable exception was when a lucrative insurance contract was given over to a firm employing a Daley son. When chided, Daley exploded with rage over the issue, insisting that it was the duty of any good father to help a son.

In 1967 Daley was re-elected for a 4th term, after running once again unopposed in the primary, he defeated Republican John L. Waner in the general election. 1968 would prove to be a turbulent year for Daley and the Democratic party.

Daley attempted to play a major role in the 1968 election, but this time not for the Kennedys but against them.

The Democratic party was in crisis, President Lyndon Johnson, despite being elected with a huge majority in 1964, was hugely unpopular due to his pro-Vietnam War policies.

In November 1967, an unknown and unremarkable Minnesota senator named Eugene McCarthy (*See chapter 14*) announced his intent to challenge Johnson for the Democratic presidential nomination.

On January 27, 1968, Daley informed President Johnson that Robert Kennedy had met him and asked for his support in the upcoming Democratic primaries. Despite being a long-term friend and ally of the Kennedy clan, Daley refused to support Robert Kennedys bid.

In March 1968, McCarthy won 40 percent of the vote in the New Hampshire presidential primary, shocking the Democratic establishment and highlighting he was a real contender in the race for the nomination.

A few days later, Senator Robert F. Kennedy abandoned his support for Johnson and entered the presidential fight himself.

On March 31st, President Johnson told a stunned American public during a televised address, that he would not seek re-election. The following month, Vice President Hubert Humphrey backed by Johnson announced his candidacy for the nomination, further dividing the Democratic party.

Rather than support Robert Kennedy, Daley attempted to engineer a ticket headed by Hubert Humphrey and bizarrely Lyndon Johnson as his vice-presidential running mate.

American politics was thrown into even more

turmoil on April 4th, 1968, when Martin Luther King Jr was assassinated at the Lorraine Motel in Memphis, Tennessee by James Earl Ray.

African Americans were a major component of the Daley coalition, providing him with his winning margin in his two closest mayoral elections. But his relationship with them deteriorated in the turbulent hours after Dr. Martin Luther King's assassination.

The African Americans communities' anger and grief spilled over into a maelstrom of rioting, arson and looting throughout Chicago's west side.

Daley was angered not only by the rioting, but also by what he perceived as a weak police response to the disorder.

Daley called in Police Superintendent James B. Conlisk and as he later reported back at a press conference, he said:

"I said to him very emphatically and very definitely that an order be issued by him immediately to shoot to kill any arsonist or anyone with a Molotov cocktail in his hand, because they're potential murderers, and to shoot to maim or cripple anyone looting."

Source: Kennedy, Eugene (1978). Himself! The Life and Times of Mayor Richard J. Daley

This statement generated significant controversy and the command provoked the wrath of the liberal news media.

Reverend Jesse Jackson, called it "a fascist's response". Daley later backed away from his words in an address to the City Council, saying:

"It is the established policy of the police depart-ment–fully supported by this administration–that only the minimum force necessary be used by policemen in carrying out their duties."

Source: Kennedy, Eugene (1978). Himself! The Life and Times of Mayor Richard J. Daley

In August 1968 Daley and Chicago hosted the 1968 Democratic National Convention at President Lyndon B. Johnson's request. Daley intended to use the occasion to highlight Chicago and his achievements to the country and the news media. Instead, the convention descended into farce and violence and Daley's reputation would soon be tarnished.

For the week of the convention violence erupted between Chicago police and Anti-Vietnam war demon-strators. Ironically, Daley had been a private critic of the Vietnam war and had urged Johnson to withdraw US forces.

At home in their living rooms, horrified Americans

alternated between watching images of police brutally beating young, blood-splattered demonstrators and Humphrey's nomination. During the nomination process, some delegates spoke about the violence. One pro-McGovern delegate Senator Abraham A Ribicoff from Connecticut referred to the police violence as "Gestapo tactics in the streets of Chicago." He went on to try and introduce a motion to move the convention to another city. Daley was pictured on tv screens shouting Ribicoff down.

Network television brought the horrors of convention week into the living rooms of America and the world with one network comparing the events in Chicago to the recent soviet invasion of Czechoslovakia.

A federal commission would later investigate the violence and the response describing it as a 'Police Riot.'

Mayor Daley defended his police force which will forever be remembered for a trademark Daley slip of the tongue.

"The confrontation was not caused by the police. The confrontation was caused by those who charged the police. Gentlemen let's get this thing straight, once and for all. The policeman is not here to create disorder. The policeman is here to preserve disorder."

*Source: Kennedy, Eugene (1978). Himself! The Life
and Times of Mayor Richard J. Daley*

Daley was renowned for his linguistic mishaps so legendary were these that his press secretary, Earl Bush would tell reporters,

"Write what he means, not what he says."

*Source: Cohen, Adam; Elizabeth Taylor (2000).
American Pharaoh: Mayor Richard J. Daley: His
Battle for Chicago and the Nation*

Public opinion polls conducted after the convention demonstrated that most Americans supported Daley's tactics. Despite this for a few years afterwards some professional societies refused to schedule their annual meetings in Chicago.

Undaunted Daley returned his attention to Chicago and in 1970, he reduced state power in Chicago by lobbying for and gaining "home rule" status, which allowed the city to impose all taxes apart from income taxes without state legislative approval.

In 1971 Daley was re-elected for his 5th term as mayor, after running unopposed in the primary and against Republican Richard E. Friedman in the general election.

He also returned to his building program to enhance

the power and appearance of Chicago. Notable projects where the Sears Tower, IBM Plaza, Marina City, Lake Point Towers, John Hancock Building, and the Water Tower Place.

These all contributed to the revitalisation of the downtown. Although the city lost several historic buildings to the trend towards new construction (including the Garrick theatre and the stock exchange building), the old public library was saved by a Daley-appointed committee and later became the Chicago cultural centre.

In 1972, Daley was dealt another blow when the Democratic National Convention refused to seat his Illinois delegation because of noncompliance with new selection rules. This was liberal revenge for the 1968 convention.

In 1975 Daley triumphed yet again at the polls winning 70% of the vote as he was re-elected as Chicago's mayor for a sixth consecutive term

Omnipotent domestically, Daley would play Democratic kingmaker one more time not for a Kennedy but another future Democratic President Jimmy Carter.

In July 1976 at Democratic convention in New York City's Madison Square Garden Daley helped Jimmy Carter secure the nomination on the first ballot.

Carter always maintained that Daley's endorsement clinched his first-ballot nomination for the presidency, but Daley failed to deliver Illinois for Carter in the election.

Just over one month after the 1976 election Daley collapsed on the city's North Side while on his way to lunch. He was rushed to the office of his private physician at 900 North Michigan Avenue.

A veil of secrecy surrounded the events of the mayor's last day. For two hours, the nature of his illness was left to unconfirmed reports of his choking on food while eating with friends to collapsing on the sidewalk. The police closed off the section around the office building as throngs of holiday shoppers on the avenue talked about the unknown illness.

Doctors from north-western University's Hospital, four blocks away, were called in and emergency equipment, including an ambulance, stood by as reports circulated that the ill mayor would be taken to the hospital. And at north-western, there were reports that medical personnel were standing by awaiting his arrival.

This went on for nearly two hours, and even when the ambulance wheeled away, its rear window covered, many persons thought it was taking him to the hospital. It was finally announced at about 4 P.M. by Mr. Kenneth Sain that Mayor Daley had died. He was 74 years old.

Daley's funeral took place in the church he attended since his childhood and had served as an altar boy the Nativity of Our Lord in his beloved Bridgeport on the city's north side.

Historians rate Richard J Daley as the sixth best

mayor in American history, but I'd rather leave you with Daley's own analysis of his political legacy:

> "I'm not the last of the old bosses. I'm the first of the new leaders."

Source: Cohen, Adam; Elizabeth Taylor (2000).
American Pharaoh: Mayor Richard J. Daley: His
Battle for Chicago and the Nation

Mayor Richard Daley, the legendary Chicago political boss and fellow Irish American, was impressed by the energy and intellect of the young Byrne and wanted her to work for him. In 1964 he appointed her to his anti-poverty initiative the Head Start programme

CHAPTER 12
JANE BYRNE
THE WOMAN WHO SMASHED THE GLASS CEILING IN THE WINDY CITY

n January 2021, history was made when America welcomed its first female Vice President Kamala Harris, I'd like to share with you the story of another woman politician who broke the glass ceiling, Jane Byrne.

Politics has always been a rough profession, especially for Irish Americans who had to fight against institutional prejudice. It gave rise to many individuals with characters of steel who changed the way America looked and worked. One such politician was Jane Margaret Byrne, the first woman to be elected mayor of Chicago the second largest city in the United States at the time, who finally broke the glass ceiling in the windy city.

Jane Margaret Burke was born on the 24th of May 1933 at John B. Murphy Hospital in Chicago to second-generation Irish American parents Katherine Marie Burke (née Nolan) and Edward Patrick Burke.

Edward was the vice president of Inland Steel so Jane would enjoy a comfortable upbringing and was raised on the city's north side. Jane attended Saint Scholastica high school. A highly intelligent young woman, Byrne spent her first year of College at St Marys of the Woods and later transferred to Barat College where she would eventually graduate with a bachelor's degree in chemistry and biology in 1955.

Whilst at college, she had met and fallen in love with a young Marine pilot William P Byrne. Shortly after her graduation, they were married, and Jane's only child Katherine C Byrne was born in 1957.

The young family would soon face tragedy when on the 31st of May 1959, William Byrne was killed. He was flying from marine Corps air station Cherry Point in Havelock North Carolina to naval air station Glenview in Illinois. Lt Byrne attempted to land twice in dense fog. After being waved off to try another landing, his plane's wing struck the porch of a nearby house and the plane crashed into Sunset Memorial Park, killing him.

Jane Byrne was now 26 and a widow with a young child to raise, but rather than utilise her degree with a career in science or research she decided that politics was what she wanted to do next.

Byrne's involvement in politics stemmed partly from the grief of her husband's air crash.

Just after the tragedy, she heard Senator John F. Kennedy talk about the loss of life due to the Cold War. Inspired she joined his campaign for president and became secretary-treasurer for the presidential contender's Chicago headquarters.

Showing the tenacity and determination that would be a hallmark of her future career she threw herself into JFK's campaign for president in 1960.

Her organisational skills and hard work impressed the Kennedy organisation so much that they offered her a job in Washington, but Byrne decided to remain in Chicago and pursue graduate studies at the University of Illinois, Chicago Circle campus. She taught for a while and was planning to pursue a career in teaching. However, it was not just the Kennedys who had noticed Jane during the campaign.

The leader of another political dynasty was also impressed, Mayor Richard Daley of Chicago.

Daley, the legendary Chicago political boss and fellow Irish American, was impressed by the energy and intellect of the young Byrne and wanted her to work for him. In 1964 he appointed her to his anti-poverty initiative the Head Start program.

A year later he promoted her to a job with the Chicago committee on urban opportunity. During this period, she studied Chicago politics and became a fiercely loyal Daley supporter.

Her reward was to be named in 1968 as the first

woman member of his cabinet. Jane became the commissioner of sales, weights, and measures. In this role Byrne attempted to uproot corruption and return her office to its original purpose, consumer protection.

In 1972, Byrne served as a delegate to the Democratic National Convention (DNC). The convention nominated Senator George McGovern of South Dakota for president and Senator Thomas Eagleton of Missouri for vice president. Eagleton withdrew from the race just 19 days later after it was disclosed that he had previously undergone mental health treatment, including electroshock therapy, and he was replaced on the ballot by Sargent Shriver of Maryland, a Kennedy in-law.

The ticket would go on to lose in a landslide to President Richard Nixon who won 49 states only losing Massachusetts and the District of Columbia.

Jane was also chairperson of the DNC resolutions committee in 1973.

Despite the strong opposition of the predominantly male Chicago democratic leadership, in 1975, Mayor Daley appointed Jane as the chairperson of the powerful Cook County Democratic central committee. This was a role that helped her learn first-hand the inner workings of the "Democratic machine."

The Cook County Democratic party was a political party which represents voters in 50 wards in the city of Chicago and 30 suburban townships of Cook County. The organisation had dominated Chicago politics and consequently, Illinois politics since the 1930s. If you wanted to thrive in Democratic politics, then you needed the Cook County committee on your side.

Cook County was created on 15 January 1831, and it was named after Daniel Cook, who had been one of the earliest and youngest statesmen in Illinois history.

By 1837, local Democrats were winning electoral victories under the leadership of William B. Ogden.

Ogden recruited Irish immigrants into the party. Their loyalty to native Democrats was established in return for political favours and an occasional elected office.

It was now under the control of Richard Daley. Daley had helped turn out the vote for John F. Kennedy in the 1960 presidential election. Kennedy won Illinois by just 8,858 votes, yet won Cook County by 450,000 votes, with some Chicago precincts going to Kennedy by over 10 to 1 margin!

Illinois' 27 electoral votes helped give Kennedy the majority he needed. Political commentator Len O'Connor described the Cook County Democratic party at the time as one of the most powerful political machines in American history.

When Mayor Daley died suddenly of a heart attack on 20th December 1976, the Democratic leadership under newly appointed Mayor Michael Bilandic quickly removed Jane from the Cook County central committee.

Never afraid of a fight, Byrne accused the mayor of a

shady backroom deal to increase regulated taxi fares which was unfair to citizens of the city.

Byrne accused the new mayor, Michael A. Bilandic, of not looking out for the public interest and "greasing" a nearly 12 percent cab fare increase for the city.

Mayor Bilandic retaliated by sacking Byrne from the city administration and her position of head of consumer affairs.

Byrne was determined to exact revenge and in August 1977, she announced her intention to challenge Bilandic in the 1979 Democratic mayoral primary, the real contest in the heavily Democratic Chicago.

Officially announcing her mayoral campaign Byrne partnered with Chicago journalist and political consultant Don Rose, who served as her campaign manager. Rose had previously served as the Chicago press secretary for Martin Luther King Jr.

During her campaign, she married Jay McMullen, a noted reporter for the Chicago Daily News and the Chicago Sun-Times.

Political observers gave Byrne short odds in ousting Bilandic. A memorandum inside the Bilandic campaign said it should portray her as, "a shrill, charging, vindictive person—and nothing makes a woman look worse".

Campaigning with funds mostly donated by her new husband, Jay McMullen, and lacking an efficient political organisation, Byrne's chances of winning seemed impossible. Even her major campaign issue, the taxicab fare increase, lost its potency when a federal grand jury found no wrongdoing. But as Harold McMillan once said the biggest impact on politics are events dear boy events and an act of weather turned the tide for Byrne. Snow, which started to fall on New Year's Eve, 1978, gave her an issue to win the mayoralty.

In January 1979, a blizzard paralysed Chicago, and the city ground to a halt, interrupting public transportation and garbage collection.

The Chicago blizzard of 1979 was a major hazard that affected northern Illinois and northwest Indiana on January 13th and 14th, 1979. It was one of the largest Chicago snowstorms in history at the time, with 21 inches of snowfall in the two-day period.

By the end of Sunday, January 14th, the depth of snow on the ground peaked at 29 inches. The blizzard lasted for a total of 38 hours.

At its peak, wind gusts reached speeds of 39 miles per hour. Five people died during the blizzard, with approximately 15 others seriously injured due to conditions created by the storm. One of the five deaths came when a snow plough driver went berserk, hitting 34 cars and ramming a man.

The inability of the mayor to devise and implement an adequate snow removal plan angered the city's residents.

Byrne would recall in her memories.

"From the airport to mass transit to simply walking down the street, Chicagoans were frustrated and buried in snow."

Source: Jane Byrne: My Chicago 1992

Byrne also received the powerful endorsement of Jesse Jackson, giving her a strong position with African Americans and Republican voters in a strange quirk of the American electoral system turned out in large numbers to vote for her in the primary.

Infuriated voters in the North Side and Northwest Side areas retaliated against Bilandic for the Democratic party's slating of only south side candidates for the mayor, clerk, and treasurer (the outgoing city clerk, John C. Marcin, was from the northwest side).

A break in the bad weather permitted a record turnout to the Democratic primary and secured Byrne the upset victory.

Turnout in the primary was among the greatest in Chicago mayoral history. By some reports, turnout was 839,443, which was 58.97% of Chicago's 1,423,476 voters.

Turnout exceeded the average mayoral primary election turnout in the years since 1955 by more than 10 percentage points. All these factors allowed Byrne to oust Bilandic in the primary 51% to 49%.

Positioning herself as a reformer in the mayoral election on the 3rd of April 1979, Jane Byrne trounced her

Republican opponent, Wallace Johnson., winning in a landslide with 82.1% of the vote, which included a sweep of all 50 wards. This gave her the largest margin of votes in the history of Chicago's mayoral contests. This is still the largest winning margin in windy city political history.

Jane Byrne had smashed the glass ceiling and was elected as the first woman mayor of America's second-largest city.

Byrne proved to be a progressive mayor. She hired the first African American and female school Superintendent Ruth B. Love. She collaborated closely with the gay community ending the police department's ongoing policy of raiding gay bars. Jane also began research into tougher gun laws which would effectively ban handgun possession with tough regulations on gun registration.

In her first three months in office, she faced strikes by labour unions as the city's transit workers, public school teachers and firefighters all went on strike.

Jane's enemies even took to describing her as 'Calamity Jane' as she speedily fired and hired people in such top jobs as police superintendent and press secretary. Many of these enemies where within her own Democratic party.

She was also finding it hard to combat the old boy's network in the Democratic party which had grown over the Daley years. In an interview after she left office, she described the beginning of her term as:

"It was chaos, like spaghetti in a pressure cooker,
it was all over the ceiling."

Source: Chicago Tribune 2004

The highlight of her first year as mayor was the visit
of Pope John Paul the 2nd to Chicago in October 1979.
At the time, Chicago had the second largest Polish
community in the world, surpassed only by Warsaw
and the visit was a great success.

As Jane found her feet as mayor, she was determined
to revitalise the city and change the way it felt and was
perceived.

Byrne championed plans for the 1992 Chicago
world's fair and used special events such as Taste of
Chicago, open air farmers markets and Chicago fest to
revitalise downtown Chicago.

Jane wrote in her 1994 book My Chicago:

"The formula was basic: The more attractions, the
more people, the more life for the city. I vowed to
bring back the crowds, to make Chicago so lively
that the people would return to the heart of the
city and its abandoned parks."

Source: Jane Byrne: My Chicago 1992

Mayor Byrne also gave permission for the film the

Blues Brothers, to be shot on location in and near Chicago in the summer and fall of 1979. She even allowed John Belushi and Dan Ackroyd's request to crash a car through a window at Daley Plaza, figuring Daley loyalists did not like her anyway.

In Byrnes turbulent first year she had dealt with transit, fire and school strikes. Ever hands on Byrne was often seen confronting striking workers on the picket lines.

Byrne used her influence to ensure that the Chicago Democratic operation endorsed Senator Ted Kennedy for president in 1980 during the Democratic primaries. However, while this may have been through loyalty to the Kennedy clan, it was a political miscalculation. Incumbent President Jimmy Carter easily won the Illinois Democratic primary and even carried Cook County and the city of Chicago.

In the first three months of 1981 a gang war resulted in 37 shootings and accounted for the deaths of 11 people in the city's infamous Cabrini Green public housing complex. Byrne had tried to stem the violence with several actions.

She first ordered the closure of several liquor stores in the area which had been identified as gang hang outs.

Then mayor Byrne demanded the Chicago Housing Authority evict tenants who were suspected of harboring gang members in their homes. This resulted in the eviction of 800 tenants, many more than Byrne had expected and a decision which soured Byrne's reputation with working class African Americans. A constituency that had given her such backing in her bid for mayor.

Determined to tackle the rise of violence in the Chicago's inner city and draw national attention to the poverty and deprivation in Cabrini Green Byrne decided to act.

She would later recall in her book:

"How could I put Cabrini on a bigger map?
Suddenly I knew I could move there."

Source: Jane Byrne: My Chicago 1992

So, she did, and on the 26th of March 1981 Jane and her husband Jay McMullen the former journalist and now her press officer decided they would move into an apartment in the notorious housing complex.

On the night of the 31st of March after attending an official engagement at the Conrad Hilton Hotel, Jane and Jay finally moved into a 4th floor apartment in Cabrini Green on North Sedgewick Avenue.

This alone immediately drew local and national attention, but the news media were more interested in the fact that just hours after Byrne moved in the police raided her building and arrested 11 gang members who were planning a shootout.

Byrne's objective of achieving national exposure to the crime and poverty in Cabrini was achieved with 3 weeks of publicity. Byrnes stay ended abruptly on the 18th of April 1981 after an Easter celebration photo op was interrupted by a protest from Cabrini residents who wanted Byrne out. They believed her entire stay was a publicity stunt and this further eroded her support amongst African American voters.

While initially standing as a progressive with enormous backing from the African American population and the endorsement of Jesse Jackson, Byrne was now tacking right. This was due to the rising popularity of Richard J. Daley now the head of the Daley political dynasty. Jane feared that Richard Daley would challenge her for the position of mayor, a job he felt he was born for.

In a move to appeal to the white base of the Democratic party Byrne dismissed many reformers who had worked diligently for her election. Jane began to work closely with Democratic stalwarts from the Daley years such as Edward

M. Burke and Ed Vrdolyak, who during her campaign she had denounced as an "evil cabal".

In a reversal from her progressive early years as mayor she angered and alienated many of these progressives and blacks that had supported her mayoral campaign by replacing black members of the Chicago board of education and Chicago housing authority board with white members, some of whom even held racist stances.

This was something she would later regret as she planned for her second term.

On November 11th, 1981, Jane Byrne was involved in a strange incident. Dan Goodwin a serial dare devil who had climbed the Sears Tower then the world's tallest building the previous spring began to scale the John Hancock Centre.

Wearing a wetsuit disguised as a Spider-Man suit and using a climbing device he designed for the climb, Goodwin scaled the 100-story building. Goodwin said he made the climb to call attention to the inability to successfully fight fires in high-rise buildings.

The Fire department didn't want Goodwin or the publicity and were determined to stop him.

To elude firemen who were descending toward him in a window-washing machine, Goodwin swung like Spiderman across the building with a rope. William Blair, Chicago's fire commissioner, had ordered his men to stop Goodwin by directing a full-power fire hose at him and by using fire axes to break window glass in Goodwin's path. They then attempted to dislodge Goodwin from the building with grappling hooks attached to long poles. Mayor Byrne intervened, allowing Goodwin to continue to the top. Byrne explained that while she did not agree with his climbing of the John Hancock Centre, she certainly opposed the fire department knocking him to the ground below and trying to kill him!

In January 1982, Byrne proposed an ordinance banning new handgun registration, which was considered controversial. The ordinance was created to put a freeze on the number of legally owned handguns in Chicago and to require owners of handguns to re-register them annually. The ordinance was approved by a 6–1 vote in February 1982.

Byrne initiated the idea for creating a unified lakefront museum campus, which was later implemented, and she also began the expansion of O'Hare international Airport.

Confident in her record In August 1982, Byrne decided that she would seek a second term as mayor.

However, two factors had now changed. The first was that demographically Chicago had changed. African American votes were now vitally important to anyone who wished to be mayor and Byrne through accident and design had alienated this important voting bloc.

Secondly, Richard Daley wanted to be mayor and was now a major player in the Cook County Democratic party.

As the re-election campaign began in July 1982, a poll by the Chicago Tribune showed that Jane trailed behind Richard M. Daley by 3%.

However, this was not going to be Daley's turn.

African American lawyer Harold Washington now entered the race. In 1979 Byrne benefited from receiving 59.3% of the African American vote, this soon flowed to Washington.

Byrne was defeated in the 1983 Democratic primary for mayor by Harold Washington; the younger Daley ran a close third. Washington won the Democratic primary with just 36% of the vote; Byrne had 33%.

Unwilling to admit defeat, Byrne initiated a write-in campaign for the general election but called it off for lack of support.

Washington went on to become the first African American to be elected as the city's mayor in April 1983 after a multiracial coalition of progressives supported his election.

However, his political struggles with a hostile city council encouraged Byrne to look forward to the 1987 election.

Byrne ran again against Washington in 1987 but was narrowly beaten. However, she did endorse Washington in the general election, where he had to run against not only a Republican opponent but 2 former Democratic supporters of Mayor Daley (Edward Vrdolyak and Thomas Hynes).

Undaunted Jane decided in March 1988 to run in the Democrat primary for the position of Cook County Circuit Court Clerk. She lost out to the Democratic parties favoured candidate, Aurelia Pucinski, who was endorsed by Mayor Washington.

Byrne's fourth run for mayor became a rematch with the younger Daley in February 1991. She received only 5.9 percent of the vote, finishing a distant third behind Daley and Alderman Danny K. Davis. This defeat effectively ended her political career.

Sadly, her husband Jay died from lung cancer just a few months later.

She through her energies into writing her side of her story and in 1992 published her book, 'My Chicago,' which covered her life and her historic political career.

Byrne entered hospice care and died on November 14th, 2014, in Chicago, aged 81, from complications of a stroke she suffered in January 2013. She was survived by her daughter Katherine and her grandson Willie.

Byrne also pulled one over on the media that once followed her so closely. After some media reported her age as 80, Kathy Byrne explained that her mother often deliberately gave the wrong year for her birth.

"She wanted to be younger," she said. "Whenever she would see the wrong age she'd say, 'I snookered them again." Her funeral Mass was held at St. Vincent de Paul on Monday, November 17th, 2014. She was buried at Calvary Catholic Cemetery in Evanston, Illinois'

Her legacy has been remembered in words and deeds. Mayor Rahm Emanuel said of her:

"The city of Chicago has lost a great trailblazer. From signing the first ordinance to get handguns off our streets, to bringing more transparency to the city's budget, to creating the Taste of Chicago, Mayor Byrne leaves a large and lasting legacy."

Former Mayor Richard M. Daley her great rival and son of her old mentor said of her:

"Mayor Jane Byrne was a woman of strength, courage and commitment. She was a pioneer in public service whose impact on this city will remain for years to come."

In a dedication ceremony held on August 29, 2014, Governor Pat Quinn renamed the Circle Interchange in Chicago the Jane Byrne Interchange.

In July 2014, the Chicago City Council voted to rename the plaza surrounding the historic Chicago Water Tower on North Michigan Avenue the Jane M. Byrne Plaza in her honour.

Perhaps her most lasting legacy is that the current mayor of Chicago is Lori Elaine Lightfoot the first openly lesbian African American woman to be elected mayor of a major city in the United States.

CHAPTER 13
DANIEL PATRICK MOYNIHAN
THE DEMOCRAT WHO WORKED FOR NIXON

D aniel Patrick Moynihan known to his friends and family as Pat, was a man who rose from humble Irish American origins in Hell's kitchen in New York to become a Harvard professor, United States Senator, Ambassador to India and Ambassador to the United Nations. He also served in the cabinets and inner circle of Presidents Kennedy, Johnson and surprising for a Democrat, Republican

Presidents Richard Nixon and Gerald Ford.

This made Moynihan the sole individual in the nation's history to be appointed, in succession, to four presidential cabinets: Kennedy, Johnson, Nixon, and Ford.

Daniel Patrick Moynihan was born on March 16th, 1927, in Tulsa Oklahoma to Irish American parents Margaret Ann (née Phipps), a homemaker, and John

Henry Moynihan, a reporter for a daily newspaper in Tulsa. The Moynihan's had roots in County Kerry. When Daniel was six John moved his family to New York City where he secured a role writing advertising copy for RKO pictures.

In 1937 John Moynihan lost his job with RKO. He had begun to drink heavily, and this took not only its toll on his home life but worse was to come. A heavy gambler, John got into fights with other gamblers to whom he owed money. When Daniel was 9 years old John Moynihan left his family and would never see his children again.

The abandoned family now lived in poverty. Living in New York's Hell's Kitchen was not easy for Daniel, and he shined shoes after school to help supplement the family income. His pitch was at the edge of Bryant Park near the corner of 42nd street and Sixth Avenue. Woody Guthrie worked just down the sidewalk, singing his songs for coins. He and his brother, Michael Willard Moynihan, spent most of their childhood summers at their grandfather's farm in Bluffton, Indiana.

Margaret Moynihan and her three children moved every year from shabby apartments around New York City, one above a bar in Hell's Kitchen. Margaret Moynihan married again, briefly, to an older man who provided temporary security and a move back to the suburbs. Margaret was vigilant about her children's education and would read to them every night.

Moynihan attended New York City Catholic and public schools and graduated first in his class from Benjamin Franklin High School in Manhattan as class valedictorian. His yearbook predicted that he would grow up to be "cussing out the labour unions and dumb radicals."

The poverty Moynihan experienced had a profound effect on his future political philosophy and he was determined to use his intelligence to rise above his surroundings.

In 1949 Moynihan wrote:

"I've lived much of my life in a jungle of broken families, watching them tear out each other's minds, watching them feasting on each other's hearts.

We used to play marbles for keeps. If you lost, you lost. It is the same way with politics, but not everybody knows this.

I owe something to the city of New York. I was raised here during the Depression. We were poor. Yet there was never a day of my life that I would have wished to be any other person. There was then, as now, a sense of building an even greater city... there is none like us."

Source: Godfrey Hodgson, The Gentleman From

New York: Daniel Patrick Moynihan –
A Biography (Houghton Mifflin Harcourt; 2000)

His children would later recall what their father thought of his childhood:

"Dad seldom spoke of his childhood, sometimes he told of his mother's struggles, how he worried for his young sister, Ellen after his father left Dad smiled when recounting adventures, he shared with his brother Michael, shining shoes and selling newspapers in Times Square. "In those days we would set up our shoeshine boxes, you had to get there on time or lose your space, make fifty cents" he said. "You could go find some lunch, and come back, your box would be right there. No one would think of stealing it. It was a peaceable kingdom."

Source: Godfrey Hodgson, The Gentleman From
New York: Daniel Patrick Moynihan –
A Biography (Houghton Mifflin Harcourt; 2000)

Moynihan worked for a while as a longshoreman on the New York docks before gaining a place in City college of New York, which offered free higher education. He told friends He took the entrance exam only to prove he was:

"As smart as I thought I was. I swaggered into test room with my longshoreman's loading hook sticking out of my back pocket. I wasn't going to be mistaken for any sissy college kid."

Source: Godfrey Hodgson, The Gentleman From New York: Daniel Patrick Moynihan – A Biography (Houghton Mifflin Harcourt; 2000)

He thought college was something for rich kids.

WW2 cut short his time at college and Daniel enlisted in the United States navy. In 1944 He joined the naval reserve attending Vermont's Middlebury college V-12 program to train for an officer position. Through the V-12 program the federal government paid tuition to participating colleges and universities for courses taught to qualified individuals, high school seniors who passed nationwide exams, naval enlisted personnel recommended by their commanding officers, and navy and marine corps members.

The men chosen for V-12 wore uniforms, underwent drills, took physical training and were paid $50 per month. Depending on past college courses, the men studied for three terms lasting four months each, followed by four months at a naval reserve midshipmen's school.

Students who wanted to then join the marine corps moved on to boot camp and then to the three-month

Officer candidate course at Quantico, Virginia. At the completion of all the training, participants received commissions as navy ensigns or marine corps second lieutenants.

In 1945 Margaret Moynihan opened a saloon on West 42nd Street in Manhattan, which she named Moynihan's Bar. The family lived upstairs above the bar.

While on leave, Daniel would work as a bar tender. In 1946 he enrolled as a naval reserve officers training corps student at Tufts University in Massachusetts, where he received an undergraduate degree in naval science in 1946. He finished his active service in 1947 aboard the USS Quirinus where he served as a midshipman and a communications officer.

On his return from the navy, he returned to New York and again worked in his mother's bar. Determined to continue his education he used funding from the GI Bill which enabled him to return to Tufts and complete a BA in Sociology.

The GI Bill in its original form, the 'Servicemen's Readjustment Act of 1944', was designed to provide benefits, including small business loans, mortgages, and education grants, to veterans following WWII.

He would go on to complete a master's degree at Tufts's Fletcher School of Law and Diplomacy in 1949.

Daniel was still conscious of his working-class roots and would later say of his fellow students at Middlebury and Tufts:

"They get my ass by the way they sit there and wallow in every kind of economic and social advantage our society has to offer and remain completely spiritually and mentally medi-ocre...they need a good swift kick in their blue-blooded asses. They need to get hurt occasionally. They need to get some feeling in them. But if I abstained from having anything to do with anyone, I think could use a kick in the ass, I didn't have many drinking companions."

Source: Godfrey Hodgson, The Gentleman From New York: Daniel Patrick Moynihan – A Biography (Houghton Mifflin Harcourt; 2000)

While studying Moynihan had to commute between Boston and New York to help in his mother's bar and was so busy he missed his graduation in 1948.

In 1950 he took summer courses at Harvard, visited Washington to look for job. But his life would change forever when he won the Fulbright scholarship for graduate study at the London School of Economics (LSE).

The Fulbright paid for his passage to England, tuition, books and £50 pounds a month. With his GI Bill benefits he had $300 a month coming in which was twice the average monthly wage in post war Britain.

A delighted Moynihan wrote to his mother and sister back in New York:

"I'm keeping well stuffed with sausage and beer,
staying up till dawn reading irrelevant books and
talking to unlikely people."

Source: Godfrey Hodgson, The Gentleman From
New York: Daniel Patrick Moynihan –
A Biography (Houghton Mifflin Harcourt; 2000)

He would go on to spend 3 years in London,
observed Queen Elizabeth II's coronation and took time
to visit parliament to hear Winston Churchill speak.

Moynihan was not called up for service in the
Korean War but took a keen interest in the conflict from
London. He observed:

"The crucial battles are at present being fought
round and about the world not with guns but
with ideas—specifically with symbols—and not
amongst the high aristocracy or the parliamentar-
ians, but amongst the sprawling, plodding,
stupid, sluggish, ugly, beautiful working people
of the world who like some great giants are
awakening from the nightmare of the 19th
century, thrashing about, and demolishing the
world that was built on their backs."

Source: Greg Weiner, American Burke: The Uncommon
Liberalism of Daniel Patrick Moynihan

Despite his working-class roots and concern for his fellow man, Moynihan was an ardent anti-communist and even took time to write for the New Statemen to counter what he perceived as support for Communist China from British socialists.

So concerned was he about British public opinion he wrote to his family saying:

> "I get the impression that Americans are not generally aware of just how fundamentally we are being opposed by a small but enormously vital element in British society...I respectfully submit that we had damn sure better get off our intellectual asses, but quick."

Source: Greg Weiner, American Burke: The Uncommon Liberalism of Daniel Patrick Moynihan

His articles and letters would lead to speaking engagements about US policy towards Asia, a role he would fill 25 years later, as ambassador in New Delhi and at the United Nations.

During his time in London, he took time to visit Ireland with his close friend and flatmate fellow student John Barry, a young lawyer from Tulsa. The two cycled around the south and west of Ireland in June 1951.

The LSE experience made Daniel a global citizen, it

gave him freedom, adventure, wisdom and bonds of friendship that sustained him throughout his life.

On his return to America in 1953 Daniel began to be involved in US politics. He volunteered on the New York mayoral campaign of Robert F. Wagner Jr, who defeated the Republican nominee, Harold Riegelman, as well as the Liberal Party nominee Rudolph Halley. In 1955 Moynihan began 3 years of service in Albany as assistant to Governor W. Averell Harriman, eventually rising to position of acting secretary and speech writer until Harriman's loss to Nelson Rockefeller in the 1958 election. That same year he would marry Elizabeth Brennan.

They met on the campaign trail, and it was love at first sight. A stricken Daniel burst into her room one night soon after they met declaring, "You are going to marry me," before passing out drunk on her floor.

She became her husband's chief advisor and handler, running his future campaigns. They had three children: Tim, a papier-mâché sculptor; Maura, a singer, actress, and writer; and John, a cartoonist.

After Harriman's defeat in the 1958 election, Moynihan returned to academia, serving as a lecturer for brief periods at Russell Sage College (1957–1958) and the Cornell University School of Industrial and Labour Relations (1959) before becoming director of government research at Syracuse University (1959–1961). He also became a member of the New York State tenure

commission and public affairs committee of the New
York State Democratic party.

In 1959, while director of government research at
Syracuse University, Moynihan published an article in
The Reporter, entitled "Epidemic on the Highways. In
this, he put forward the position that that prosecuting
motor collisions as criminal offenses did not increase
auto safety. His assertion was that the rise in highway
deaths was an epidemiological issue, and that compul-
sory use of seat belts was a more effective means of
reducing accidents.

Moynihan wanted to write a book on the subject and
a deal was even offered, but politics was now in his
blood, and he secured a position as a Kennedy New
York delegate to the 1960 Democratic National Convention in Los Angeles which nominated John F Kennedy
for president and Lyndon Johnson for vice president.

By now an influential and well-connected member
of the New York Democratic party Moynihan abandoned his book idea and threw himself into the 1960
election. While not yet in the inner circle of the
Kennedy's his intellect was highly valued, and he
wrote several policy papers for the Kennedy
campaign.

On Kennedys victory Moynihan was asked to come
and serve at the new Camelot.

A rising star in Democratic politics Moynihan joined
the Kennedy Administration firstly as a special adviser

and then assistant secretary to labour secretaries Arthur J. Goldberg and W. Willard Wirtz.

Given his strong academic background, he did not have operational responsibilities. Instead, he devoted his time to trying to formulate national policy for what the press would dub the war on poverty.

In September 1963, Moynihan Published with Nathan Glazer, the sociologist and fellow Kennedy administration adviser "Beyond the Melting Pot: The Negroes, Puerto Ricans, Jews, Italians, and Irish of New York City".

Moynihan and Glazer set out to challenge the concept of the big society and asserted that the United States was a homogeneous society in which ethnic differences become less important over time.

Unsurprisingly in the era of Martin Luther's I have a dream speech only a month before publication, the book created a maelstrom of controversy. The book did garner praise for denying the inevitability and desirability of cultural homogenisation, but it was heavily criticised for allegedly elevating ethnicity over class, for conflating ethnicity and race, and for maligning the African American family especially African American males as family role models.

No matter the controversy, it would soon be dwarfed by events that would not only shake America but the world.

At 12.30 on November the 22nd President Kennedy

was assassinated in Dallas Texas. Moynihan's reaction to this terrible event is best viewed in his own words in a memorandum he penned to himself regarding the slaying of JFK.

"Bill Walton, Charlie Horsky and I were just finishing lunch at Walton's house—in the grandest good mood with Walton leaving for the Russian tour that afternoon—I was talking about Brasilia and the phone rang. Oh no! Killed! No! Horsky's office had phoned for him to return. We rushed upstairs. Television had some of it, but the commercials continued. Bill began sobbing. Out of control. Horsky in a rage. Clint, Jackie's agent had said the President is dead. Walton knew this meant it was so. He dressed more or less, and we went directly to the White House from George-town. On the way the radio reported that Albert Thomas had said he might be living.
We went directly to the President's office which was torn apart with new carpets being put down in his office and the cabinet room. As if a new President were to take office. No one about save Chuck Daly. McGeorge Bundy appeared. Icy. Ralph Dungan came in smoking a pipe, quizzical, as if unconcerned. Then Sorensen. The three together in the door of the hallway that leads to the Cabinet room area. Dead silent. Someone said

"It's over. Mary McGrory said "We'll never laugh again. I replied to Mary, we'll laugh again, but we'll never be young again.""

Source: Godfrey Hodgson, The Gentleman From New York: Daniel Patrick Moynihan – A Biography (Houghton Mifflin Harcourt; 2000)

Moynihan was concerned like were many in the Kennedy administration to get the alleged shooter Lee Harvey Oswald into secure federal custody rather than held by the Dallas police.

On November 24, Oswald was brought to the basement of the Dallas police headquarters on his way to a more secure county jail. A crowd of police and press with live television cameras rolling gathered to witness his departure. As Oswald came into the room, Jack Ruby emerged from the crowd and fatally wounded him with a single shot from a concealed .38 revolver. Ruby, who was immediately detained, claimed that rage at Kennedy's murder was the motive for his action. Some called him a hero, but he was nonetheless charged with first-degree murder.

When Moynihan found out that Oswald had been shot, he is reported to have pounded his head against the wall in frustration and anger.

Moynihan was grief stricken for the fallen president and his daughter would later recall:

"I watched my mother arrange her black veil and gloves for the president's funeral. Five year later I would watch her do the same for Senator Robert Kennedy's funeral. Something changed forever in my father's heart, as in everyone who lived through it. I could see that something more than the president had been killed. The promise of the Democratic party, a belief in America leading the world, with a vision of hope and unity, was shot down."

Source: Godfrey Hodgson, The Gentleman From New York: Daniel Patrick Moynihan – A Biography (Houghton Mifflin Harcourt; 2000)

Daniel Moynihan was no conspiracy theorist, but he wanted, as did the American public to know why Kennedy had been assassinated and his assailant murdered.

Moynihan believed that JFK had been "my" president in a way that happens only once. He passionately believed with great insight it must be said, that unless the murder of Kennedy and of his assailant was remorselessly investigated, a cloud of suspicion would envelope the national government, darkening its moral authority, for a generation to come.

In his quest for answers, he would later say:

"At best, we encountered incomprehension; at worst, the suspicion that we thought there was a conspiracy. We did NOT; we were merely convinced that a large amount of the public would believe there was one unless the inquiry went forward with this preeminent concern in mind."

Source: Godfrey Hodgson, The Gentleman From New York: Daniel Patrick Moynihan – A Biography (Houghton Mifflin Harcourt; 2000)

While the trauma of the assassination drove many of his friends from Washington. Moynihan grieved for the fallen president, but he still believed in the power of government to do good. He became the only member of Kennedy's cabinet who remained in electoral politics. For the rest of his life, he kept a photograph of President Kennedy near to his desk.

Despite carrying on his government role he was never quite trusted by the new administration of President Lyndon Johnson.

Again, without operational responsibilities. He devoted his time to trying to formulate national policy for what would become the war on Poverty. Moynihan's research of labour department data demonstrated that even as fewer people were unemployed, more people were joining the welfare rolls. These recipients were families with children but only one parent (almost invariably the mother). The laws at that time permitted such families to receive welfare payments in certain parts of the United States.

A proud New Yorker Moynihan was appalled when in 1964 the Penn Station in New York City, was demolished to make way for Madison Square Garden.

Moynihan deplored its destruction and sought funds for converting the beaux arts Post Office building on 34th Street into a new Pennsylvania Station. Advocates wanted the new building to be known as Moynihan Station.

In 1965 he published the controversial The Negro Family: The Case for National Action, now commonly known as the Moynihan Report. The report called for policies "directed to a new kind of national goal: the establishment of a stable 'Negro' family structure."

This focused on the deep roots of African American deprivation in the United States and controversially concluded that the high rate of families headed by single mothers would greatly hinder progress of African Americans toward economic and political equality.

Moynihan was attacked by African American and civil rights leaders for displaying a patronising attitude and cultural bias. Some African American leaders also accused him of racism.

As a supporter of Robert Kennedy, (he had Served as campaign adviser to Robert F. Kennedy in his successful

'64 campaign for the Senate from New York) his position was already difficult in the Johnson administration. The powerful backlash to his report ended his role in the administration.

His partying shot was to call for a formal alliance between liberals and conservatives and he hoped the next administration would be able to unite the nation again. As we shall see these words proved to be prophetic.

Moynihan returned once again to teaching as a Harvard professor. He did not give up politics and he ran for office in the Democratic party primary for the presidency of the New York City council, a position now known as the New York City public advocate. However, he was defeated by Queens district attorney Frank D. O'Connor.

1968 was to prove a monumental year in US politics and offered a new opportunity for Moynihan.

On the 31st of March President Johnson appeared on national television and announced that he was partially halting the US bombing of Vietnam, and that he had decided not to seek his party's nomination for president. "There is division in the American house now," Johnson declared.

Moynihan immediately threw his support behind Robert Kennedy.

On April the 4th The Rev. Martin Luther King Jr. was

assassinated in Memphis, Tennessee bringing more race riots in US cities.

On June 5th, 1968, at the Ambassador Hotel in Los Angeles. Following dual victories in the California and South Dakota democratic primaries, Robert Kennedy spoke to journalists and the crowd. A 24-year-old Sirhan Bishara Sirhan shot him multiple times with a handgun. Kennedy died in the Good Samaritan hospital 26 hours later.

In November the Republican nominee, former vice president Richard Nixon, defeated the Democratic nominee, incumbent vice president Hubert Humphrey, and the American Independent Party nominee, Governor George Wallace. A conservative was now in the White House, and he was about to make an offer the liberal Moynihan would find hard to refuse.

Moynihan, the Democratic intellectual joined the Republican President Nixon's administration in 1969, as an assistant to the president for domestic policy. Later that year he was promoted to become a presidential counsellor. His friends and family were stunned by his alliance with Nixon, and his wife Elizabeth refused to move to Washington with their 3 children.

Moynihan and Nixon were political opposites, Moynihan was a noted liberal with a focus on policy development who flitted between government and academia sometimes at the same time, while Nixon was a centre-right politician for whom politics was life itself.

It was a bit of a shock that Nixon tapped Moynihan to be a domestic policy advisor, but Nixon was persuaded that the social problems of the time required Moynihan's insight and experience.

Moynihan's created an energetic group of young liberals whose ideas on societal change pushed Nixon and his conservative advisors.

However almost all proposals submitted by Moynihan's team had to be scrapped because money was so tight.

As one of the few people in Nixon's inner circle who had done academic research related to social policies, he was very influential in the early months of the administration. While working for Nixon, Moynihan pushed for an aid package for poor families, but the program went nowhere. So did Moynihan's suggestion that the United States end the war in Vietnam.

The perplexing problem that Nixon had to tackle was how to reform the welfare system as he had campaigned on, but to do it in a manner that was soft in delivery, did not increase the deficit and was acceptable to the Democrat majority in Congress.

Moynihan and Nixon put together a Family Assistance Plan (F.A.P.) that functioned as a universal basic income, with a guaranteed income for the poor, including the working poor.

The Moynihan-Nixon F.A.P. was a plan to stop the

programs of LBJ's Great Society but keep the money flowing.

The Nixon-Moynihan F.A.P. rolled out with near universal support. It breezed through the House but stalled in the Senate. The odd combination of Nixon-Moynihan was checked in place by an even odder coalition of very conservative Senators and very liberal organisations and interests. Disheartened by a lack of progress he returned to Harvard in 1970.

Later that year he served as a member of the US delegation to the twenty-sixth general assembly of the United Nations. He was replaced by John Ehrlichman, who would later be sent to prison for his role in the Watergate scandal.

In 1973 he accepted Nixon's offer of US Ambassador to India. He played a significant role in n negotiating an end to India's huge food aid debt to the United States.

He proposed that part of the burdensome debt be written off, part used to pay for US embassy expenses in India, and the remaining converted into Indian rupees to fund an Indo-U.S. cultural and educational exchange program that lasted for a quarter of a century.

On February 18th, 1974, he presented to the government of India with a check for 16,640,000,000 rupees, then equivalent to $2,046,700,000, which was the greatest amount paid by a single cheque in the history of banking. The "Rupee Deal" is logged in the Guinness Book of World Records for the world's largest check, written by Ambassador Moynihan to Prime Minister Indira Gandhi.

In June 1975 he became the United States' ambassador to the United Nations a position which also included a rotation as the president of the security council. In this role, he became famous for his blunt replies to criticism of the United States by other countries.

President Ford who had replaced the disgraced Nixon continued Americas anti-communism stance and as Ambassador Moynihan reflected the policy of the White House at the time. He was also a strong supporter of the state of Israel, condemning UN resolution 3379, which declared Zionism to be a form of racism.

In December 1975, Indonesia invaded East Timor, President Ford considered Indonesia, then under a military dictatorship, a key ally against communism, which was influential in East Timor.

Under White House direction Moynihan ensured that the UN Security Council took no action against the larger nation's annexation of a smaller country. The Indonesian invasion caused the deaths of 100,000–200,000 Timorese through violence, illness, and hunger.

Moynihan would later regret this policy which he called a defence of a shameless policy dictated by the cold war fight against communism with East Timor the loser.

Moynihan's views towards communism and the Soviet Union evolved during his term at the UN.

Viewing the machinations of world politics at first hand, he began to view the Soviet Union less as an expansionist enemy and more as a failed state in terminal decline.

Demoralised, by what he perceived as an aggressive US policy Moynihan resigned from what he would subsequently characterise as an "abbreviated posting" in February 1976.

He would later state that he was:

"Something of an embarrassment to my own government, and fairly soon left before I was fired."

Source: Stephen Hess, The Professor and the President: Daniel Patrick Moynihan in the Nixon White House (2014)

Daniel Moynihan had served 4 presidents, but he now wanted to represent the people of New York State and in 1976 he ran in the Senate election in New York.

Moynihan's controversial defence of Israel as United States Ambassador to the United Nations did him no harm with the large Jewish population in New York and he was easily elected, a position he would hold until 2001.

Throughout his long term in the Senate, he was famous for his criticism of all four presidents under whom he served. His first act as a new senator was to evaluate his assumption that the state of New York was paying out more in Federal taxes than it was receiving in return from Washington.

His assumption proved correct, and he issued a report called "The federal budget and New York State,"

In this he argued that the wealthier taxpayers of his state subsidised social programs and public works benefitting the rest of the country.

He would go on to make this an annual exercise.

As a renowned writer and no stranger to expressing controversial and at times unpopular opinions, Moynihan was an enthusiastic believer in the right to free speech and the freedom of the press.

In 1978 Myron A. Farber a reporter at the New York Times was jailed for contempt and the newspaper fined, ending up spending 40 days in jail with fines of $285,000.

This was because of his involvement in what became known as the 'Dr X Case.'

In June 1975, the paper received a letter from a woman claiming that as many as 40 patients had been murdered at a hospital by its chief surgeon.

Farber's investigations led to the identification of Dr. Mario Jascalevich as the hospital's chief surgeon. While Jascalevich's surgical patients routinely survived, those of a new surgeon were dying at a significantly high rate. This new surgeon, together with directors of the hospital, opened Jascalevich's locker on October 31st, 1966, and found 18 near empty vials of curare, a powerful muscle relaxant that could cause death if not administered in conjunction with artificial respiration.

Jascalevich's defence attorney Raymond A. Brown accused other doctors at the hospital of framing Jascalevich to cover up their own ineptitude. They went as far as to imply that Farber had conspired with prosecutors to advance their respective careers by pointing the finger of blame at Jascalevich.

After Brown subpoenaed the reporter, Farber testified in the case but cited the First Amendment of the United States constitution, when he refused to turn over thousands of pages of his notes that the defence had requested, citing a compelling right to protect the identity of the sources used in the articles from individuals who had spoken to him with the expectation that their confidence would be maintained.

For his refusal, Farber was eventually imprisoned, whilst he would later be pardoned, he did spend a period of 40 days in jail.

This appalled Moynihan, who in an August 7th, 1978, speech to the Senate, following the jailing of M. A. Farber, highlighted the possibility of Congress having to become involved with securing press freedom and that the Senate should be aware of the issue's seriousness.

Moynihan was always proud of his Irish roots and in 1981 he was instrumental with fellow Irish American politicians Senator Ted Kennedy, New York Governor Hugh L Carey and House Speaker Tip O'Neil in setting up The Congressional Friends of Ireland, or Friends of Ireland.

This was a bipartisan group of senators and representatives opposed to violence and terrorism in Northern Ireland and dedicated to maintaining a United States policy that promotes a just, lasting, and peaceful settlement of the conflict. It would go onto play a significant role in the Anglo-Irish Agreement of 1985 and the Good Friday Agreement in April 1998.

As UN Ambassador he had the view that the Soviet Union was on borrowed time and this in interest in foreign policy did not end in the Senate, where he sat on the Select Committee on Intelligence.

Whilst anti Soviet, he was convinced of their decline and when the Reagan administration supplied support to the Contras in Nicaragua, Moynihan was a vehement critic of the policy.

He argued there was no active Soviet-backed conspiracy in Latin America, or anywhere. He suggested the Soviets were suffering from massive internal problems, such as rising ethnic nationalism and a collapsing economy. In a December 21st, 1986, editorial in The New York Times, Moynihan predicted the replacement on the world stage of communist expansion with ethnic conflicts. This would prove a prophetic warning that future presidents should have heeded.

Moynihan introduced Section 1706 of the Tax Reform Act of 1986, which cost certain professionals (like computer programmers, engineers, draftspersons, and designers) who depended on intermediary agencies (consulting firms) a self-employed tax status option, but other professionals (like accountants and lawyers) continued to enjoy Section 530 exemptions from payroll taxes.

On the face of it, a boring piece of legislation, but it would have a dramatic impact 7 years after his death, when Andrew Joseph Stack III deliberately crashed his single-engine Piper Dakota light aircraft into Building I of the Echelon office complex in Austin, Texas, killing himself and Internal Revenue Service (IRS) manager Vernon Hunter.

Thirteen others were injured, two severely. Stack, a 53-year-old software engineer, left a long, rambling biographical suicide note that expressed anger at US tax laws especially Section 1706.

In 1990, Moynihan supported the appointment of Sonia Sotomayor to federal district judgeship. He would later be instrumental in first recommending Ruth Bader Ginsburg for the Supreme Court and then helping secure her confirmation.

In 1992, Governor Bill Clinton of Arkansas defeated President Bush in the presidential election. One of Moynihan's first engagements with the new president elect was to send him a memo on ethnic problems in the

Balkans after a journey to the former Yugoslavia. Again, this would prove prophetic as President Clinton would authorise the bombing of Serbia in March 1999.

When President Bill Clinton sought to establish a national health insurance program, Moynihan was against the bill, saying that the administration should first reform welfare.

On other issues though, he was much more progressive. He voted against the death penalty, the flag desecration amendment, the balanced budget amendment, the private securities litigation reform act, the defence of marriage act, and the North American Free Trade Agreement. He was critical of proposals to replace the progressive income tax with a flat tax. Moynihan also voted against authorisation of the first Gulf War.

In 1994, Moynihan defeated Reverend Al Sharpton in the Democratic primary and went on to win re-election with 55% of the vote. A year later in a great PR coup he persuaded. President Clinton to return Governors Island to New York for just $1.

In 1998 he Published Secrecy: The American Experience, it would be his last book.

Shortly after he announced that he would retire at the end of his fourth six-year term, in 2000. However, there was to be some excitement before that.

On December 19th, 1998, the US house of Representatives voted to impeach President Clinton on charges of lying under oath to a federal grand jury and obstructing justice in the Monica Lewinsky affair. The two allegations of "high crimes and misdemeanours" now went to the Senate for trial.

President Clinton was acquitted by the Senate of all charges and Daniel Moynihan voted for acquittal.

Daniel endorsed the first lady, Hillary Rodham Clinton, as his replacement for his Senate seat.

In 2000, President Clinton awarded Moynihan the Medal of Freedom, the United States' highest civilian honour. He retired from the Senate a year later.

Daniel Moynihan died on March 26th, 2003, because of complications arising from a ruptured appendix.

Moynihan was buried at Arlington Cemetery with full military honours. He was a tenured professor at Harvard, US Ambassador to India and to the United Nations. From 1976 to 2000 he won four terms in the US Senate from New York—the lone survivor of John F. Kennedy's cabinet to remain in electoral politics. He produced 19 books, innumerable reports, articles and studies and received 69 honorary degrees.

An amazing journey and series of achievements for a poor boy from Hell's Kitchen and County Kerry, who shined shoes on the streets of New York.

CHAPTER 14
EUGENE MCCARTHY
THE GREAT LIBERAL WHO BACKED REAGAN

E ugene McCarthy ran for the presidency 5 times and never secured the nomination. As a liberal he was not afraid to call out the anti-communist paranoia of Senator Joseph McCarthy and helped end the presidential career of Lyndon B. Johnson when he ran on an anti-war platform in the 1968 democratic presidential primaries. He was also one of the most prominent 'Reagan Democrats,' who endorsed the Republican presidential candidate, Ronald Reagan.

Eugene Joseph McCarthy was born on the 29th of March 1916 in Watkins in rural Minnesota. His parents were Anna a home maker of German descent and Michael a postmaster and cattle farmer, whose family had emigrated to Canada from county Cork.

His mother had a deep Roman Catholic faith, and she would have a major influence on the future political, and moral philosophy of her son. He attended St. Anthony's Catholic School in Watkins. The young Eugene enjoyed both the academic and sporting aspects of his schooling. He particularly enjoyed baseball and ice hockey. He would also spend long hours leafing through and reading his aunts large collection of books.

He attended Saint John's Preparatory school and Saint John's University where he was heavily influenced by the monks who taught him. He received a bachelor's degree in 1935 which was followed by graduate studies at the University of Minnesota, where he received a master's degree in sociology in 1939.

In between, Eugene started his career teaching social sciences in public schools in both his native Minnesota and neighbouring North Dakota.

In 1940 he returned to Saint John's University where he became professor of economics and education. Indulging his love of sport, he coached the hockey team for one season.

Eugene had a deep faith instilled in him by his mother and in 1943 he assessed his calling by experiencing the contemplative life of a monk by becoming a Benedictine novice at Saint John's Abbey.

Despite his faith, the religious life was not for Eugene, and he left the monastery after nine months and enlisting in the US Army. He would serve out World War 2 in Washington as a code breaker for the military intelligence division of the war department.

Eugene worked under the direction of the famed cryptologist, William Frederick Friedman.

After the war ended Eugene returned to Minnesota to start a post teaching sociology and economics at the College of St. Thomas in St. Paul, Minnesota.

Shortly after his return the would-be monk met and fell in love with a fellow teacher Abigail Quigley. They married in 1945 and would go on to have four children. In 1945 he became a sociology instructor at the College of Saint Thomas, in Saint Paul. He and his wife would have 4 children: Margaret, Michael, Mary and Ellen.

Eugene was now developing an interest in politics and was an active member of the Minnesota Democratic Farmer Labour Party in the Saint Paul area, which was affiliated to the Democratic party. He now set his sights on the national stage and planned a run for Congress. In 1948 he ran for Congress in Minnesota's traditionally Republican Fourth Congressional District (East St. Paul). Powered on by a coalition of Catholic and labour voters he won by 25,000 votes.

McCarthy was now in the House of Representatives where he would serve five terms before moving to the Senate in 1958.

As a congressman he was best known there as the leader of 'McCarthy's Marauders', a caucus of young midwestern liberals.

During the 1950s McCarthy worked on labour and agricultural issues and maintained a liberal voting record. On numerous occasions in the House, he attempted to curtail the activities of the Central Intelligence Agency (CIA).

McCarthy supported the US intervention in favour of South Korea during the 1950-53 Korean Conflict.

In 1952 he famously engaged the much-feared Wisconsin Senator Joseph McCarthy (no relation) in a nationally televised debate in which he parodied the senator's arguments to "prove" that General Douglas MacArthur had been a communist pawn.

Joseph McCarthy was best known for his heavy-handed and wide-ranging investigation of Communism in the US government and in society at large. (*See Chapter 15*).

Senator Joseph McCarthy made accusations of treason and communist activity in the United States throughout his career. One of his most famous moments came in 1950, in Wheeling, West Virginia, where he claimed to have a list of 205 individuals in the State Department that were known to the Secretary of State as being members of the Communist party. Although he refused to produce any names and was never able to provide any evidence, McCarthy created general fear in America. McCarthyism, or the Red Scare as it came to be called, dominated American politics in the 1950s, damaged many people's careers and distracted the voting population from other pressing issues.

In 1957, Eugene established an informal coalition of

members of Congress, later formally organised as the 'House Democratic Study Group', to counter anti–civil rights actions of southern Democrats.

> But by 1958 McCarthy had grown tired of the House. "The House," he remarked, "is not a home."
>
> *Source: Eugene McCarthy Up Til Now: A Memoir*
> *(1987)*

He had decided his new home would be the US Senate.

In 1958 McCarthy was elected to the US Senate and became a respected legislator in the upper house. However, he was often overshadowed by his more high-profile fellow Minnesota senator Hubert H. Humphrey.

He chaired the special committee on unemployment. The committee dedicated itself to studying the causes of unemployment and ways to alleviate them, holding hearings in McCarthy's native Minnesota, as well as in Michigan and Pennsylvania.

"Unemployment," he said in 1959, "is first of all a human and social problem, affecting the welfare and happiness of individual workers and of their families." He was critical of the government's lack of urgency about maintaining full employment. He said, "there has been no real recognition of the basic fact that to be strong and healthy and secure an economy must expand and grow dynamically."

Source: Walter Reuther Library, Wayne State University, Detroit, MI.

Increasingly, he gained a reputation as a loner, although he generally voted with his party's liberal faction.

McCarthy supported Hubert Humphrey in the 1960 Democratic primaries and his national profile was raised when he nominated Adlai Stevenson for president at the 1960 Democratic National Convention in Los Angeles.

McCarthy gave a passionate speech in praise of Stevenson when he said:

"Do not reject this man who made US all proud to be called Democrats!"

Source: Eugene McCarthy Up Til Now: A Memoir
(1987)

He even joked about his own merits as a candidate telling the convention:

"I'm twice as liberal as Hubert Humphrey, twice

as intelligent as Stuart Symington, and twice as Catholic as Jack Kennedy."

Source: Eugene McCarthy Up Til Now: A Memoir
(1987)

This was to no avail as the die was cast for John F. Kennedy who secured the Democratic nomination with Lyndon B. Johnson as his vice president.

However, the quite man from Minnesota was now on the national stage and a player in the Democratic party.

In early August 1964 McCarthy supported the Gulf of Tonkin Resolution which authorised President Lyndon Johnson to "take all necessary measures to repel any armed attack against the forces of the United States and to prevent further aggression" by the communist government of North Vietnam.

It was passed on August 7th, 1964, by the US Congress after an alleged attack on two US naval destroyers stationed off the coast of Vietnam. The Gulf of Tonkin Resolution effectively launched America's full-scale involvement in the Vietnam War.

This support did him no harm, later in August at the 1964 Democratic convention in Atlantic City, New Jersey where Eugen was considered as a possible running mate for Lyndon Johnson in the 1964 election.

President Johnson generated publicity during the

convention by floating Eugen's name for the vice-presidential slot on his re-election ticket only to see fellow Minnesota Senator Humphrey chosen for that position.

Until the selection of Humphrey as the vice-presidential nominee in 1964, many Democratic leaders had considered McCarthy the logical choice for the nomination. President Lyndon Johnson himself had even led McCarthy to expect it.

Along with Ted Kennedy, Eugene co-sponsored the Immigration and Nationality Act of 1965.

The law overhauled America's immigration system during a period of deep global instability. For decades, a federal quota system had severely restricted the number of people from outside Western Europe eligible to settle in the United States. Passed during the height of the Cold War, it erased America's longstanding policy of limiting immigration based on national origin.

The popular bill passed the House, 318 to 95. The law capped the number of annual visas at 290,000, which included a restriction of 20,000 visas per country per year. But policymakers had vastly underestimated the number of immigrants who would take advantage of the family reunification clause. In particular, the law created new opportunities for immigrants from Asian nations to join relatives in America. Following the act, annual immigration jumped to nearly a half million people, and only 20 percent came from Europe.

McCarthy later expressed regret about its impact and

became a member of the federation for American Immigration reform.

In 1965, McCarthy joined the Senate Foreign Relations Committee, which was to become the focal point of opposition to the Vietnam War.

McCarthy became convinced that peace in Vietnam required a political settlement with the Vietcong. He began to oppose American participation in the war at every turn.

In January 1966, McCarthy and 14 other senators signed a public letter urging Johnson not to resume the bombing of North Vietnam after a brief holiday truce. From that first public criticism of the Vietnam war McCarthy now became a thorn in the Johnson administrations side and one of the most veracious critics of the US engagement in Vietnam.

In 1966, he voted to repeal the Gulf of Tonkin Resolution, which effectively gave the president unlimited authorisation to use American military forces in Southeast Asia.

Beyond the war itself, McCarthy objected to the Johnson administration's disregard for the Senate's role in shaping foreign policy. Reminiscent of his time in the Congress he was also critical of the Central Intelligence Agency's influence in policymaking and sought to reduce US arms sales abroad.

Over the next two years McCarthy came to the fore as the leading critic of Johnson's Vietnam War policies.

In 1967 he summarised these opinions in 'The Limits
of Power', a thoughtful, but critical book that
condemned reckless American military and political
intervention in other nations' affairs.

The opposition to the Vietnam war was growing
slowly, McCarthy and Oregon Senator Wayne Morse
gave regular speeches ion the Senate denouncing the
conflict. Several Oregon Democrats encouraged
Robert Kennedy to challenge President Lyndon B
Johnson in the 1968 democratic primaries. Eugene
also spoke to Kennedy and urged him to
run.Kennedy refused and the group now turned to
McCarthy.

Eugene McCarthy announced his candidacy for president on November 30th, 1967, saying:

"I am concerned that the Administration seems to
have set no limit to the price it is willing to pay
for a military victory."

Source: Eugene McCarthy Up Til Now: A Memoir
(1987)

Political pundits saw Eugene's campaign as an interesting insurgency designed to raise anti-war awareness,
but with little chance of success.

In December McCarthy addressed the conference of
concerned Democrats in Chicago, accusing the Johnson

administration of ignoring and bungling opportunities for bringing the war to a conclusion.

This passion still did not ignite his campaign, but this all changed in January 1968 when the North Vietnamese Army launched the Tet Offensive from January 30th until the 23rd of February.

The Tet Offensive was a coordinated series of North Vietnamese attacks on more than 100 cities and outposts in South Vietnam. The offensive was an attempt to foment rebellion among the South Vietnamese population and encourage the United States to scale back its involvement in the Vietnam War. Though US and South Vietnamese forces managed to hold off the attacks, news coverage of the massive offensive shocked the American public and eroded support for the war effort.

The public backlash to the Tet Offensive resuscitated McCarthy's flagging campaign and he was now at the forefront of the 'Dump Johnson' movement.

An outpouring of support by largely unpaid, politically inexperienced student volunteers on college campuses across the country captured national attention and gave McCarthy's candidacy political momentum.

Several anti-war college students and other activists from around the country travelled to New Hampshire to support McCarthy's campaign. Some anti-war students who had the long-haired, counterculture appearance of hippies chose to cut their long hair and shave off their beards in order to campaign for McCarthy door-to-door, a phenomenon that led to the informal slogan "Get clean for Gene".

The efforts of this "Children's Crusade" proved decisive in the campaign's first primary, held in New Hampshire on 12th March. Winning a surprising 42 percent of the vote, McCarthy demonstrated that Johnson was vulnerable. President Johnson had narrowly won the popular vote in New Hampshire, but the delegates' response was a devastating blow for an incumbent president.

Robert Kennedy announced, that he would enter the race on March 16th, this was a blow to Eugene as most Democrats and the political commentariat saw Kennedy as a far stronger candidate than himself.

McCarthy and his supporters viewed this as opportunism, creating a lasting enmity between the campaigns.

The shock waves from New Hampshire led to Johnson's withdrawal from the race on the 31st of March. After Johnson's withdrawal, Vice President Hubert Humphrey announced his candidacy on April 27th.

Humphrey, long a champion of labour unions and of civil rights, entered the race with the support of the party "establishment", including most members of Congress, mayors, governors and labour union leaders

Robert Kennedy was successful in four state primaries (Indiana, Nebraska, South Dakota, and California) and McCarthy won six Wisconsin, Pennsylvania,

Massachusetts, Oregon, New Jersey, and Illinois. However, in primaries where they campaigned directly against one another, Kennedy won three primaries, Indiana, Nebraska, and California and McCarthy won one, Oregon.

Humphrey did not compete in the primaries, leaving favourite sons to collect favourable surrogates, notably United States Senator George A. Smathers from Florida, United States Senator Stephen M. Young from Ohio, and Governor Roger D. Branigin of Indiana.

The Humphrey campaign concentrated on winning the delegates in non-primary states, where party leaders controlled the delegate votes.

Kennedy defeated Branigin and McCarthy in the Indiana primary, and then defeated McCarthy in the Nebraska primary. However, McCarthy upset Kennedy in the Oregon primary becoming the first man to beat a Kennedy brother in an election.

After Kennedy's defeat in Oregon, the California primary on June 4th was seen as crucial, both men knew this result would be decisive.

Lacking a stark contrast over issues, the Democratic primary race began to focus on more personality rather than policies. The Kennedy forces portrayed McCarthy as an aloof intellectual; the McCarthy supporters painted Kennedy as a ruthless opportunist. Against his opponent's flash and charisma, McCarthy presented a subdued reasonableness that held considerable appeal in affluent suburban areas.

The Californian contest proved to be a bitter election. On the stump in San Francisco, McCarthy stated that Robert Kennedy "played a prominent role in formulating policies which resulted in disastrous adventures," including the Vietnam War. He also criticized his opponent for relying too much on private enterprise to reduce poverty in America's inner cities, favouring a more activist government approach that included job-linked housing programs outside the ghetto.

This latter issue became a point of contention during the two candidates' televised debate on 1st June.

Robert Kennedy accused Eugene of proposing to "take 10,000 black people and move them into Orange County (a wealthy Los Angeles suburb)," a charge with decidedly racist overtones.

McCarthy responded poorly and performed below par in the debate and lost resoundingly to the more telegenic and well-prepared Kennedy.

In the election three days later, Kennedy defeated McCarthy by five percentage points. Kennedy also won the South Dakota primary held the same day.

McCarthy, however defeated Kennedy in New Jersey and refused to withdraw from the presidential race. He defiantly announced he would fight Kennedy in the upcoming New York State primary, where McCarthy had large support from anti-war activists.

However, tragedy was to strike the campaign.

Minutes after giving his victory speech at the Ambassador Hotel in Los Angeles, California, Kennedy was assassinated in the kitchen service pantry in the early morning of June 5th.

A Palestinian immigrant with Jordanian citizenship named Sirhan Bishara Sirhan was arrested. Senator Robert Kennedy died 26 hours later at Good Samaritan Hospital.

After winning the New York primary on 18th June, McCarthy conducted what some supporters viewed as an erratic, indifferent campaign. He appeared downbeat and self-absorbed, uncertain of how to proceed against Humphrey, who was rolling up enough delegates to secure the Democratic presidential nomination.

Even though political polls indicated that McCarthy, rather than Humphrey, was the strongest candidate against the likely Republican nominee, Richard Nixon, old-guard Democratic professionals remained opposed to his candidacy.

The late entrance of Senator George McGovern into the race as a second anti-war candidate complicated matter further.

Despite strong showings in several primaries, he won more votes than any other Democratic candidate, McCarthy garnered only 23% of the delegates at the 1968 Democratic National Convention, largely due to the control of state-party organisations over the delegate-selection process. After Kennedy's assassination, many Kennedy delegates, remembering his bitter war of words with McCarthy, chose to support George McGovern rather than McCarthy

On the eve of August's Democratic convention in Chicago, McCarthy acknowledged that his chances were all but hopeless. Humphrey easily triumphed over McCarthy on the first ballot but never recovered from the ill-will between his party's factions. The violence committed by Chicago police against demonstrators outside the convention hall further soured McCarthy's supporters from casting their lot with Humphrey. This was termed a "police riot" by Democratic mayor Richard M. Daley's law enforcement operations targeting the army of anti-war protesters. CBS reporter Dan Rather was even punched in the stomach on-camera by a Chicago plain-clothes detective, which was one of the nadirs of American politics.

Although he discouraged his supporters from launching an independent campaign on his behalf, McCarthy refused to endorse the Democratic ticket until Humphrey turned away from Johnson's war policies. He finally gave his support on 29th October, after the vice president announced his willingness to suspend bombing in North Vietnam. This last-minute gesture failed to save Humphrey from a narrow defeat by Nixon. Third-party candidate George Wallace, an Alabama Democrat, had siphoned-off support from traditional Democratic demographic groups by running on an anti-integrationist platform.

Capitalising on the "politics of rage", Wallace effectively split-off parts of the old party base, the heart of the solid south and many working-class Democrats, by a blunt appeal to racism. It effectively handed the election to Nixon, who won with less than half the popular vote.

While McCarthy did not win the Democratic nomination, the anti-war "New Party", which ran several candidates for president that year, listed him as its nominee on the ballot in Arizona, where he received 2,751 votes. He also appeared on the Oregon ballot as the New Party candidate. In 1969, after 24 years of marriage McCarthy separated from his wife Abigail, but the two never divorced. The children stayed with their mother after the separation. According to McCarthy biographer Dominic Sandbrook, McCarthy was involved in a romantic relationship with CBS News correspondent Marya McLaughlin that lasted until McLaughlin's death in 1998.

McCarthy did not seek re-election in the 1970 Senate election, ironically the defeated Democratic candidate ex Vice President Hubert Humphrey won his seat.

After leaving the Senate in 1971, McCarthy became a senior editor at Harcourt Brace Jovanovich Publishing and a syndicated newspaper columnist, he also devoted much of his time to writing, including poetry.

He ran for the Democratic presidential nomination four more times, in 1972, 1976, 1988 and 1992, but never came close to generating the enthusiasm of his first campaign.

After his 1972 campaign, where he fared poorly in the New Hampshire and Wisconsin primaries and soon dropped out McCarthy left the Democratic Party.

In 1976 he ran as an independent candidate for president. Conducting what appeared an eccentric campaign but which included policies now favoured by many mainstream politicians he took a libertarian stance on civil liberties, promised to create full employment by shortening the working week, and even came out in favour of nuclear disarmament. He eventually won 0.9% of the popular vote and Democrat Jimmy Carter was elected president.

In 1980, dismayed by what he saw as the abject failure of Jimmy Carter's presidency, he said,

"He was the worst president we ever had".

Source: Eugene McCarthy Up Til Now: A Memoir
(1987)

He also appeared in a campaign ad for Libertarian candidate Ed Clark and wrote the introduction to Clark's campaign launch. He would eventually endorse Republican candidate Ronald Reagan.

In 1982, McCarthy ran for the US Senate but lost the Democratic primary to businessman Mark Dayton, 69% to 24%.

In the 1988 election, McCarthy appeared on the ballot as the presidential candidate of a handful of left-wing state parties, specifically the Consumer Party in Pennsylvania and New Jersey and the Minnesota Progressive Party in Minnesota. In his campaign he supported trade protectionism, Reagan's strategic defence initiative and the abolition of the two-party system. He received 30,905 votes.

In 1992, returning to the Democratic fold, he entered the New Hampshire presidential primary and campaigned for the Democratic nomination, but was excluded from the first televised debate by its moderator, Tom Brokaw of NBC.

McCarthy staged protests and took unsuccessful legal action in an attempt to be included in the debates. Unlike the other excluded candidates, McCarthy was a longstanding national figure and had mounted credible campaigns for president in previous elections. He won 108,679 votes in the 1992 primaries.

Besides seeking office, he spent his post-Senate years lecturing at universities and writing books. His published works have included everything from political studies to children's stories and collections of poetry.

After leaving active politics, McCarthy concentrated

on teaching, political commentary, and poetry writing. In 1998, he published No-Fault Politics: Modern Presidents, the Press, and Reformers. In 2001, a documentary film titled, I'm Sorry I Was Right: Eugene McCarthy was released. In the film, McCarthy discussed his past experiences, extrapolates on lessons learned from the Vietnam War, warned against the growing power of the military-industrial complex, and recited some of his poetry.

In 2003, McCarthy continued to write, to travel the country, and to speak out against the war in Iraq. McCarthy was a critic of President George W. Bush, whom he considered an "amateur", and Bush's subsequent war in Iraq.

McCarthy died of complications from Parkinson's disease at age 89 on December 10th, 2005, in a retirement home in Georgetown, Washington, D.C., where he had lived for the previous few years. Former President Bill Clinton gave his eulogy.

In 2009, his alma mater, St. John's University, honoured McCarthy by establishing the Eugene McCarthy Distinguished Public Service Award.

McCarthy believed that the Democratic Party greatest achievements were the Civil Rights Act of 1964 and the enactment of the national health insurance programs "Medicare" and "Medicaid" as part of LBJ's vision of the "Great Society". However, he blamed the ratcheting up of Vietnam War by Johnson for the failure of part of the Great Society agenda, as it took the focus of revitalising America. Not surprisingly, it was this opposition to the war in Vietnam that gave McCarthy his national prominence.

However, he was more than an anti-war campaigner his liberal progressive polices were the product of a man whose roots were in the roman catholic faith and the hard-working Irish of Minnesota and the Midwest.

Eugene McCarthy is a man who should be remembered for so much more and who earned his place in American political history.

CHAPTER 15
JOSEPH MCCARTHY
THE ANTI-COMMUNIST SENATOR OR OPPORTUNIST?

Despite being allies during the 2nd world war as the post war political environment developed a cold war erupted between America and Russia and in the US these tensions drove many prominent politicians to attack what they saw as communist infiltration. For a period in the early 1950s, America was gripped by a paranoid fear of all things actual and allegedly soviet.

Many innocent men and women were smeared with the tag of communists or soviet sympathisers. One man personified that era, even giving his name to the tactics used to out and ostracise alleged communist party members.

This man was Senator Joseph McCarthy and his reckless and, in many cases, unsubstantiated accusations and public attacks on fellow politicians, actors, film makers and government officials would become known as McCarthyism.

Joseph Raymond McCarthy was born on the 14th of November 1908 on a farm in Grand Chute in rural Wisconsin. He was the fifth of nine children born to his Irish working-class parents. His Father Timothy was the son of an Irish father and a German mother while his mother Bridget was a Tierney from county Tipperary.

Despite being a bright child, Joseph dropped out of school when only 14 to help on the family farm and to work in a local grocery store to earn more money for the family.

Ambitious, he didn't abandon academia and McCarthy returned to education when he was 20 and attended Little Wolf high school in Manawa Wisconsin.

He then went on to Marquette University in Milwaukee, to study engineering before switching to a law degree. A popular student Joseph was elected the president of his class and he received a Bachelor of Laws degree in 1935.

Admitted to the bar that same year, Joseph supplemented his law income by playing poker. He had a vision of where he wanted to go and that involved politics. He tried unsuccessfully to lobby to become a district attorney as a Democrat. He then ran for the nonpartisan but elected post of 10th district judge in 1939. Joseph successfully defeated the incumbent Edgar

V. Werner to become at 30 the youngest circuit judge in Wisconsin state history.

In a taste of what would later become a McCarthy trait, Joseph was ruthless during the campaign and lied about his opponents age to create an impression that his opponent was too old and infirm to continue as a judge. McCarthy claimed Werner was 73 when he was in fact 66.

The smear had traction as Werner was renowned as being unpopular with lawyers and many of his judgements had been reversed by the Wisconsin Supreme Court. Werner was also notoriously disorganised and had built up a considerable backlog of cases.

Despite his youth and inexperience, McCarthy soon earned a reputation as a no nonsense and efficient judge with a fast paced and common-sense approach to justice. He made up for his lack of experience as a jurist by demanding precise briefs from the contesting attorneys. He then digested these, dispensing swift justice. He was not fond of overseeing long cases or delivering wordy judgements. He soon became famous for dealing with cases quickly, some in a matter of minutes.

Despite this his judgements held up and he had a low percentage of cases reversed by the Wisconsin Supreme Court. However, he was censured in 1941 for having lost vital evidence in a price fixing case.

When the United States entered the war in December 1941 McCarthy deliberated about joining up. His position as district court judge exempted him from military service but when his great friend and future campaign manager Urban P Van Susteren extolled the future political benefits of enlistment, Joseph made up his mind, took a leave of absence from the bench and joined the United States marine corps. His college degree qualified him for a direct commission, and he entered the marines with the rank of first lieutenant.

He was posted to the Solomon Islands and Bougainville where he served as an intelligence briefing officer for a dive bomber squadron.

Conscious that active service looked far better on a political resume than a desk job he volunteered for combat missions as a gunner observer. He would eventually fly in 12 such missions which were generally low risk.

After a particularly uneventful mission Joseph was allowed to use the machine gun and fire as many bullets as he wished. After destroying many innocent coconut trees, he was given the nickname by combat veterans 'Tail Gunner' Joe.

McCarthy ended the war with the rank of Captain, he would remain in the marine corps after the war eventually attaining the rank of Major.

McCarthy was still on active duty in 1944 when he decided to run for the Senate as a Republican. He was defeated in the Wisconsin primary by the incumbent

Alexander Wiley. Undaunted he prepared to run again in 1946.

After McCarthy left the marines in April 1945, five months before the end of the Pacific war in September 1945, McCarthy was re-elected unopposed to his circuit court position.

Determined to carve out a political career and seeing the Senate as his preferred route, McCarthy began the groundwork to ensure he did not repeat the mistakes of his failed 1944 attempt to secure the Republican nomination. He began creating a political operation and ground game in readiness for the 1946 primaries. As part of this campaign, he secured the support of the Wisconsin Republican party boss Thomas Coleman. While this was a major plus he needed all the help he could get he was going up against a tough opponent in three term Senator Robert M. La Follette Jr.

La Follette not only benefited from incumbency, but he also had an impeccable political pedigree. A political heavyweight who had founded the Wisconsin Progressive Party he had politics in his genes, as the son of former senator and popular Wisconsin Governor Robert M. La Follette Sr.

The 1946 Republican primary proved to be a bare-knuckle fight but a one-sided affair. McCarthy played heavily on his own war record and attacked his opponent for not enlisting to fight in the conflict. This was an outrageous smear, as La Follette was 46 when war broke out and too old for active service. Despite this the accusation stuck and damaged his opponent. McCarthy also began to use his war time nickname "Tail-Gunner Joe", using the slogan, "Congress needs a tail-gunner".

This was not the only smear used during the campaign, McCarthy also accused his rival of not only avoiding the fight but actually profiting from the war making massive gains on his investments while he was away defending his country. The truth was McCarthy himself had made more money on his investments during the war, but the mud stuck, and the damage was done impacting on the fading Le Follette campaign.

Another factor which influenced the campaign was the influence of the Communist party who rode in behind McCarthy which was ironic given the future direction of his Senate career.

In the primary McCarthy won the Republican nomination by 207,935 votes to 202,557. This was largely in part because of his negative campaigning and the support of the communist controlled United Electrical Radio and Machine workers unions.

In the 1946 Senate election McCarthy faced off against his Democratic opponent Howard J. McMurray. Joseph won in a landslide securing 61.2% of the vote and at the age of 38 he was now the youngest member of the US Senate. 'Tail gunner Joe,' was now off to Washington.

McCarthy's early Senate career was relatively low

key, and he gained a reputation as a moderate Republican when he was active in issues such as housing legislation and sugar rationing. It was in this area that he first attracted controversy when he received a $20,000 personal loan from a Pepsi bottling executive, earning the Joseph the derisive nickname "The Pepsi-Cola Kid".

In July 1946 McCarthy displayed a maverick streak and a disregard for being liked which would be a hall mark of his future career when he lobbied for the commutation of death sentences given to a group of Waffen-SS soldiers convicted of war crimes for carrying out the 1944 Malmedy massacre of American prisoners of war.

On December 17th, 1944, the 1st SS Panzer Division of the Sixth Panzer Army, commanded by Colonel Joachim Peiper, was heading west from Büllingen, Belgium. This movement was part of the general German advance during the Battle of the Bulge. At the same time, a US convoy of thirty vehicles and nearly 140 men of Battery B of the 285th Field Artillery Observation Battalion was heading south from Hürtgen Forest toward Ligneuville.

The two forces converged just before noon at the crossroads hamlet of Baugnez, two and a half miles south of Malmedy. Combat Group Peiper (Kampfgruppe Peiper) (part of the Waffen SS) immediately began firing upon Battery B. The US troops panicked. Those who did not escape, including medical personnel, quickly surrendered. After being searched and relieved of their personal possessions, the US troops were lined up in eight rows in a field at the crossroads. Then for reasons that are unclear, Combat Group Peiper fired on the GIs. German troops walked among the bodies and shot any who was alive. Survivors of the atrocity recalled being fired upon several times, and even hearing laughter as the Waffen SS troops killed the Americans.

When the Germans left the site, at least 84 US soldiers were dead. Just over 40 Americans survived the incident, now known as the Malmedy Massacre, either by fleeing into the woods or pretending to be dead.

The Malmedy Massacre was one of a series of atrocities committed by Peiper's division. US prosecutors claimed officials believed that his unit was responsible for killing some 350 unarmed American soldiers and about 100 Belgian civilians over a one-month period in Belgium as well as other atrocities on the eastern front.

The discovery of the SS crime led to a concerted manhunt by US military authorities to locate and prosecute the killers. After the war, they succeeded in tracking down some 400 members of the Waffen SS unit, who were taken to a prison in Schwäbisch Hall, near the German city of Stuttgart. From December 1945 to April 1946, US Army war crimes investigators interrogated the prisoners to gather evidence and confessions. Subsequently 74 of the SS men were selected to stand trial for the Malmedy Massacre and the killings of non-combatant Belgian civilians. The US Army then transported them to the former Dachau concentration camp, where US military tribunals were holding war crimes trials.

On May 16th, 1946, the trial of 74 SS members who had taken part in the Malmedy Massacre and other killings during the Battle of the Bulge began. All the defendants were charged with violation of the laws and usages of war and with deliberately participating in the killing, shooting, and torturing of US soldiers and unarmed civilians. The prosecution argued that the defendants committed these war crimes as part of premeditated Nazi conspiracy to wage a ruthless campaign against Allied forces and civilians during the German military offensive of December 1944. This policy of killing prisoners of war, it was charged, had been ordered by Hitler and willingly executed by Peiper.

The defense counsel did not dispute the fact that US Army soldiers had been killed but argued that the shootings occurred in the heat of battle, not because of a criminal conspiracy.

On July 16th, the military tribunal found all the defendants guilty. Forty-three were sentenced to death by hanging (including Peiper) and twenty-three were sentenced to life in prison, with the rest receiving either ten-, fifteen-, or twenty-year prison terms.

During the proceedings, Peiper claimed that the American war crimes investigators had beaten the defendants, coerced them into signing confessions, given them mock trials, and intimidated their families. These accusations, which became the subject of heated dispute, haunted the trial. The chief American defense counsel, Colonel Willis

M. Everett, appealed to the US Supreme Court as well as other bodies to have the executions halted and the matter of "fraudulently-acquired confessions" and other legal improprieties thoroughly investigated.

News of the defense claims leaked out to the press and generated criticism of American war crimes trial procedures both in the United States and Germany. Leading German clerics, including some who had been imprisoned by the Nazis in concentration camps, condemned the Malmedy proceedings.

Despite opposition from his fellow Senators across the political spectrum, McCarthy was critical of the convictions because the German soldiers' confessions were allegedly obtained through torture during the interrogations.

The United States Congress also launched investigations into the claims raised by the defense team, but the findings largely exonerated American authorities in Germany.

Under popular pressure amid the Cold War between the western powers and the Soviet Union, all the sentences of the Malmedy defendants were commuted, including those sentenced to death. By 1956 all the convicted had been freed from prison.

McCarthy's defence of the SS soldiers did nothing to add to his already poor reputation among his fellow Senators who viewed him as a loner with a quick temper and prone to irrational and violent verbal outbursts. He was viewed as completely unlikable with little or no friends and allies in the Senate. In 1949 he was even voted the worst senator currently in office by Washington political journalists.

Outside the Washington political bubble, his reputation could not have been more different, he was the darling of the cocktail party set and viewed as gregarious and great company. Perhaps this was because drink was involved and his socialising and frequent drinking in his office in the Senate led to accusations that Senator McCarthy was fast becoming an alcoholic.

Joseph McCarthy's life changed forever on February the 9th 1950, when he gave a sensational Lincoln Day speech to the Republican women's club in Wheeling West Virginia. While no audio record exists of this speech, its incendiary contents were soon reported across America. During the speech McCarthy attacked the rise of communism and its danger to America.

McCarthy produced a list which he waved above his head exclaiming that it contained the names of 205 known members of the communist party who were actively shaping policy in the US state department.

This sensational claim was soon spread coast to coast by the US media and McCarthy was brought to national prominence as the fear of communist infiltration gripped America.

This paranoia was driven by recent events such as the victory of the communists in the Chinese civil war, the development of a nuclear bomb by the Soviet Union and the fallout from the recent trial of Alger Hiss accused of spying for the Soviets during the 30s.

McCarthy despite the outlandish nature of his claims was genuinely surprised by the media reaction to his accusations and the uproar it created. He was soon accused of revising both his claims and the number of supposed communist infiltrators. Just days after his speech the number had reduced to 57, and on the Senate floor on February 20th, 1950, he further revised the figure to 81. Realising his credibility was under threat and to maintain his newfound celebrity status, McCarthy embarked on a length speech in which he preceded to outline the case against each of the 81 names on his revised list.

Naturally, people wondered where had the previously obscure junior senator from Wisconsin obtained his list of alleged communist infiltrators. McCarthy claimed he had received the information from some good, loyal Americans in the State Department. As with most things with McCarthy, the reality was different to his claims. He had just recycled his allegations from the so-called "Lee list", a report that had been compiled three years earlier for the House Appropriations Committee.

This committee had been led by Robert E. Lee, a former FBI agent and they reviewed the security clearance documents on State Department employees and had determined that there were "incidents of inefficiencies in the security reviews of 108 employees.

In reciting the information from the Lee list cases, McCarthy consistently exaggerated, representing the hearsay of witnesses as facts and converting phrases such as "inclined towards communism" to "a communist".

Despite the fluctuating numbers in McCarthy's accusations, the Senate voted unanimously to investigate his allegations.

The Maryland Senator Millard Tydings was appointed to head up a subcommittee of the Senate committee on foreign relations to investigate Joseph McCarthy's early claims of Communist penetration of the federal government and military.

Tydings is reported to have said before the hearings began:

"Let me have McCarthy for three days in public hearings and he'll never show his face in the Senate again."

The charge laid before the committee was that the defeat of the Kuomintang regime in China by the communists had been caused by the actions of alleged Soviet spies in the State Department.

McCarthy also alleged that Owen Lattimore a China expert in the State Department was a "top Russian agent."

The hearings began in March 1950 and were marked by partisan infighting throughout. Tydings and the Democrats were incensed by McCarthy's attack on the State Department during a Democratic presidency and were determined to discredit him and repudiate his allegations. The Republicans rode in behind McCarthy and supported his claims.

As McCarthy took the stand, Tydings interrupted him 85 times with questions and demands for substantiation, which despite McCarthy's colourful allegations never came. This enraged McCarthy whose notorious hot temper exploded when he condemned Tydings as an "egg-sucking liberal".

During the proceedings, the Washington Post cartoonist Herbert Block coined the term 'McCarthyism 'in a cartoon in the March 29th edition of the paper. For McCarthy's opponents the term was a synonym for baseless defamation, mudslinging and political demagoguery. However, McCarthy ever the showman embraced the term and declared:

"McCarthyism is Americanism with its sleeves rolled up"

He would also go on to publish a book in 1952 called McCarthyism: the fifth for America.

In July 1950, the Tydings committee published its report, concluding that McCarthy's accusations were spurious and condemning his charges as an intentionally nefarious hoax.

However, McCarthy may have lost in the Senate, but in the court of public opinion fanned by the media he was the victor, and he was determined to continue his anti-communist crusade not only that he also began to demand that investigations be held into alleged homosexuals working in the forging policy bureaucracy, who were according to McCarthy susceptible for blackmail by soviet agents.

Again, the media promoted McCarthy's agenda and his approval ratings increased and he gained a powerful national following and platform.

McCarthy set out punish his political opponents especially Millard Tydings by accusing them of being communist sympathisers and in some cases actual communists. During the 1950 Senate elections McCarthy and his supporters campaigned against Tydings accusing him of protecting communists and shielding traitors.

McCarthy's staff even went as far as producing a doctored picture which showed Tydings in conversation with known communist leader Earl Browder. McCarthy denounced the picture but did not fire the staffers involved and Tyding lost his election by over 40k votes and claimed McCarthy and his accusations were to blame.

McCarthy also campaigned against other prominent Democrats and in each race, he was involved the Republicans won.

During the 1952 presidential election, the Eisenhower campaign toured Wisconsin with McCarthy. In a speech delivered in Green Bay, Eisenhower declared that while he agreed with McCarthy's goals, he disagreed with his methods.

With his victory in the 1952 presidential race, Dwight Eisenhower became the first Republican president in 20 years. The Republican party also held a majority in the House of Representatives and the Senate.

After being elected president, Eisenhower made it clear to those close to him that he did not approve of McCarthy, and he worked actively to diminish his power and influence. Still, he never directly confronted McCarthy or criticized him by name in any speech, thus perhaps prolonging McCarthy's power by giving the impression that even the President was afraid to criticize him directly

McCarthy was now recognised as a key Republican campaigner, and he was now regarded as one of the most powerful men in the Senate. Very different from the undistinguished early years where the loner was disliked and tolerated at best. His Republican colleagues now looked upon him with newfound respect or was it fear?

In 1952 he was also awarded the Distinguished Flying Cross; this was after he deliberately falsified his participation in 32 aerial combat missions. Despite his superiors knowing these claims were false, they feared his political power and wanted his influence in Washington, so they awarded him his medal and war hero was added to his growing reputation. McCarthy even claimed to have a war wound, lingering pain from a badly broken leg which resulted from various stories of aircraft crashes to enemy fire. He had indeed broken his leg during the war, but during a party aboard a ship crossing the equator for the first time. However, critics who knew of his various embellishments of his war time valour and wounds would mockingly refer to him in Washington by his war time nickname 'Tail Gunner Joe."

McCarthy also won re-election in 1952 with 54% of the vote, defeating former Wisconsin State Attorney General Thomas E. Fairchild.

In 1953 McCarthy married Jean Fraser Kerr, a researcher in his office, the couple would later adopt a baby girl and give her the name Tierney Elizabeth McCarthy.

In 1953, at the beginning of his second term as senator, McCarthy was put in charge of the Senate Committee on

Government Operations. President Eisenhower and other Republican leaders had grown increasingly worried about the methods that McCarthy was adopting and the sweeping allegations he was making. They believed that by giving him the chairmanship of what they perceived to be a mundane committee, they could side-line him and put him where they felt he could do little harm.

This would prove to be a costly mistake, McCarthy a master of Senate procedure knew that his committee also included the Senate permanent subcommittee on investigations, and he used this mandate to launch a series of expansive probes into what he claimed was communist infiltration into the US government.

McCarthy now appointed 27-year-old Robert F Kennedy as an assistant counsel to the subcommittee. Robert Kennedy would resign after six months ostensibly because of disagreements with McCarthy and the committee counsel Roy Marcus Cohn; however, I tend to think a shrewd political operator such as Robert Kennedy perhaps saw the damage McCarthy was causing and decided that his future career would be best served by disassociating himself from the investigations.

One Kennedy who was closer to McCarthy was the patriarch of the family Joseph, who saw McCarthy as useful to his sons future presidential ambitions. Joseph

Kennedy knew that anti Catholic prejudice had ended the presidential dreams of Al Smith and he threw his support behind McCarthy as a popular national Catholic politician who might pave the way for a younger Kennedy's presidential candidacy.

That younger Kennedy would be John F. Kennedy who served with McCarthy in the Senate from 1953 onwards. JFK never attacked McCarthy even at the height of his investigations, when asked about this he once replied:

"Hell, half my voters in Massachusetts look on McCarthy as a hero".

Throughout the next two years McCarthy continued his communist witch hunt. In hearing after hearing, he aggressively interrogated witnesses in what many came to perceive as a blatant violation of their civil rights. Despite a lack of any proof of subversion, more than 2,000 government employees lost their jobs because of McCarthy's investigations.

His browbeating tactics destroyed careers of people who were not involved in the infiltration of our government. His freewheeling style caused both the Senate and the subcommittee to revise the rules governing future investigations and prompted the courts to act to protect the constitutional rights of witnesses at Congressional hearings.

The subcommittee even turned its eye towards the overseas library program of the International Information Agency. McCarthy's aide Roy Marcus Cohn toured Europe examining the card catalogues of the State Department libraries looking for works by authors he deemed inappropriate.

On his return, McCarthy then recited the list of supposedly pro-communist authors before his subcommittee and the press.

The State Department bowed to McCarthy and ordered its overseas librarians to remove from their shelves "material by any controversial persons, communists, fellow travellers, etc."

Some libraries went as far as burning the newly forbidden books. Shortly after this, in one of his few public criticisms of McCarthy, President Eisenhower urged Americans:

"Don't join the book burners. Don't be afraid to go in your library and read every book." At the end of 1953, McCarthys committee turned its attention towards a new target but one they would find more difficult to attack, the United States Army. McCarthy was so eager to begin he returned early from his honeymoon and opened an investigation into the Army Signal Corps laboratory at Fort Monmouth.

The press lapped up these new allegations of a dangerous communist spy ring which had been established among a group of army researchers.

However, despite weeks of testimony and allegations, McCarthy and his committee was unable to produce any hard evidence to substantiate their claims.

With the press turning against him, McCarthy sought a new target and turned his attention to Irving Peress a former dentist from New York who had been drafted into the army in 1952 and subsequently promoted to Major.

After his promotion, it had come to light that Peress had declined to answer questions regarding his political affiliations (he was a member of the left wing American Labor Party) because of this the US military decided to discharge him from the service within 90 days. When this came to McCarthy attention, he alerted the press that he was going to subpoena Peress to appear before his committee on January 30th, 1954.

Major Peress did not answer any of the questions or allegations thrown at him, he declined to make any statement other than claiming his rights to silence in order not to incriminate himself under the fifth amendment.

An infuriated McCarthy contacted the Secretary of the Army Robert T. Stevens and demanded that he arrange for Peress to be courtartialled. Peress was one step ahead of McCarthy and asked for his pending discharge from the army to be affected immediately.

This request was granted by his commanding officer Brigadier General Ralph W. Zwicker who gave Peress an honourably separation from the army.

McCarthy encouraged his supporters to demand who promoted Peress and it soon became a rallying cry among his anti-communist supporters. Once again, the reality did not reflect well on McCarthy as Peress had been promoted to major automatically on his enlistment because of the Doctors Draft Law of which McCarthy himself had been a strong supporter and for which he had voted!

Thwarted once again, McCarthy was the centre of controversy in March 1954 when the prominent television documentary series 'See It Now' hosted by Edward R. Murrow ran a show highlighting the methods McCarthy had been using in his numerous anti-communist investigations.

Edward R. Murrow became famous for his radio broadcasts from London during the second world war. On Christmas Eve 1940, during the blitz, he finished his programme: "Merry Christmas is somehow ill-timed and out of place, so I shall just use the current London phrase, so long and good luck." The variant "Good night, and good luck" became his sign-off in later television reports.

On the show broadcast on March 9th, 1954, titled "A Report on Senator Joseph R. McCarthy", Murrow painted a picture of a man whose recklessness with the truth and ugly attacks on his critics had contributed to a climate of deep fear and repression in American life.

At the end of the show, Murrow turned to the

camera and delivered a long monologue, which read, in part:

> "This is no time for men who oppose Senator McCarthy's methods to keep silent, or for those who approve. We can deny our heritage and our history, but we cannot escape responsibility for the result. There is no way for a citizen of a republic to abdicate his responsibilities. As a nation we have come into our full inheritance at a tender age.
>
> We proclaim ourselves, as indeed we are, the defenders of freedom, wherever it continues to exist in the world, but we cannot defend freedom abroad by deserting it at home."

Source: "See It Now – A Report on Senator Joseph R McCarthy", March 9th, 1954

Further controversy for McCarthy was to follow later that month when the US army in retaliation for his attacks on army personnel and senior officers accused McCarthy and his chief counsel, Roy Cohn, of improperly pressuring the army to give favourable treatment to G. David Schine, a former aide to McCarthy and a friend of Cohn's, who was then serving in the army as a private. McCarthy claimed that the accusation was made in bad faith, in retaliation for his questioning of Peress and Brigadier Zwiger.

The Senate Permanent Subcommittee on Investigations, usually chaired by McCarthy himself, was given the task of adjudicating these conflicting charges. Republican senator Karl Mundt was appointed to chair the committee, and the Army–McCarthy hearings convened on April 22nd, 1954.

The hearings lasted for 36 days and were broadcast on live television by ABC and DuMont, with an estimated 20 million viewers. After calling 32 witnesses and two million words of testimony, the committee concluded that McCarthy himself had not exercised any improper influence on Schine's behalf, but that Cohn had engaged in "unduly persistent or aggressive efforts".

The Murrow expose had dented McCarthy's popularity but many of those who witnessed the Army–McCarthy hearings saw him as bullying, reckless, and dishonest, and press coverage was also negative towards him. In Gallup polls of January 1954, 50% of those polled had a positive opinion of McCarthy. In June, that number had fallen to 34%. In the same polls, those with a negative opinion of McCarthy increased from 29% to 45%.

The tide of public and political opinion was now turning against Joseph McCarthy. Once the darling of the Republican conservative wing he was now seen as a volatile individual whose reckless accusations mostly without any foundation was fast becoming not only a liability to the Republican party but to the anti-communist movement.

Once a political movement, McCarthyism was now a synonym for witch-hunting and the denial of civil liberties. Senate opposition to McCarthy was growing and on June 1st Vermont Republican Senator Ralph E. Flanders compared McCarthy to Adolph Hitler, accusing him of spreading "division and confusion" and saying:

> "Were the Junior Senator from Wisconsin in the pay of the Communists he could not have done a better job for them."

> *Source: John G Adams, . . Without Precedent: The Story of the Death of McCarthyism (1983)*

Later that month Flanders introduced a resolution to have McCarthy removed as chair of his committees.

Despite the growing opposition to McCarthy there was no clear majority supporting this resolution. The main reason for this was not support for McCarthy but the concern about usurping the Senate's rules regarding committee chairs and seniority.

Undaunted Flanders next introduced a resolution to censure McCarthy himself.

This resolution was initially written without any

reference to particular actions or misdeeds on McCarthy's part. As Flanders put it, "It was not his breaches of etiquette, or of rules or sometimes even of laws which is so disturbing, but rather his overall pattern of behaviour."

A special committee, chaired by Senator Arthur Vivian Watkins, was appointed to study and evaluate the resolution. This committee opened hearings on August 31st.

After two months of hearings and deliberations, the Watkins Committee recommended that McCarthy be censured on two counts: his contempt of the Subcommittee on Rules and Administration, which had called him to testify in 1951 and 1952, and also his abuse of General Zwicker in 1954. The Zwicker count was dropped by the full Senate on the grounds that McCarthy's conduct was arguably "induced" by Zwicker's own behaviour. In place of this count, a new one was drafted regarding McCarthy's statements about the Watkins Committee itself.

The two counts on which the Senate voted were:

- That McCarthy had "failed to co-operate with the sub-committee on Rules and Administration", and "repeatedly abused the members who were trying to carry out assigned duties ..."
- That McCarthy had charged "three members

of the [Watkins] Select Committee with 'deliberate deception' and 'fraud' ... that the special Senate session ... was a 'lynch party'", and had characterised the committee "as the 'unwitting handmaiden', 'involuntary agent' and 'attorneys in fact' of the Communist Party", and had "acted contrary to senatorial ethics and tended to bring the Senate into dishonour and disrepute, to obstruct the constitutional processes of the Senate, and to impair its dignity".

On December 2nd, 1954, the Senate voted to "condemn" McCarthy on both counts by a vote of 67 to 22.

The only senator not on record was John F. Kennedy, who was hospitalised for back surgery; Kennedy never indicated how he would have voted.

McCarthy was eventually stripped of his chairmanship and condemned on the Senate floor on December the 2nd 1954, for conduct "contrary to Senate traditions." That turned out to be the final nail in the coffin of the McCarthyism era, and Joseph McCarthy himself fell from the public eye though he continued to serve in Congress.

His career as a major public figure, however, had been ruined. His colleagues in the Senate avoided him; his speeches on the Senate floor were delivered to a near-empty chamber or they were received with intentional and conspicuous displays of inattention and some cases out right contempt.

Joseph McCarthy died in the Bethesda Naval Hospital on Thursday, May 2, 1957, at the age of 48. His death certificate listed the cause of death as "Hepatitis, acute, cause unknown"; previously doctors had not reported him to be in critical condition. It was hinted in the press that he died of alcoholism (cirrhosis of the liver), an estimation that is now accepted by modern biographers.

He was given a state funeral that was attended by 70 senators, and a solemn Pontifical requiem mass was celebrated before more than 100 priests and 2,000 others at Washington's St. Matthew's Cathedral. Thousands of people viewed his body in Washington. He was buried in St. Mary's Parish cemetery, Appleton, Wisconsin, where more than 17,000 people filed through St. Mary's Church to pay him their last respects.

Robert F. Kennedy attended the funeral in Wisconsin. McCarthy was survived by his wife, Jean, and their adopted daughter, Tierney.

So ended the life of the junior senator from Wisconsin who saw communist infiltrators everywhere in an era of paranoia and cold war fear and whose lasting legacy is lending his name to describe unjust persecution, McCarthyism.

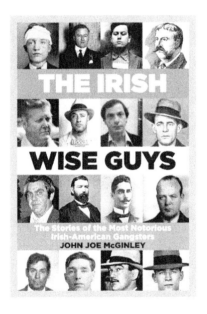

Printed in Great Britain
by Amazon

78709720R00231